LEADERSHIP WITHIN REACH

Personal Stories of Success from 88 Central Ohio Leaders

Chip Chapman,

Allison West and Rebecca Chapman

Leadership within Reach
PERSONAL STORIES OF SUCCESS FROM 88 CENTRAL OHIO LEADERS

ISBN-13 978-0-9790327-0-7
ISBN-10 0-9790327-0-9

Published by The Knowledge Group, Inc.
1464 Manning Parkway
Powell, Ohio 43065

Available at quantity discounts for bulk purchases.
For information, call 1-800-536-4TKG

Printed in the United States

To order additional copies of this book, visit
www.LeadershipWithinReach.com

Dedication

We dedicate this book to the young leaders in our family—Joseph Chapman, diagnosed with type 1 diabetes in December 2004, and his loving and supportive older sister, Emily—and to all the other wonderful children and families we've met who lead the charge for a cure while managing diabetes every day, too.

Love,
Dad, Mom and Aunt Allison

ACKNOWLEDGEMENTS

We gratefully acknowledge the following:

- All the inspirational leaders who took time from their busy schedules to share their personal stories, thoughts and comments for the book
- Staci Perkins, executive director of the Mid-Ohio Chapter of JDRF, and her super staff who wholeheartedly supported us from the beginning
- The Minds On and Lacelet crew—Tom and Gina Augustine, Doug Stitt and Randy James—who provided inspiration and helped us with concept, title and cover design
- Our editorial board—Jack Jackson, Colleen Pyron and Richard S. Webster, Ph.D.—who helped us improve the flow and clarity of the stories
- Dr. Paul Otte, who shared his wisdom and experience on leadership and writing books
- Lisa Peterson and the patient staff at Studio 6 Sense who helped us create a clean professional layout
- Jackie Ness, of Finesse Editing, for reviewing all final content
- The team at Globus Printing who created a fantastic-looking final product
- The leaders at the Columbus Chamber of Commerce, Experience Columbus, The Entrepreneur Institute and Leadership Columbus who agreed to help us by taking a leadership role in promoting the book

Contents

PART II: ENTREPRENEURS

Part III: Corporate Movers & Shakers

Part IV: All in the Family

ABOUT COLUMBUS

I grew up in Columbus bored to tears.

We had a pretty good zoo, a 47-floor skyscraper called LeVeque Tower and a storybook Christmas shopping experience at Lazarus Department Store downtown, a trip which was always highlighted by the irresistible aroma of roasting nuts at the Planters shop just up the street. We'd hit the Ohio State Fair every August and would sometimes catch a minor league baseball game at Jet Stadium.

Honestly, that was about the extent of the city scene in Columbus, which is why my childhood buddies and I somehow felt compelled to use our extended spare time to fight, play pick-up games of football and baseball, and plunder the neighborhood.

As I think back on those days I hardly recognize the place today. The city grew up right along with me, and I am so proud to call Columbus my hometown.

Old, historic neighborhoods like German Village, Italian Village, Victorian Village, the Brewery District, the Arena District and the Short North have been restored and now serve as major entertainment centers. Downtown looks like a real downtown. Professional sports have arrived on the scene by way of the Columbus Blue Jackets (hockey) and the Columbus Crew (soccer), while The Ohio State University fuels an unmatched passion for Big 10 sports. The shopping at Easton Town Center, The Mall at Tuttle Crossing and at Polaris Fashion Place is as good as it gets. And art buyers in the know fly in regularly to scour the galleries for another great find.

But best of all, Columbus has an undeniable international feel, thanks mostly to the university, among the largest campuses in the world. The melting pot that is Columbus, the 15th largest city in the United States, is also due in part to the fact that so many corporations are headquartered here. SARCOM, Huntington Bancshares, White Castle, Worthington Industries, Nationwide Insurance, Cheryl & Co., *Highlights for Children*, and Battelle are just a few.

Arriving on the heels of these international students and professionals are the restaurants that cater to them, which in itself has profoundly impacted the feel (and taste) of the city.

As much as Columbus has changed, Broad and High streets still mark the center of the city. Everything the city offers ripples out from that point on the map. Not surprisingly, the Ohio Statehouse anchors this prime piece of real estate.

A National Historic Landmark and a masterpiece of 19th-century Greek Revival architecture, the Ohio Statehouse was completed in 1861 and restored to its original grandeur in 1996. It is a beautiful building inside and out, and the daily guided tours point out the thousands of tiny details that make Ohio's capitol building such an amazing place.

There are so many stories wrapped up in the history of this building. For example, underground tunnels once ran between the capitol and the downtown hotels. No doubt, the tunnels served to keep state legislators out of Columbus' always-unpredictable weather.

Another story often told is that the building of the statehouse led to the imprisonment of many of the city's Italian stonecutters. The old Ohio Pen, which once stood just a few blocks away, supplied much of the labor in the building of the statehouse. As the story goes, the skilled Italian stonecutters were thrown in the slammer for the tiniest infractions and then sent to work at Broad and High.

While I can't verify the truth of that story, I do know that Columbus has been piling up some enviable rankings in recent years:

- #11 Best American places to live and work, *Employment Review*
- #10 City in the nation for campus scenes that rock, *Rolling Stone*
- #1 Best super specialty museum in the country for children (COSI Columbus), *Child Magazine*
- #24 Best place for business and careers, *Forbes*
- #12 Top arts destinations, A*mericanStyle Magazine*
- #4 Cleanest city in the United States, *Reader's Digest*
- #12 Best walking city, *Prevention* magazine

I'm telling you, there's a lot to love about Columbus.

William J. Purpura
Editor, *Home & Away* magazine

"My colleagues from other community leadership programs across the country are envious when they hear me describe the open and welcoming environment that exists here for those that want to participate and be involved in guiding the city's agenda. We are indeed fortunate that Columbus recognizes the depth and breadth of talent in our community and listens closely to all the voices that have a perspective that can help make this a better city for all. This is a rare look at the inside stories of our community's best and brightest—who, individually are talented and compassionate leaders and collectively, help make Columbus one of the best communities to live in, work and raise a family."

Laurie Marsh, Executive Director - Leadership Columbus

"In 2006 *Money* magazine ranked Columbus as the eighth best big city in America in which to live. The phrase that was used to distinguish Columbus is that we are within 600 miles of half of the U.S. population, but we are so much more than that. Ohio's capital city is one of the few in the northeast quadrant of the country whose economy and population have grown steadily over the past three decades. Here you'll find excellent arts and entertainment, attractions, sports, and a quality of life that make the city one of the best places in the Midwest to live, work, raise a family and visit. Columbus is on a roll, with smart, talented and dedicated civic and business leaders who are optimistic about the future and determined to get things done. This book provides valuable insight into those individuals who have helped our city to thrive and have made it a place that is valued and enjoyed by residents and visitors alike."

Paul Astleford, President and CEO - Experience Columbus

"At the Chamber we do a lot of benchmarking against other communities. It's no surprise to us that the Columbus region stands strong against so many places. We have tremendous assets, the kind that attract new businesses to our community and help local businesses start and grow. Perhaps our region's greatest strength is its attitude. Here, people and businesses get connected. We are collaborative, and that's what it takes to be successful in today's competitive environment."

Ty Marsh, President and CEO - Columbus Chamber

FOREWORD

If you Google books on leadership, you'll find about 93,600,000 "hits." Searching for just books, you'll find approximately 1,920,000,000. The point is two-fold; First, leadership books account for 5 percent of all books; and second, if your goal is to write a unique leadership book, you have a difficult task.

Add to that the decision to interview leaders as a foundation for your book, and you can appreciate the challenges it creates. The authors of "Leadership Within Reach" accepted the challenge for two reasons: One, to raise funds and awareness of juvenile diabetes; and two, to show that leaders emerge at any age and come from all walks of life.

Selecting which leaders to interview was a daunting task in itself. There will be readers who question who was included and who was not. The answer is simple: The leaders interviewed had some things in common. They were located in central Ohio, and their names were known by many in the area, including the authors. They were willing to meet with the authors and answer a series of rather personal questions.

To all the leaders who were not included, I am sure the authors would say it was just a matter of time and accessibility. To those who might question who was included, I would join with the authors and encourage you to read the profiles and discover the reasons why.

Over the years, I have noted how few books or articles on leadership actually define "leadership." At Franklin University, a common definition is "a relationship between a leader and a follower in the accomplishment of a positive goal." Your personal definition may differ from this, and that's fine. The important point is that you approach this book, and your own leadership, with the understanding that the conclusions you reach are often based on your beginning definition.

The authors based their questions on their definition of leadership. The common thread to the questions was "success"—how the leader defines it and was motivated to it, how it changed over the years, and who helped on the journey. They also asked about each individual's strongest leadership qualities as well as examples of leadership situations and how they reacted to them.

The results from the interviews may surprise you. While some common responses occurred, the most significant results may be found in the differences. As predicted, there are no clear pathways to success. Readers must find their own way by learning from other successful leaders.

Let's return to the driving force behind the authors' efforts and what gave them the purpose for this book. Chip Chapman's son has diabetes, and being a leader himself, Chapman wanted to do something about it—to show his son how he could lead by example. He couldn't cure diabetes—that's best left to the medical professionals. He couldn't take the diabetes on himself, as much as he may have wanted. Instead, he put his efforts and resources into this book, with the profits going to the Juvenile Diabetes Research Foundation (JDRF). Chapman's hope is that in some way, he can make the cure come faster, reduce the impact of the disease, or just make a day or even an hour easier for his son and others with diabetes. In this way, Chapman personifies leadership.

Of course, each reader will contribute to the cause through the purchase of this book and any other support they can provide. So both the authors and readers are leaders in the effort.

As part of our work at Franklin University's Leadership Center, we have identified five higher-level themes of leadership (1). These levels are not intended to identify or be applied to leaders only in higher-level leadership positions. They are found in leaders at all levels who have taken their leadership to a level higher than others.

These levels of leadership are: seeing the possible over the probable, staying focused despite uncertainty, remaining conceptual, having commitment, and having a sense of presence. At Franklin, we've found these themes have been tested and reinforced in business, community, government and educational institutions.

To further understand leadership, let's look at those who demonstrate these levels every day and are the motivation behind this book—those with diabetes, especially young children. Every day they must put the probable aside, choosing instead to see the possibility of a cure. They have learned to live with the uncertainty of this disease and to stay focused on their treatment.

Those with diabetes remain conceptual, forced to see things through a "10,000-foot view," while maintaining the details of everyday treatment. To be successful, they must have a commitment to their treatment, day in, day out, never wavering. And unlike those of us who are just observers, they understand the concept of a sense of presence of their disease in both place and time. They can never put it aside.

How do I know about the levels of leadership applied by those with diabetes? Because my own son, now a successful adult leader, has lived with diabetes since he was 17. As I watch him, I admire his leadership—just as I am sure Chapman admires his son, and any reader does who is directly or indirectly affected by this disease. Together, we know these are the real leaders who go beyond being the motivation of the book to become examples of leadership we can all follow!

Dr. Paul J. Otte
Executive Director of the Leadership Center
and President, Franklin University

(1) From "The Conflicted Leader and Vantage Leadership," Franklin University Press, 2006.

INTRODUCTION

Studying the practice and philosophy of renowned leaders and entrepreneurs has always appealed to me. In fact, the concept for this book came to me as I was reflecting on several leadership events that I'd recently attended. The questions in my mind were: How does one become a successful leader? Are leaders born or can they be developed? What motivates some people and not others to take action and step forward into a leadership role?

These questions stemmed from several thought-provoking experiences. Early in 2006, I attended the President's Forum sponsored by The Entrepreneur Institute in Columbus and witnessed 200-plus local business leaders soak up the personal success stories of Cheryl Krueger, founder of Cheryl's Cookies; Phil Urban, CEO of Grange Insurance; and Laconda Dager, third-generation leader of Velvet Ice Cream. I'd also heard Paul Astleford, CEO of Experience Columbus, express his concerns to my Rotary Club about Columbus' lack of national presence, despite being the nation's 15th-largest city. And, I'd recently browsed the "Power 100 List of Local Leaders," compiled annually by *Columbus CEO* magazine.

With this background for inspiration, I found motivation from a painful personal experience to pursue the questions in my mind and write this book. My son, Joseph, nearly 5 at the time, was diagnosed with type 1 diabetes (also called juvenile diabetes) in December 2004. After getting over the initial shock, my family learned to manage Joseph's insulin-dependent lifestyle.

Then, Joseph asked me if he would always have to take insulin injections to live. I reacted by doing what a lot of parents would do (especially fathers)—I looked for a way to "fix" the problem.

I soon learned that "fixing" diabetes requires research, which in turn requires significant dollars. After our son's diagnosis, my wife and I joined the local chapter of the Juvenile Diabetes Research Foundation (JDRF). Its mission is to find a cure for juvenile diabetes, and it devotes 85 percent of the funds it raises to research. It's a highly respected organization that operates on a lean budget so that it can invest heavily in world-class scientists and research projects. That's why the profits from this book will be given to JDRF.

"Leadership Within Reach" also reflects the positive, entrepreneurial spirit of another family we met through JDRF. Tom Augustine, whose daughter is diabetic, wanted to find a "fix" for her as well, so in 2005 he created the Lacelet to raise awareness and funds for diabetes research. In the spirit of the Lance Armstrong "Live Strong" bracelet, the Lacelet is a tie-on for shoelaces, drawstrings or necklaces, emblazoned with the words "Within Reach," signifying that a cure for diabetes is achievable. You can read more about the Augustines' inspiring story on page 134.

Having shared all this background with you, I hope it helps you gain even more pleasure in owning and reading "Leadership Within Reach."

Writing the book was a labor of love for me, my wife, Rebecca, and her sister, Allison West. We worked with the unconditional support and love of our entire family. And we enjoyed a warm reception from every single leader we approached—a unique quality of our Midwest community. We wish time and space allowed us to include stories from even more of our accomplished, inspiring local leaders.

I need to tell you that many of the leaders we spoke with were both humbled and inspired by the challenging questions we asked. Many had not been asked to consider some of these issues in quite a while. After you read the stories, I encourage you to spend some quality time thinking about your own leadership experiences, goals and potential. You'll find a special section at the back of the book that will guide you through this process.

I believe we have delivered on our goal to share personal glimpses into the lives, journeys, motivations and inspirations of 88 Central Ohio leaders. I hope you will derive as much enjoyment and inspiration from reading these stories as I did in hearing the stories firsthand. As you read these vignettes, you may find some common threads that tie them together. You may also realize, as I did, that there is no simple answer or direct path to take in becoming a successful leader today. However, I believe this book demonstrates that great leadership is certainly "Within Reach" if you have the desire to learn and the willingness to take action.

Chip Chapman,
President, The Knowledge Group, Inc.

Part I
Helping Others

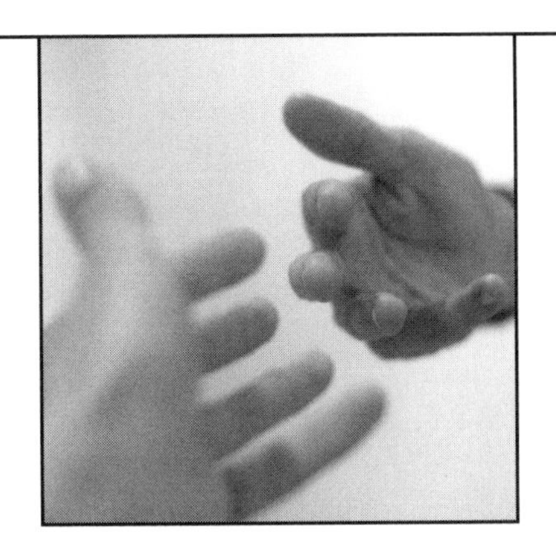

Yvette McGee Brown

President, The Center for Child and Family Advocacy

Words to live by:
"Be prepared. Pursue excellence. There's no substitute for hard work."

Hometown: Columbus, Ohio
First job: 14 years old, working with children in a summer program
Hobbies: traveling, reading, being home with family
Favorite book: "Slaves in the Family," Edward Ball
Favorite movies: "The Color Purple," "Roots," anything with Denzel Washington
I am: "Passionate."

Yvette McGee Brown wants her life to be significant. She doesn't worry about how successful she is—for her, it's more about making a difference and knowing that her work matters. Leading the Center for Child and Family Advocacy (CCFA) at Children's Hospital enables her to make progress on these goals every day. "I'm very cognizant that being in this position is an honor. I don't want to disappoint all the people who came before me who didn't have these opportunities," she said.

McGee Brown; Children's Hospital CEO Dr. Thomas Hansen; and Columbus businesswoman, philanthropist and chair of Children's Hospital board of directors Abigail Wexner developed the vision for CCFA and researched similar programs nationwide to ensure it reflected best practices.

The Center opened in 2005 and is the first nationwide to offer comprehensive services for both abused children and victims of domestic violence under one roof. Services include intervention, prevention and long-term treatment. Thanks to generous benefactors, McGee Brown said, CCFA operates mortgage-free in its 42,000-square-foot building. The Center needs the space: Each year in Columbus, more than 7,000 children are reported as abused and/or neglected.

To promote top-quality service, McGee Brown said, "I tell everyone to operate as if everything we do will be reported on the front page of the newspaper. I try to inspire others with my passion." Her personal mantra is to pursue excellence and integrity. Perhaps that's why she thinks other people may find her demanding.

McGee Brown tackled equally demanding children's issues before joining CCFA as a judge in the Domestic Relations and Juvenile Division of the Franklin County Common Pleas Court. At the time, she was 32 and the youngest elected judge in Ohio. "I loved being a judge. The work was far more grueling than I could have imagined. I know I made a difference. I really did hold people's feet to the fire, especially because we were working for children."

Nine years on the bench took their toll. McGee Brown admits that she'll feel lifelong effects from many cases over which she presided. In one, a 14-year-old boy had shot and killed another 14-year-old. The victim's mother sat in court every day, holding an 8" x 10" photo of her son. After the verdict (seven years' imprisonment in the juvenile system), the victim's mother began writing to Brown annually on the anniversary of her son's death.

There were positives, too. For example, when McGee Brown left the bench, she received a letter from a drug-addicted young mother whom she had helped. It said, "I never knew somebody like you could care about somebody like me."

Many caring people shaped McGee Brown's life. Like many of those she's helped, she was born to a teenage mother. Her father disappeared after her birth. She admires her mother and grandmother for having "an inner strength to keep going. Like the everyday people I admire, they made it work, with a small income, a family and no public accolades."

"I really believe there are angels directing my path," she said. One "angel" was a female African-American professor at Ohio University in Athens, who asked McGee Brown what she planned to do with her journalism degree. After hearing that she wanted to work in Washington, D.C., her professor said to become an attorney. "I told my grandmother about it, and it was a done deal. There was no going back."

After earning her law degree, McGee Brown entered public service with a job at the Ohio Attorney General's office. There she met and interviewed with Janet Jackson, currently head of the United Way for Central Ohio. "I was so mesmerized by her. I remember she wore this wonderful purple suit and shoes, and she told me I had to pay some dues before I could dress like that!" McGee Brown laughs.

Next, McGee Brown worked for the Ohio Department of Rehabilitation and Corrections and then the Ohio Department of Youth Services, both of which courted her to be chief legal counsel.

"It's the journey that makes all of us," she said. "I believe in blessings." Describing herself as a painfully shy girl, McGee Brown was gifted with an avid desire to read. She was inspired by Harriet Tubman and Martin Luther King, Jr. As an adult, McGee Brown read Rick Warren's "The Purpose-Driven Life," which she said changed her life because its message prompted her to contact her estranged father.

She also feels blessed with her husband, Tony, whose first call to ask her out was veiled by a request to pick up bumper stickers to help promote her campaign. They married six months after McGee Brown took the bench. Together they raised two daughters from Tony's first marriage (his first wife died of cancer) and a son.

"I define success like Ralph Waldo Emerson did—it's having the respect of people in high places and the friendship of many. It's about making a difference, " McGee Brown said. She wouldn't change anything in her life: "All my experiences have contributed to who I am today."

"I believe in excellence—never settle for less."

MICHAEL CARROLL

CEO,
AMERICAN RED CROSS OF GREATER COLUMBUS

Words to live by (from his father):
"Anything worth doing is worth doing well."

Hometown: Rutland, Vt.
First job: running a playground at a recreation department
Hobbies: golfing, traveling
Favorite movies: "Deer Hunter," "Philadelphia"
I am: "Adaptable."

American Red Cross CEO Michael Carroll traveled a winding road—literally—to his professional destination. After college graduation, he joined a friend in his Volkswagen van and "aimlessly" traveled the country throughout the 1970s. "We were just like 'On the Road,'" Carroll explains, referring to the 1959 novel by Jack Kerouac describing his cross-country travels.

Perhaps these diverse experiences fueled Carroll's ability today "to see the big picture out of the stuff," as he puts its, and "to set concepts for groups that enable them to get engaged around an issue quickly." Carroll also describes himself as a situational leader and an "incrementalist," apt titles for a man who must make solid decisions in times of crisis and often with less-than-optimal resources.

"You have to be flat-out adaptable and assess what's possible on the fly," Carroll said. His work at the Red Cross began in Maryland in the late 1970s, after his "counter-culture" travels. He first did case work, but found a passion in so-called "disaster courses" that prepared him to do field work. Promotions carried him to the state headquarters in Baltimore and then to the national offices in Alexandra,

Va., where he headed East Coast disaster operations.

"By then I was in my early 30s, and I saw my career dead-ending. I caught a big break when the Miami chapter merged with the local blood bank, and I was invited to apply for chapter manager," Carroll said.

Miami remained home to Carroll, his wife, Glenda (whom he married in 1990 at the age of 40), and their son until 1992 when Hurricane Andrew convinced them it was time to leave. As CEO of the Dade county chapter, Carroll stayed behind at the disaster headquarters to guide the relief efforts. Carroll accepted his current job in part because of how well the Columbus community supported nonprofits.

At the Columbus chapter, Carroll manages 54 full-time paid staff and 600 volunteers and a budget of nearly $6 million. With these resources, the chapter serves more than one million people in Franklin, Fayette, Pickaway and Madison counties.

Managing this organization is just part of Carroll's service to the Red Cross. After Hurricane Katrina devastated Louisiana and parts of other southern states in 2005, Carroll led the Red Cross operations for Texas, Arkansas and Oklahoma. He describes his time in Houston as "the most difficult, intense professional circumstance I'd ever faced. I got up every morning and did my best. It was more intense and ambiguous than Hurricane Andrew. We were making it up on the fly, and the exchange with government was not always friendly."

This "situational" leader also defines success case by case: "Sometimes shelters are comfortable and sometimes they're not. Many times sleeping cots and eating hot meals is as successful as sleeping on the floor and eating peanut-butter sandwiches." Carroll keeps moving forward because "people count on me, and I have a little bit of personal pride in that. I can't let people down who are loyal to me and doing their best. I think it's a vanity, but I'm aware that people think I'm a leader, and I wouldn't want it any other way."

Born in Glens Falls, N.Y., Carroll grew up across the border in Rutland, Vt., the state's second-largest city with 20,000 residents. The oldest of five children, he attended the same Catholic grade school as his father and grandfather. After high school he tried studying at American University in Washington, D.C., but homesickness pulled him back to the University of Vermont.

While in college, he found civil-rights disturbances eye-opening, and he had serious concerns about the Vietnam War. "I always thought my country cousins were hicks, but after those experiences I thought, 'Who's the hick now?'" Carroll may have felt a certain naiveté at the time, which doubtlessly evolved as he traveled the country with his college friend.

"One time, I thought I'd joke about those years on my résumé. I wrote that from '72 to '79 I was 'doing research into the counter culture.' At an interview, I had someone say how interesting that must have been, and did I write a paper about it?" Carroll laughingly recalled.

Carroll obviously embraces all of his life's travels and experiences. He admires "people you can count on—who won't leave you holding the bag when times get tough." In particular, he credits former colleague Ben Evans with helping without expecting anything in return, and never compromising on issues of character. Evans once said of Carroll that he would fight a lion, to which Carroll responded, "I don't walk away. I can't walk away. But now I apply more strategy to the fight."

Carroll explained: "I recognize that I can rub people the wrong way, so I tell myself to listen more. And I know that not talking is not the same as listening! As I've matured, I am more genuinely interested in what other people say. I want to always be open to learning."

ED COHN

CEO, BIG BROTHERS BIG SISTERS OF CENTRAL OHIO

Words to live by:
"Don't confuse your net worth with your self worth."

Hometown: Columbus, Ohio
First job: paper carrier
Hobbies: spending time with family, playing with his son on their all-terrain vehicles
Favorite books: "Good to Great," Jim Collins, "The Present," Spencer Johnson
Favorite movies: "Forrest Gump," "Flatliners"
I am: "Determined."

Spend just a few minutes with Ed Cohn and he'll sweep you up in his vision for the community. He envisions entire neighborhoods rallying to help children, schools reaching unprecedented levels of achievement, and community organizations coordinating plans and resources. Give Cohn a little more time, and he'll outline how this vision can be accomplished. It starts with the one-to-one mentoring for which Big Brothers Big Sisters is famous.

"We have a great brand, but it needs to change to reflect new strategies," Cohn said. Even though the traditional mentoring program boasts 74 years' success in Columbus, a new school-based mentoring program has reached many more children in the last two years.

Cohn aims to reach students in all of the Central Ohio schools in need—namely, 89 of the 311 area schools identified as being at-risk academically by the state education department. Currently, Big Brothers Big Sisters works with 33

Columbus-area schools, reaching about 23 students at each school, for a total of nearly 760 kids.

Central Ohio operates the fourth-largest metropolitan agency in the country out of 425 agencies nationwide.

"We've got a lot of smart kids out there. They're just burdened with other issues, and they need somebody to talk to," Cohn explained. He said that when adult mentors help students manage family and peer issues, as well as offer academic tutoring, dramatic academic gains can be made.

Cohn continued: "Our goal is to saturate the schools with mentors. We'll see a dramatic impact on the students' quality of life and the quality of our schools. But once we reach the 'tipping point' with mentoring and tutoring, the entire community will step forward. Eventually, kids will step forward to help other kids."

Creating a community vision and leading people toward it are skills Cohn developed in, of all fields, banking. After earning degrees in finance and accounting from The Ohio State University, he worked for two large national banks. At that point, he knew he wanted to make a more personal impact, so he accepted the role of CEO at County Savings Bank, a privately owned community bank in Columbus and Newark. When the owners wanted to sell, Cohn managed its merger with community banks in Zanesville, Canton and Dayton, Ohio.

Finally, in July 2004, Cohn directed the sale of Unizan Bank to Huntington Bancshares. By then, he'd also served the community via the Boy Scouts, the American Heart Association and, in 1999, Big Brothers Big Sisters. He was instantly enamored with the program. When the CEO left in 2004, Cohn accepted the lead role, despite "flattering opportunities" offered by Huntington president Tom Hoaglin if he were to stay with the bank after the merger.

It was a tricky transition. Cohn promised the Unizan chairman that he'd stay until the sale was final; he also told Big Brothers Big Sisters that he'd start right away. A few months' delay in the bank deal turned into nearly 20 months. In order for Cohn to begin his new role, the bank showed overwhelming and unprecedented support by reducing his duties, allowing him to work part-time at the agency, paying his salary, and making a monthly contribution to Big Brothers Big Sisters. Finally, in March 2006, the bank sale was final, and Cohn began working full-time at the agency.

"I figured I was doing the best I could if the bank, my family and Big Brothers Big Sisters were equally unhappy with me during that transition time," Cohn laughed. Even though his reduced bank duties freed up half of his regular work schedule, he still put in 40 hours a week at the bank and another 35-40 with his new job.

While discussing his new role at Big Brothers Big Sisters, Cohn told Hoaglin, "I might be crazy, but I believe our community can realize this vision." Hoaglin told him that the community needs "people who think 'crazy' and not just incrementally." Cohn acknowledges that they hand out a lot of "band-aids" for short-term, necessary help, but that his community vision will also provide a long-term strategy for sustainable, transformational results.

The youngest of three children, Cohn credits his family for influencing his priorities and perspectives. His German father and Romanian mother, both Holocaust survivors, met when the concentration camps were liberated at the end of World War II. They immigrated to the United States in 1949 with their two-year-old daughter, sponsored by the Yenkin family, owners of Yenkin-Majestic Paints.

"My parents were very family focused. They always assumed their children would go to college, and have successful careers and happy families," Cohn said. Married for 25 years, he and his wife have a 12-year-old son. Cohn nearly lost his wife and son when she was pregnant and developed a life-threatening liver disorder. Because of it, the Cohns' son was born three months early, weighed one-and-a-half pounds, was not breathing and had no heartbeat.

All of his experiences help Cohn value and enjoy his family. They live in a log home tucked in the woods, which gives him and his son plenty of space to enjoy their all-terrain vehicles. "We have a blast together. He's keeping me young," Cohn said.

In fact, Cohn hopes his legacy evolves from his love of his own child and his desire to serve others. He aims to lead his agency in mentoring an entire generation of children, thereby breaking the negative cycles. "I love to see people succeed. To do that, I have to lead by example and challenge people to do their very best."

GENE HARRIS

SUPERINTENDENT, COLUMBUS PUBLIC SCHOOLS

Words to live by:
"Find something you can be passionate about and enjoy—that enables you (where you can) to contribute to more than your own bottom line."

Hometown: Columbus, Ohio
First job: cleaning crystal chandeliers at Sims Electric for $1.25/hour
Hobbies: traveling, church activities, gardening, golfing
Favorite books: "On Becoming a Leader," Warren G. Bennis, John Grisham novels
Favorite movie: "Raiders of the Lost Ark"
I am: "Passionate."

Gene Harris lived an idyllic childhood. At home she grew up with a loving, extended family—parents, brother, sister, grandparents, aunt and uncles. In her community she enjoyed "wonderful people and families who fed you too much, too often!" she laughed.

Harris' family gave her a solid foundation as a young girl that continues to sustain her today. She said of her parents, now 80 and married for 59 years: "I watched a good marriage. They showed me what a long-lasting marriage looked like. I always knew I wanted to be married forever, watching them."

A strong education at Columbus Public Schools prepared Harris for her future as one of the first women to attend Notre Dame University. She credits three educators for providing unique motivation: A middle-school teacher who accepted only her best effort, a high school librarian who revealed the world of African-American literature, and a superintendent and mentor who saw promise in her as a principal.

Today as superintendent, she leads the schools she loved as a child, and where she found inspiration from her teachers at Garfield School. "I thought I was born to be a teacher. I never lost the zeal for it, not through junior high or high school," Harris said.

"I admire people who are always looking ahead," she explained, instead of those who focus on past missteps. "I also admire folks who can see what many think on the surface would be impossible—like Martin Luther King, and people who do things even when they don't have to."

When measured against these qualities, it's clear Harris passes the test.

In her quest to be an educator, Harris always moved forward. She began her career teaching junior-high English and drama, married her husband, Stan, and embarked on a breathtaking path. She finished graduate school in 1979 while still teaching; then gave birth to her son, Wade, in early 1980; and returned as a principal-in-training that fall. Promotions advanced her from assistant principal to principal (the district's youngest at the time), supervisor of principals, and assistant superintendent of curriculum.

Harris then left the school district to serve as assistant superintendent at the state Department of Education. She resigned in 1998 to finish her dissertation and earn her doctoral degree. After some consulting work and a return to Columbus schools as assistant superintendent, she achieved her goal of becoming superintendent in 2001.

That year, Harris overcame many personal and professional challenges. She lost her sister to lupus. Her husband had open-heart surgery. Her son had left home to study at Howard University in Washington, D.C. And she helped the school district handle student and staff reaction to Sept. 11.

Like those she admires, this exuberant leader looks beyond the surface for meaning and possibilities. "Success is about achieving personal and professional satisfaction, making a contribution and seeing the results," Harris said. "Early on it meant making a certain amount of money, which couldn't be farther from where I am right now."

Harris strives to motivate others. "People need to be inspired. Life is tough sometimes, and jobs are hard," she said. "I'm willing to listen to people in unusual places. Everyone's voice counts and should be heard."

Others may call her impatient to get a job done, she said, or say she tackles more than she should or doesn't delegate enough. But Harris said people know she's committed to her work and is willing to "walk through fire" for her students.

For many, it's a challenge to do things they don't have to. Harris felt this pull when she wasn't chosen to lead the Columbus schools the first time she applied. "It felt like a personal failure. But, I decided to be very open and offer my help to the new superintendent in any way she needed."

"I believe there are no random acts. Everything happens for a reason," she said. She searched for a reason underlying her battle with cancer in 1989, when she was 36, married and mother of a young son. "I went through six months of treatment. I really understood 'reflection' for the first time," she recalls. "My family, my fabulous husband and my faith got me through it all."

In addition to becoming a mother, Harris said the best day of her life was her wedding day. In fact, she and her husband share a lifelong romance: They met in eighth-grade health-science class and stayed together ever after. She followed him to Notre Dame their sophomore year—she would've gone sooner, but the college wasn't yet accepting women.

Clearly the legacy she hopes to leave in the Columbus schools is children who are achieving, moving forward on the right track, and living successful lives. Harris summarized: "I meet my current and former students everywhere. Many are doing great things—and some aren't doing so well. I'm motivated because I see what has been achieved, and what hasn't happened, and therefore what our challenges are. I want to establish a culture that says everyone is valuable and has to learn."

Cynthia C. Lazarus

President and CEO, YWCA Columbus

Words to live by:
"See the possibilities."

Hometown: Louisville, Ky.
First job: babysitting
Hobbies: reading, knitting, sports
Favorite book: "Kristin Lavransdatter," Sigrid Undset
Favorite movie: "Sophie's Choice"
I am: "Paradoxical."

Cindy Lazarus is making a difference. Whether it's through her political endeavors (including three terms on the city council and 10 years as a judge), her many community service projects, or by her service on numerous boards and committees, she's built her life around serving others. CEO and President of YWCA Columbus, Lazarus also sits on the boards of the Columbus Bar Foundation, The Leo Yassenoff Foundation and the Columbus Marathon.

Obviously, Lazarus doesn't sit idly by on the sidelines. "There's more to life than making ourselves happy. I'm a very competitive person so my need to achieve is very strong," she said.

Taking care of others was a lesson Lazarus learned early. Back home in Louisville, Ky., Lazarus was the third eldest of 10 children in an Irish-Catholic household. "We were raised modestly, but the one thing we always had in abundance was babies. To this day, I'd do anything to take care of newborn babies," she said.

In addition to babies, reading and sports were also integral parts of her childhood. "Catholic educators believed that a tired kid was a good kid. Athletics were primary in helping me make good choices."

After high school, Lazarus stayed in Louisville and entered Bellarmine College in 1965, where she received a degree in philosophy. She had no idea what type of work she would find with the degree. "I studied philosophy because it was the most interesting thing I'd heard of. I wasn't thinking in terms of a career or what I'd do with it. I was totally unprepared for the job market," she said.

The next 10 years were unhappy ones spent moving and changing jobs. "I moved around a lot because I thought that if I could change something on the outside, I'd be happier on the inside," she said. Her journey started in Louisville in a position at the welfare department. Lazarus married and followed her husband to Chicago, where she took a Civil Service exam to widen her job opportunities.

Lazarus described her next job in a state psychiatric hospital for emotionally disturbed children and adolescents as an extraordinary experience. "I helped care for families who were in extreme distress. Never again did I want to feel that unprepared for a job," she said. She returned to school and earned a master's degree in social work from The University of Chicago.

Still unhappy, she divorced and moved again to northern Minnesota and then to New Orleans. Lazarus finally returned home and earned a law degree from The University of Kentucky in 1979. That same year she sought treatment for alcoholism. Lazarus had secretly been drinking excessively since she was 21 years old.

What's amazing even now to Lazarus is the fact that she accomplished so much while being an alcoholic. She'd started drinking in college and continued through law school. Her family never believed she had a problem. She said, "They thought I was just being a drama queen."

"I wish I would have had a more-affirming childhood. I grew up unprepared to be an adult who took good care of herself. My alcoholism fit into this. Even though I passed the bar exam, I was still unhappy. But I was out of excuses. So I got help and stopped drinking."

Lazarus came to Columbus in 1980, accepted a job for an advocacy agency, and studied for the Ohio bar exam. The job fell through due to lack of funding, so she hung up her own shingle instead. "There was a real interest in female attorneys back then. I never had trouble finding clients, just ones who could pay," Lazarus said.

New to the city, Lazarus wanted to meet more people, so she entered the political realm. She ran for Franklin County prosecutor in 1985. She lost the race but was appointed to the Columbus City Council later that year and was re-elected in 1989 and 1993.

Her political star was on the rise. In 1994 Lazarus was elected to serve as judge in the U.S. 10th District Court of Appeals. It was a period of introspection for Lazarus. "I thought about what I was going to do with the rest of my life. I loved my time on the bench, but at the same time I realized that the court wasn't the best place to use the gifts I had. I wanted to work with the community."

In 2005 Lazarus joined the YWCA Columbus. Throughout its history, the YWCA has served to empower women. Today it exists to eliminate racism and create opportunities for women's growth, leadership and empowerment. As CEO, Lazarus is continuing the charge. Just after she came on board, the group opened the YWCA Family Center for homeless families, a $6.5 million facility.

"I had been involved with the Y for years. Although I'd never been on the board, I'd been invited to participate in different programs. The Y had every woman of significance in town affiliated with their board. It was like the all-star team."

Lazarus believes her leadership at the YWCA is characterized by a willingness to work hard, a sense of humor ("at myself as well as others"), and an interest in learning. "But I don't feel like I have to know it all."

Fighting her alcoholism has been the hardest thing Lazarus has ever faced. "Early in life, success was external. When I achieved some of those markers, I realized that wasn't really success. Now success is the ability to make change happen. Through effort and determination, I've made my life better."

Lazarus says the best time of her life has been motherhood. Her daughter will enter Kenyon College in the fall of 2006. "She laughs at me because I have all these clichés that I use. One of them is, 'If you don't need stitches, get back on the field and suck it up.' And I believe in the principle of owning it, of taking responsibility for your own life."

TONY R. WELLS

PHILANTHROPIST, TONY R. WELLS FOUNDATION

Words to live by (from his grandfather): "If you don't have the cash to buy it, you don't need it."

Hometown: Middleburg, Ohio
First job: working on the family farm
Hobbies: running, investments, wine
Favorite book: any book that I actually finish!
Favorite movie: "Hoosiers"
I am: "Tenacious."

Philanthropist and entrepreneur Tony R. Wells grew up tending cattle, pigs, chicken, sheep and crops on his family's farm in Middleburg, Ohio. "When you grow up cleaning out pig pens, you just want to run away from it. I remember I couldn't wait to get off the farm," Wells said.

"Growing up I was very jealous of others who had material things. I dreamed of motorcycles, cars, jets and having money," Wells reflected. "Neither of my parents had careers outside a factory or the farm, so my exposure to professional careers was limited. I didn't know what I wanted to be when I grew up.

"As a kid I loved competing, negotiating and making money. I would challenge anyone to play Monopoly," he continued. "I loved to compete for recognition, but only if I knew I could dominate."

After graduating from high school in 1979, Wells used his life savings to leave the farm and attend Wilmington College, where he planned to study agricultural engineering. He felt one of life's ironic twists when he sought a campus job to help pay the bills and was hired to clean pig pens on the college farm.

Anxious to enter a more profitable career than farming, Wells followed his college counselor's advice and entered the then-emerging field of computer science. Although he didn't earn a college degree, Wells, who retired at age 39, says it never held him back. "I was never that great a student anyway."

After working successfully for other firms for a decade, Wells and his wife, Dana, created their own company in 1992, called Knowledge Development Centers. The firm provided high-quality training and meeting facilities and meeting-management services for international clients.

The pending the birth of their second child (11 years after their first) prompted the Wells to plan the sale of KDC in 1999. "It was time to play family," Wells said. "It wouldn't be any fun to run the company without Dana. I'm the visionary and she's the implementer."

Selling KDC enabled Wells to retire at an early age in 2000. However, retiring young does not mean success for him. "Success is a goal you never quite get to—it's a moving target. You can't rely on your past accomplishments. You pack them in a box, set it aside and start all over again."

Soon after retiring, Wells again teamed with his wife to indulge their passion for working with nonprofits. They created the Tony R. Wells Foundation, which provides technology and social-enterprise grants to nonprofit groups in the Columbus area. Today the Foundation and the United Way of Central Ohio sponsor the GroundWorks Group to help nonprofits achieve their missions through information management and technology.

"I see challenges every day that don't get addressed because they're too hard. I don't have a problem polarizing people to get them to the table to make decisions," Wells said. He often strives to break the stereotypes that business owners and nonprofits hold of each other; namely, that businesses see nonprofits as mismanaging money, and that nonprofits see businesses as misunderstanding the work in the trenches.

Wells understands both sides well, given his entrepreneurial efforts and his service on many nonprofit boards. He currently serves on boards for Goodwill Columbus, Adventure for Wish Kids, Easter Seals, Community Research Partners and GroundWorks Group.

A self-described "driven overachiever," Wells says he has the "passion of an evangelist" and a commitment to complete what he sets out to do. His four guidelines for living are simple and direct: Always do what's right; if you mess up, fix it; tell your wife you love her every day; and never stop dreaming.

Wells doesn't know what his leadership legacy will be. "To me, that's a story someone else will have to tell. Someday when my kids fill out their leadership profile, if they mention me, then I guess I did OK."

Mark Real

President and CEO, KidsOhio.org

Words to live by:
"Find out what you're good at, and hone your analytic and writing skills."

Hometown: South Bend, Ind.
First job: mowing lawns
Hobbies: traveling, bicycling, hiking
Favorite books: "Undaunted Courage," Steven Ambrose
Favorite movie: "Casablanca"
I am: "Tenacious."

As president and CEO of KidsOhio.org, Mark Real is fervent about discovering the real issues behind the most pressing problems in Ohio schools. "Our purpose isn't to push any political agenda or pound on anyone. We just want to find the facts so we can address the problems constructively. It's how you say something that counts."

Addressing misconceptions and presenting facts in a way that people can embrace is Real's mission. "Part of leadership is solving the real problem, as opposed to what you think the problem is," he said.

He points to a misconception in Columbus Public Schools that teenagers were committing the majority of violent offenses. A 2005 KidsOhio.org analysis of discipline found, in fact, that in a year's time, 57 percent of all students in that school remained incident-free, and just 7 percent of kids committed half of the offenses that resulted in filed charges.

Surprisingly, the majority of these charges were filed against first-, second- and third-grade students who committed assaults on other students and teachers at an elementary school. Real explains: "We found that these younger children are coming to school with basically no impulse control. Their parents are very young, in their late teens, and their experiences have been very different than those of more educated parents who had their children in their late 20s and early 30s. Much of what these kids hear at home is negative, and as a result, they're hungry for support and structure. This is a new challenge for education."

KidsOhio.org, started in 2002 by Real and Columbus businesswoman and philanthropist Abigail Wexner, is an Ohio-led, nonpartisan, nonprofit organization working to improve the lives and education of Ohio's nearly three million children, especially those who are disadvantaged. Their agenda includes improving early reading programs, increasing academic achievement for disadvantaged children, and building new schools that can also serve as community centers.

"This could be a 150-hour a week job. My issue has always been maintaining a balance with my family and my work. I wish I had more balance. Fortunately, my wife, Sue, and daughter, Megan, are very supportive."

Real believes his Catholic upbringing in Mansfield, Ohio, ultimately led to his life of service. He remembers his early activism: "When I was in high school, I joined the Young Christian Students. Its purpose was to look at social problems, judge them in light of Christian principles and take some action. The national debate about civil rights also was going on at the time. My father, who was a member of the liberation forces at the Buchenwald concentration camp in 1945, was appointed to the Mayor's Committee for Civil Rights. I joined the Youth National Association for the Advancement of Colored People. I learned a lot about people who were different from me. These experiences had a direct impact on my career choices later."

While in the Youth NAACP, Real became acquainted with an African-American attorney whose child had gotten sick—and later died—because a hospital emergency room in the South had turned them away. "I remember thinking how incredible it was that he could tell the story with such great sadness and rage, but revenge didn't guide his life—justice did," Real said.

His other life-changing relationship occurred as a consequence of his membership in the Interfaith Youth Exchange, where Real met a local rabbi who lost his entire family in the Holocaust. "I remember his sense of humor and perspective on life—he wasn't defeated by his experience. He was still hopeful."

"Both of these men worked for the things they believed in. They both had these very powerful, negative, experiences, but it didn't put them on the sidelines," he said.

Real's experiences and faith led him to study for the priesthood, which he left after two-and-a-half years in order to pursue a law career. "Law always had some appeal for me, and my Catholic upbringing emphasized service to others. My work today to change social policy enables me to help a greater number of kids than I could by helping them one by one as an attorney."

After earning his law degree from Cleveland Marshall Law School, Real went to work for the Greater Cleveland Interchurch Council. He left in 1981 to start an Ohio branch of the Children's Defense Fund in Columbus. In 2002, he and Wexner started KidsOhio.org.

His work in the city schools has had its share of heartaches—his hardest times have been those involving a death or injury of a child. Real said, "I remember visiting a classroom when a teacher pulled me outside and started to cry. She had baked a birthday cake for a third-grade boy who came from a troubled home. That day, she discovered he'd been beaten with an electrical cord by his mother's boyfriend. The social workers took him to the hospital before she could serve his cake. She told me, 'What kind of person would beat a 9-year-old boy?'"

However, Real receives new inspiration every day by watching people work with children. "Whether it's a bus driver, a teacher or a probation officer, they do extraordinary work and have so much patience. It's crucial for kids to have relationships with adults who treat them with respect and challenge them."

Real believes his ability to see problems with a unique lens and understand other points of view, plus his tenacity, are his top leadership skills. "I will not give up on children."

Success for Real is "making a difference. I've been able to apply my skills as an attorney to be a voice for those who may not have otherwise been heard. I hope we can earn respect as a group which helped the poorest kids in our community."

Rick Vincent

President and CEO, The Ohio Osteopathic Heritage Foundations

Words to live by:
"Be honest, trustworthy and comfortable with yourself."

Hometown: New Holland, Ohio
First job: working on a farm
Hobbies: traveling, spending time with grandchildren
Favorite movies: "The Godfather" (I and II)
I am: "Sensitive."

It's hard to imagine that Rick Vincent, a highly successful, motivated executive, dropped out of college on his first try. But you won't hear him apologize for it. "I had a blast!" he explains.

Vincent enrolled in The Ohio State University after graduating from high school, but this small-town boy was quickly overwhelmed by Columbus' and Ohio State's size. "You have to understand, I came from a town of 600 people, and Ohio State had around 47,000 students. I lasted two quarters before they asked me to leave. They put me on academic probation because my grades were terrible. I very seldom went to class."

After leaving OSU, Vincent found a new start in the U.S. Air Force. He spent four years as an Air Force medic, and then returned to Columbus to graduate from Franklin University. It was during this time that he also landed his first job at Doctors Hospital as the assistant to the nurse coordinator, where he helped improve morale and reduce turnover. "For some reason, I thought I'd try and get a job as an officer at a bank. But when I was about to graduate, things started progressing at Doctors, so I decided to stay. And I never left."

Vincent held several key positions at the hospital from 1971 through 1998. He laughingly describes himself as "the Horatio Alger of Doctors Hospital—I had a skill set that provided me many opportunities to do things that hadn't been done before. Doctors Hospital was really great in giving me opportunities to do new things. There was only one job at the hospital that wasn't created for me. I never replaced anybody until I became CEO."

Vincent describes the uncomfortable circumstances of this appointment to CEO as the worst time in his life. Not only did he replace his own boss to earn the new title, he found out about his new position at a board meeting that he attended with his predecessor. The promotion was a complete surprise. "I remember that I didn't know what to say to him at first. He was my good friend and mentor. I thought there would be one day when I would be a CEO, but I didn't expect it when it happened. But things happen for a reason. We've remained friends. He's OK today, and I'm OK today, too."

Today Vincent is in charge of The Ohio Osteopathic Heritage Foundations, which has assets in excess of $275 million and makes grants of approximately $10 million each year. The Foundations fund health care and quality-of-life initiatives in local communities and numerous medical research projects and endowments for faculty chairs at several colleges of osteopathic medicine.

Vincent defines his top leadership qualities as being a visionary, being unafraid to try new things, and teaching others it's OK to try new things. Vincent said, "I think people would say I'm a nice leader—they feel comfortable that I know they're doing what they need to do and can just do it. I stay out of the way."

Where did Vincent get his early inspiration? "My mother instilled the need in me to do the best I could all the time. She provided my concept of family—she kept our family together." Vincent was born the youngest of seven children in Columbus, Ohio. His parents divorced when he was 5 years old, and his mother took him and two of his brothers to live in Bloomingburg, a small town in Fayette County.

The most difficult situation he faced personally was "the decision to separate from my first wife, and the aftermath of that. It needed to be done, both for her and myself." Vincent describes the best time of his life as "when I married my second wife, Karen." He credits her with providing his motivation. "She's incredible. She helped raised my son and her three sons. And she graduated from medical school when she was in her 40s."

Today Vincent describes success as "being comfortable with what you've done. Regardless of your position in life—whether you have a lot of money or no money—if you're comfortable with yourself, then you're successful." He said this definition hasn't changed over the years, adding, "I wouldn't do anything differently.

"I hope that my leadership legacy will be that people say I was a nice guy who left something better than it was when I found it—and didn't hurt anybody along the way."

PAUL THOMPSON

EXECUTIVE DIRECTOR, RONALD MCDONALD CHARITIES OF CENTRAL OHIO

Words to live by:
"Measure your success in smiles rather than dollars."

Hometown: Columbus, Ohio
First job: Golden Point Drive-In, Columbus
Hobbies: golfing, spending time with children and grandchildren, jogging
Favorite book: "1776," David McCullough
I am: "Fair."

Paul Thompson held 37 jobs during his 37-year career at Nationwide Insurance. "It was a good thing because I got to do a lot of things. It advanced my career very nicely. I was a utility player, and I got to do a lot of fun assignments."

A Columbus, Ohio, native, Thompson came from a family of railroaders. After high school graduation, he joined his father and grandfathers to work the rails, too. As a railroader, Thompson was somewhat of a rebel because he was anti-union. "That really was my demise because after so long you had to join, and I wouldn't. They told me I couldn't work there any more if I didn't join." Unbeknownst to him, his mother paid his union dues. "All I knew was the heat came off," he said.

He quit the railroad one year later to work at Nationwide as a file clerk. As he rose through the ranks, Thompson became well known for bringing others up along the way. He's understandably proud of the mentoring work he did with women and minorities. "I've always had a good eye for talent, but a better eye for diverse talent," he said.

Thompson's career progression led to the top when he became vice president of sales. But his success didn't come without a cost. "I was very career-focused for many years. I traveled a lot and spent a disproportionate amount of time on my career instead of my family. I count as a blessing today that I'm as close to my kids as I am," he said.

When he retired from Nationwide, his peers were incredulous that he was leaving during his peak earning time. But in Thompson's view, money doesn't define success. "Success is when your contributions are valued and recognized by others," he said.

Thompson instead chose to follow his heart and honor a lifetime personal commitment to retire at age 55 so he could focus on giving back to the community. He was already serving on the board of directors for Ronald McDonald House when it began the search for a new executive director. "It seemed like the right time," Thompson reflected, "so I left Nationwide."

One of Thompson's early successes at Ronald McDonald Charities of Central Ohio was the opening of a new House across the street from Children's Hospital in March 2005. The new facility operates with six full-time employees and 200 volunteers to provide housing for 37 families with seriously ill children. It operates at 100 percent capacity. "I get satisfaction from helping families at a time of need," Thompson said.

Thompson admires others, such as Nelson Mandela and Elizabeth Dole, whose life work centers on helping others. "They have a conviction for life and for helping people," he said. They also demonstrate leadership qualities that guide Thompson today: "Listening, caring and integrity, and leading by example. It's important to understand that people will follow leaders who care about other people."

His personal guidelines are well-aligned with these leadership skills. "I believe in living by the Golden Rule, managing by your heart, and believing that people are basically honest," Thompson said.

He added, "Don't settle for second place. Think of your goal as always to win."

John Bickley

President and CEO, YMCA of Central Ohio

Words to live by:
"Be open-minded. Accept others who are different."

Hometown: Johnstown, Pa.
First job: packing groceries
Hobbies: watching sports, working out, vacationing in Australia
Favorite movies: "Forrest Gump," "Field of Dreams"
I am: "Passionate."

Not many people can claim that they work for the organization that invented Father's Day, basketball, softball, racquetball, resident camping and resistance training. But John Bickley can. "We're a fascinating organization. I'm a history buff of the Y. Every time I pick up a book, I learn something new about this organization. We even had a Nobel Peace Prize winner in 1946.

"I had no other dream than to work for the Y," Bickley said.

Bickley's passion and belief in his work at the YMCA are reflected in every word he speaks. "We have an obligation to serve the community. And I'm most proud of the fact that we're open to all. We're one of the most diverse organizations you could be involved in. I believe this is one of our greatest strengths and one of the reasons we've stayed relevant."

The YMCA of Central Ohio celebrated its 150th anniversary in 2005. That year it served over 150,000 members and provided $4 million in assistance to 42,000 people. "I get excited about kids in programs and in our growth," Bickley said.

His love for the organization started when he was just 7 years old. His family had just moved to Johnstown, Pa., from Tuscaloosa, Ala. "When we moved to Johnstown, I really didn't have a lot of friends or much to do, so I started going to the local YMCA." Bickley remembers that first summer he went to camp and the kindness of one counselor, Rich White. "He's part of the reason I ended up working for the Y."

In addition to his family, Bickley says he was also influenced as a child by the late Roberto Clemente of the Pittsburgh Pirates. "He was a great athlete and also a great humanitarian. I admired how he lived his life. Family values were incredibly important to him."

After high school, Bickley entered college to earn a degree in physical education, but his education was interrupted by the Vietnam War. He spent four years in the U.S. Air Force, which included two years at Lackland Air Force Base counseling veterans who had become drug abusers. After the war, Bickley earned his degree and went to work for the YMCA as a swimming instructor and camp counselor.

Bickley defines success as "satisfaction in what I do." He said, "I like the staff to challenge me. I don't like to be comfortable. I think when you get comfortable, you get lazy. You should have a certain amount of anxiety to do a job well. I don't expect any less of myself than I do of the people who work with me." He models his own personal guidelines after the YMCA's core values of caring, respect, honesty and responsibility.

When he thinks about the people who helped him along his 32-year career path at the YMCA, he names the late Eldon Ward, the first African-American Chairman of the Board in the 1980s. "He was always willing to give me advice, whether I wanted to hear it or not," Bickley admits.

Another instrumental person in Bickley's life is his youngest daughter. She was born in 1983 with a rare disease called Cohen's Syndrome that causes mental retardation and other physical impairments. Although her birth was his most difficult time, Bickley says, "If mankind could be more like her, there would be no wars and no hatred. She's never met someone she didn't love. She's changed my life and made it better."

The best time of his life is right now. Bickley describes himself as a passionate leader. "I trust people and have confidence in them. And I'm very open-minded and willing to try new things." He may also be seen as a risk-taker. "I will back my staff through anything," he added.

Though Bickley would not change anything along the way, he expressed one regret. "I would probably be a little more vocal in telling the story of our organization. It's truly remarkable."

He hopes his leadership legacy will be that the YMCA is "respected and known as the 'go-to' organization when people need help. Personally, I hope I'm remembered as passionate, caring and hard-working."

JANET E. JACKSON

PRESIDENT AND CEO, UNITED WAY OF CENTRAL OHIO

Words to live by:
"Don't be afraid to take risks."

Hometown: Randolph, Va.
First job: church janitor, working on the family farm
Hobbies: gardening, reading, golfing
Favorite book: "The Measure of My Success: A Letter to My Children and Yours," Marian Wright Edelman
I am: "Passionate."

"I'm a trailblazer," said Janet Jackson. It's an appropriate description for a woman who has been "the first" in many things throughout her personal and professional life.

Jackson grew up in southern rural Virginia in a large, loving family, surrounded by aunts, uncles and cousins. She was the oldest, and admittedly the bossiest, of six children who helped out on her family's working farm. Jackson had very little contact with white people. "I led a very segregated early life," she said. But that changed when she became one of the first black students to integrate the all-white Randolph-Henry High School.

"My mother would say that that was my decision," said Jackson. "I would say it was a decision that was definitely influenced by my elementary school teachers. My teachers were big supporters of mine. I was a good student. They knew what was coming. And the reality was the white system had things the black system didn't have. And my mother had talked college from Day One."

Jackson continued: "It wasn't pretty. The Klan was meeting up from our home on Saturday nights. I rode a bus as the only black child with all white children who had been taught to hate. They did everything they could. I endured it. When I was a junior, the school was completely integrated so things changed somewhat. I kept my mouth shut. I read all the time and worked in the library."

Jackson had discovered Wittenberg University while visiting her aunts in Ohio. She enrolled there to study library science, but instead earned a history degree in 1975.

Jackson received her law degree in 1978 from George Washington University in Washington, D.C. "My first year of law school was the pits," she said. "I didn't like D.C. I didn't like the people. It was third-generation lawyers; silver spoon; entitled. It wasn't about race, but there was real classism there," she said.

Out of law school, she worked for the Attorney General's office in Columbus for four years before moving to Cleveland in 1982 to work for a law firm. She kept the Cleveland position for just 11 months before returning to Columbus and the Attorney General's office. "I just missed the public sector too much," she said.

This move marked the beginning of many "firsts" in her career. In 1987, she became the first African-American woman to serve as a Franklin County Municipal Court judge, a post she held for nearly 10 years; in 1997, she became the first woman appointed to Columbus City Attorney. Later that year, Jackson was the first African-American elected to the office, which she held for six years.

"Success when I was a young lawyer was about money and position. For me now, it's living out my passion. Plus, it goes back to something from my 'shero' Marian Wright Edelman—'Service is the rent we pay for living. It is the very purpose of life and not something you do in your spare time.' If I live up to that, then I'm a success," Jackson said.

Jackson joined the United Way of Central Ohio in January 2003, again being the first woman and first African-American woman to lead the organization. "I'm not the typical United Way executive because I didn't grow up in the system," she said.

Why did she accept the new role? "I spent 10 years of my life having a great vantage point as a judge to observe what was happening in Columbus. I could see what happened to people if they weren't educated. I could see the effects of poverty. I was there trying to fix things at the end with punishment. I decided to be proactive," Jackson said.

"When I was on the United Way board we changed our business from fund raising to community impact. We had to figure out what the critical needs were and do something about them. Fund raising was the strategy to attack this. When we decided this, I knew this is where I wanted to be," she said.

Jackson found it challenging to give up the discretionary decision-making authority she'd enjoyed on the bench to the United Way's board of directors. "It took awhile, even in speeches, to go from the 'I' of an office holder to the 'we' of the organization."

About her leadership style, Jackson says, "I'm a quick study. I'll listen, but it doesn't take me forever to make a decision." She also believes strongly in treating others with fairness, honesty and candidness. "I am well-grounded. I know exactly where I come from," she said. "I really try very hard to treat people like people."

"The Lord did not bless me with a poker face. You know where I'm coming from. I have a very strong personality, and I don't try and hide it," Jackson said. "I'm not a 'yes' person. I'm respectful, but I'm going to fight for what I believe in."

Harland Hale

Judge, Environmental Division, Franklin County Municipal Court

Words to live by:
"Set goals that are realistic. Figure out an alternative plan to get there if your first one doesn't work. Take a step forward every day, and you can get wherever you want in life."

Hometown: Pemberville, Ohio
First job: 12 years old, cleaning hog barns, weeding corn from bean crops at a local farm for $1/hour
Hobbies: wood working, watching sports, art collecting and appraisal
Favorite book: "Memoirs," Andrei Sakharov
Favorite movie: "Sound of Music," "Patton"
I am: "Reliable."

The Honorable Harland Hale is an accomplished man who credits his success to a blue-collar work ethic, persistence and his broad perspective on life. In 2003 he earned the endorsement of many public-service, professional and community groups to win election to the bench. He and his wife, Janet, whom he describes as "a very principled lady, who has beauty and brains," enjoy their 16-year-old son, Harrison, and many close friends and associates. Name a topic, and Hale probably has a great joke to share about it.

Despite his formidable legal skills and supportive network, Hale wasn't always sure of his own capabilities. "In my 20s and 30s I lacked confidence, which to some extent you could interpret as self-esteem. It hindered my development because I declined opportunities. I considered myself a 'second-class citizen.' It took a while for me to realize you could be a decent, first-class person and yet not be 'Attila the Hun,'" Hale reflected.

Growing up in a northwest Ohio farming community, Hale heeded his father's advice: "Always do your best. Know that perfection is impossible." His hard-working father set a high bar; he was active in civic affairs, real estate and politics, and worked as a food chemist and business manager.

Early on, though, the Hale family was very poor; in fact, Hale and his three siblings used an outhouse through grade school. "Of course, you didn't realize how poor you were because that's just how things were," he said.

However, financial issues never held Hale back from actively participating in life. He played baseball, football and basketball; cared for many pets, including a wild fox; and participated in Boy Scouts, 4-H and "just about anything else you can think of," he said.

Hale's life was not all play and no work. "My parents were very demanding of me academically. They pushed me exceptionally hard because they saw my ability," he explained. Unlike many schoolmates, he graduated from high school with honors and went on to college at 17, earning a bachelor's degree in just three years from Otterbein College in Westerville, Ohio. Then, he and a best friend from Pemberville, Bob Kuhlman, entered the University of Toledo Law School. In 1979, when Hale finished his studies at the unusually young age of 23, he passed the bar exam on his first attempt.

At that point, the young attorney envisioned becoming a 30-year-old millionaire who was married with no children and traveled the world in a yacht. However, "real" life taught him to value other things. "Nothing in our lives is better than Harrison," Hale said. Now 50, he says, "I used to live to work. Now, I know there's more to life."

These days, Hale enjoys balancing life and work while serving in his long-sought role as judge. Leading the Environmental Division of the Franklin County Municipal Court in Columbus, Ohio, is a lifelong dream come true. Governor Bob Taft appointed Hale to the post in February 2003, when he was chief litigation attorney in the civil division of the Franklin County Prosecutor's Office. Hale won election to the post later that year. In his court, he presides over civil and criminal cases related to building, housing and zoning; land, water and air pollution; and animals or pets.

Three years earlier, Hale was defeated in his 2000 bid to become judge of Domestic Relations. "I'm a type-A person, very high-strung," he explained. "The loss was a shock—I was very upset. I'd given the race my all, I was endorsed by most of the community, and I knew I was qualified."

Such challenging times for Hale have been more than offset by positive ones. "My youth was the best time," he said, matched by marriage and fatherhood. Many role models influenced Hale, including former Ohio House Speaker and gubernatorial candidate, Charles F. Kurfess. Hale clerked for Kurfess' law firm, accepting an old Pontiac in lieu of salary. When Hale suggested a lower sale price be put on the title to save Kurfess some tax money, he learned "The Kurfess Principle"—"He told me to play by the rules always, never to bend them," Hale remembers.

The advice paid off. Hale believes others see him as fair, reliable and willing to "'get my hands dirty.' My blue-collar work ethic helped me when I started wearing a white shirt." He experienced hard manual work as he supported himself through college and law school as a dishwasher, survey crew member, home builder, railroad gandyman and radiator assembler.

A dynamic, outgoing leader, Hale aims to lead by example, reaching out to others through humor—though he admits his jokes don't always hit their mark. He sees himself as a "draft horse—the Maytag man." He hopes to be remembered as an honest man who knew what he was doing, who did his work well, and who understood the compassionate side of the law, including its impact on affected families.

"I'm probably one of the few people who came to town broke and rose through the political ranks," Hale summarized. "No matter the situation, I always treat people with respect, and I never sacrifice quality for quantity."

Bea Wolper

Founder, Women's Business Board

Words to live by:
"Live with integrity. If you have it, you have everything. And if you don't, you have nothing."

Hometown: Scarsdale, N.Y.
First job: shelving library books
Hobbies: reading, traveling, cooking
Favorite movies: the Harry Potter movies
I am: "Funny."

When asked to define her single most difficult life experience, Bea Wolper laughed and said: "Just pick one! I guess it was more of a realization than anything. I found out that the things that happened to me had nothing to do with me. It wasn't that I was good or bad, lovable or unlovable. It's not that I caused anything. I realized how lonely I'd been for the first 20 years of my life."

Wolper is partner at the Columbus, Ohio, law firm of Chester Willcox & Saxbe, where she specializes in helping family- and women-owned businesses. She serves on numerous professional and community boards and is a lecturer and author.

Growing up in Scarsdale, N.Y., "I was the poor little rich girl," Wolper said. "My mother was a world-famous artist. She painted the Queen of England, the Duke and Duchess of Windsor, the Vanderbilts, and she traveled all over. My dad was a real estate partner with Zeckendorf and Trump in New York. He had his own apartment in New York City. He was never home."

The family housekeeper supervised Wolper and her older sister, Diane, who at age 13 developed a brain tumor that kept her permanently functioning as a 13-year-old. "I was the only one responsible for her from the time I was 8 until I was 16 years old," Wolper recounts. "I could never leave her alone because she had grand mal seizures. She smoked, and I was afraid she'd burn the house down. I couldn't go anywhere without her."

Wolper remembers the isolation of that period in her life. "I didn't have anybody. I had books. They were my escape." Wolper became an avid reader at an early age. Even her first job at age 11 revolved around books, re-shelving them in a library. "That was one hour when I didn't have to be with my sister. I remember that when I would come home from the library, our housekeeper would have a quart of milk and a box of Oreo cookies ready for me. That was my bribe."

Wolper is still a voracious reader. "I still read two to four books a week. I read everything. I read bestsellers like they're candy," she said.

When she was 15, a family friend told Wolper she should go away to college. "But I didn't think I could do that, because who would look after my sister? But something must have clicked, because when I turned 16, I went to Grand Central Station—by myself, with a trunk—and got on a train for Tucson, Ariz.

"Within five months, my sister was hospitalized in a state institution," she said.

As with many family issues, Wolper dealt with her grief about her sister alone, while studying at the University of Arizona. Wolper thought she'd be an anthropologist and geologist, so she completed fieldwork in the Bahamas. Ultimately, she earned degrees in geology and math.

During her years in Arizona, Wolper also married and had two daughters. The marriage didn't last. She eventually divorced and moved her daughters to Cincinnati where she attended Chase College of Law.

"I went to school at night, worked full-time during the day, and raised two daughters as a single parent. I didn't sleep for about four years."

Wolper started her legal career in Cincinnati in oil and securities law; she moved to Columbus, Ohio, and met and married attorney Dick Emens. As a partner, she had the flexibility to shift her legal focus to represent women business owners at her firm. "I think of my two daughters and work hard to make sure they'll never have to go though what I did. I have tremendous passion for what I do. I feel very deeply the need to help people not make the same mistakes that I did," Wolper said.

Specific leadership qualities help Wolper achieve this desire: "I think about what other people want, I surround myself with a great team, and we attempt to solve the problem." Wolper says others would describe her as "relaxed yet intense." She continued, "You only go around once. It's important to instill faith in others. People need faith that you'll keep their confidences."

Additionally, Wolper says, "You must have a passion; and if you're lucky enough to get paid for it, you can't get any better than that."

Wolper defines success as "smiles—you feel good. You have balance." She wouldn't change anything about her choices and her life's journey. "What if you were to change one thing and it changed something else that was great? I've made tons of mistakes along the way. It's amazing how many I've made and still I'm OK."

She continued: "I have a great life. I have a loving husband and wonderful children. I love my practice. It's not like some Pollyanna-type thing, like I come in and every day is great. But overall I love it. I also love traveling and taking care of my kids and grandchildren."

"I hope that my legacy will be that women in business will be in a better position than when I started representing them in the 1980s; that they'll have access to capital; and that they'll be able to make the choices they want, including staying at home."

Part II
Entrepreneurs

John H. McConnell

Founder, Worthington Industries

Words to live by:
"You can be anything you want to be in this world, if you're honest and willing to work for it."

Hometown: Pughtown, W. Va.
First job: 10 years old, hoeing corn for 10 cents an hour
Hobbies: playing golf, watching the Columbus Blue Jackets hockey games, visiting his ranch in Colorado
Favorite books: anything by Ayn Rand or Allan W. Eckert
Favorite movie: "Lonesome Dove"
I am: "Humble."

Worthington Industries is the country's leading intermediate steel processor and manufacturer of metal-related products. With yearly sales of approximately $3 billion and 8,000 employees in 59 facilities across 10 countries, the company has been hailed for its financial success, business philosophy and employee relations.

Founder John McConnell says he owes the acclaim, in part, to his parents and grandparents, who taught him to value honesty. "I'm still looking for the honest man, someone you can shake hands with and have a deal," he said.

Incredibly, McConnell could have had a career in soap sales. Near graduation with a business degree from Michigan State in 1949, McConnell had participated in a number of on-campus job interviews. He was offered a sales position with Procter and Gamble, starting at $400 a month plus a car. A professor discouraged him from taking the offer. McConnell heeded the advice and returned to West Virginia to work at Weirton Steel for $250 a month as an inside sales rep. "The training was great. I learned the business and saw them build the mill of the future," said McConnell.

The steel mill wasn't entirely foreign to McConnell, who grew up in the small village of Pughtown, W. Va. By the time he graduated from Chester High School in 1941, he had already worked with his father as a laborer at Weirton Steel, saying, "You either worked in the steel mills or the pottery factory." Although he had a scholarship offer to play football at West Virginia University, "My dad warned me that war was coming, and if I got hurt playing ball, he wouldn't be able to help me financially," McConnell said.

When World War II broke out later that year, McConnell tried to enlist, but was told to wait for the draft. Fortunately, his grandfather was on the draft board, so when McConnell was drafted early in 1943, he was able to get into the U.S. Navy, his first choice. While he waited in San Francisco for his deployment, McConnell played football for the Navy. That, coupled with his completion of gunfire control school, earned him his choice of assignments.

During the next two years, McConnell saw action aboard the U.S.S. Saratoga. He remembers a particularly harrowing experience in February 1945. The ship was hit by kamikaze pilots as it provided cover for the marines during the first day of landings on Iwo Jima. "We survived but had a lot of damage, including more than 120 casualties." McConnell should know—he worked the guns from the highest point on the ship.

After college, McConnell spent five years with Weirton Steel, maker of large-coiled steel. From his position in the order department, McConnell recognized that although Weirton was catering to larger clients, there was probably room in the market to re-process steel for smaller markets. He took a position in outside sales with another company in Pennsylvania to learn the new process. He did so well that he decided to open his own business. "I earned enough commission from my southern Ohio territory that first year that I thought, Why not do this for myself?" McConnell recalled.

In 1954, McConnell and two partners set up shop in a 6,000 square-foot space in the Columbus suburb of Whitehall. He eventually bought his partners out, and as part of the deal, stayed for the term of the lease and cut their steel for free. By that time, the company had grown to capacity, so McConnell moved to a new location in Worthington—and Worthington Industries was formed.

Today Worthington Industries is ranked as one of the top 100 U.S. companies in which to work. "Most businessmen wouldn't think my style would be successful, but I proved them wrong," he said.

Some aspects of his style could indeed be considered controversial. For example, McConnell placed all his employees on salary starting in the 1960s. He explains: "I think recognition of people is the strongest motivating force you can have. 'Be honest and always treat employees as human beings' is the basis of 'Our Golden Rule.' I wrote that philosophy in the early '60s, and it's never been changed. I was raised that way and it's a way life for me. We're a good example that shows what can happen when you treat your employees differently. You get honesty and loyalty in return."

McConnell's view of success has evolved over time. "In the early days, I just wanted to do the best I could for my family, and success was about achieving what you set out to do. I don't need anything, and my family is all taken care of. Now I just want to help other people."

And he's done just that. The most recognizable example of his contributions is the McConnell Heart Hospital at Riverside Hospital in Columbus, which provides the community with a high level of treatment and prevention. Through his ownership of the National Hockey League team, the Columbus Blue Jackets, he's established the Blue Jackets Foundation, which uses the unique resources of its athletes and coaches to improve quality of life throughout Central Ohio

In 1996, McConnell handed the leadership reigns of the company over to his son, John P. McConnell. "He grew up in the business, and maybe I put him in a bad position, following me, but he has done just a great job." And so, McConnell's legacy continues.

BLANE WALTER

CHAIRMAN AND CEO, INCHORD COMMUNICATIONS

Words to live by:
"Find that marriage between what you're good at and what you enjoy. Keep it fun."

Hometown: Columbus, Ohio
First job: paper carrier
Hobbies: golfing, skiing, exercising, listening to music, hunting, reading periodicals
Favorite book: "Confessions of an Advertising Man," David Ogilvy
Favorite movie: "Hotel Rwanda"
I am: "Creative."

He's incredibly modest about his company's robust success. Blane Walter, chairman and CEO of inChord Communications, says, "I'm a big believer that people who are successful are people who found that unique marriage between what they like doing and what they're good at."

Clearly he found the right match, because under Walter's leadership, inChord grew from around 50 employees at one company in 1994 to nearly 1,000 people at 12 firms worldwide. Specializing in health-care and wellness issues, inChord is the 31st largest marketing organization in the world, with offices in 13 countries. Its annual revenues have grown an average of 35 percent in each of the last seven years.

This explosive growth stemmed from the decision in 1997 by Eli Lilly and Company to hire Walter's company, then known as Gerbig, Snell/Weisheimer, for the majority of its marketing efforts. Their new client's needs required the agency to add 180 employees—nearly double the existing roster—in about 120 days. "It was profoundly exciting and risky, on both sides," Walter says. "Adding that number of people was difficult yet exciting. It was a test on our recruiting, our existing clients, our systems and procedures, and our culture."

A strong, positive work culture ranks high on Walter's list of corporate values. He strives to create an environment of collaboration and trust. "I want to drive people to believe in a destination, and to get excited about what it means to get there," Walter said. Also important is to "keep it fun. People can spend more mental energy on their work, and get greater rewards and more innovative ideas, when they're enjoying what they do."

Walter is the middle child of Robert Walter, chairman and CEO of Cardinal Health Inc., which is Ohio's largest public company, based in Dublin. The younger Walter appreciated how his father involved him in his work by discussing business decisions, particularly the process of making Cardinal a publicly traded company in 1983, when Walter was a teenager.

"It was incredible exposure, even when, admittedly, we didn't understand everything that was going on," Walter said. "I knew I wanted to go into business, like my dad, but I knew I'd be independent from anything my father was doing. I have a ton of respect for my dad, but I wanted to do my own thing."

Robert Walter also equipped his three sons with the support of a close adult mentor outside the family. The senior Walter's good friend, Bob Gerbig, became Walter's mentor when he was 10 years old. Gerbig owned the marketing firm Gerbig/Snell Weisheimer (now GSW Worldwide), where Walter would eventually work.

First, however, Walter earned a degree in marketing and finance from Boston College. He then worked for Smith Barney on Wall Street for two years, ensuring he had the financial skills necessary to support a successful marketing business. At age 24, he returned to Columbus to work for Gerbig, eventually buying the business. In 2001, after overseeing the acquisitions of several complementary businesses, Walter led the launch of inChord, GSW's parent company.

"Bob gave me the real-life perspective on how somebody brings a culture to a company, how to treat people and be a real motivator," Walter said.

"Nobody does anything on their own. It's always a team," he continued. Walter recruited a group of 15 key managers with diverse backgrounds to lead the business units within inChord. "They're wonderful to work with. You can think with an open canvas," Walter explains.

In addition to his father and Gerbig, Walter credits his mother for exerting a great influence. "My mom was literally the backbone of the family. She was the strong voice for believing in yourself, for personal commitment and for having interests other than just business," Walter said.

Perhaps that's why Walter believes it's important for him to keep a balance among family (he and his wife have three young children), work and friends. He envisions his work legacy this way: "I'd like to build a company based on a culture of capability that serves clients successfully decades from now."

Dave Bianconi

President and CEO, Progressive Medical, Inc.

Words to live by:
"Don't neglect your faith and family ...they are your foundation."

Hometown: Wolfhurst, Ohio
First job: pulling weeds
Hobbies: gardening, landscaping, playing guitar
Favorite movies: "The Godfather," "Crash"
I am: "Determined."

Dave Bianconi is a down-to-earth kind of guy who credits his small-town roots and close family ties with keeping him that way. "Because I have been blessed with a humble upbringing, I'm able to keep things in perspective."

It would be easy for Bianconi to boast. He founded Progressive Medical in 1986. In its early days, the three-employee, $165,000 company sold medical equipment and supplies in Ohio. Today the Columbus company has evolved into a national, managed care and health-care cost-containment company that coordinates care for workers' compensation, auto-no-fault and personal-injury protection cases.

The company grew at such a rapid pace from 2000 to 2006 that Bianconi added 300 additional employees. In 2005 the company recorded $140 million in sales, a six-fold increase since 2000. They're on track to achieve $170 million in revenue in 2006.

What's the secret to his amazing success? "I'm not a micromanager. I delegate. I enjoy letting people do their own work, and I realize there's more than one way to do something. I believe others would say I'm very generous. I try to be almost too fair with everybody."

His family taught him a good work ethic, Bianconi said. "My father worked very hard, and my grandfather was always tinkering around with something and staying active. My mother worked hard at home. They instilled in me a sense of doing the right thing and the ability to let people see you laugh at yourself."

Bianconi grew up in a small town called Wolfhurst, near Bridgeport, Ohio, right in the middle of eastern Ohio steel country. After high school graduation, he didn't know yet what direction his work would take, so Bianconi tried millwork himself. The experience taught him what he did not want to spend his life doing.

"All I knew was that there weren't going to be a lot of opportunities around my small town besides millwork. Most of those guys had been there for 40 years," he said.

That's why Bianconi decided to enter The Ohio State University to study pharmacy. "I couldn't get past organic chemistry, so I switched to business. My uncle was an accountant who had his own firm," Bianconi said.

Bianconi earned his degree in 1976 and then worked for Harrop Industries for seven years. He took his next job at Medical Designs Company. "We sold a chronic-pain-management tool that was very effective for low-back pain. As a result, we got into workers' compensation," he said.

Bianconi recalls a particularly difficult business situation at another previous employer when he had to fight the Internal Revenue Service to make the payroll. "I came into the company, and it owed the IRS $250,000 in trust-fund taxes. Although I'd had nothing to do with how that happened, I worked out a payment plan and was following it when they came in and seized all our money.

"We had $50,000 in the bank that was already spent. Without it, I couldn't make our next payroll. So I went to the local IRS office and told them we were honoring our agreement, and that they were going to put 50 people out of work with their actions. They gave me the $35,000 I needed to make the payroll."

Bianconi hasn't needed that kind of bravado at Progressive. Because the company deals with the insurance industry—which is well known for its bureaucratic approach to claims payment—he set up a special system that gets Progressive's bills to the right people for payment.

Professional and personal ethics continue to guide him. "I saw everyone in my childhood always trying to do the right thing, so when I don't see that in business, I want to change it. I ask, 'Is it ethical? Is it self-serving or company serving?'"

If he could change one thing along his path, Bianconi said, "I would have liked to have been a doctor because I always wanted to help people. We do give people a better life here at Progressive."

Success for Bianconi comes from loving his work. "Money does alleviate some pain, but it's not happiness. Feeling that you're contributing to the well-being of people around you is success."

Randy Wilcox

Founder and Board member, SARCOM

Words to live by:
"Go for it—life is not a dress rehearsal."

Hometown: Charleston, W.Va.
First job: paper carrier
Hobbies: golfing, traveling, gardening, fitness
Favorite books: "Hedgehogging," Barton Biggs, "Fooled by Randomness," Nassim Taleb
Favorite movie: looking forward to the new movie, "We Are Marshall"
I am: "Active."

Randy Wilcox's career has been similar to the country roads in his home state of West Virginia—lots of surprise curves and more than a few ups and downs. An entrepreneur and salesman at heart, his passion for customer service started in the third grade, when he identified a need for a community newspaper in his neighborhood—and started it on his own.

"I remember teaching myself to type on an old manual typewriter so I could interview our neighbors and type their stories. Then I'd make 20 copies with a hectograph my grandmother had bought me," he remembers. Wilcox proudly sold subscriptions to these little papers for five cents each.

His passion for customer service eventually led him to start SARCOM in 1983 in Columbus, Ohio. The company sells, installs and maintains computer systems for business customers throughout the country. It also offers services such as asset management, product procurement, consulting, integration and technical support.

Although Wilcox is no longer involved in the day-to-day operations of SARCOM, he serves on its board and assists the management team. "I hope my legacy is that I revived customer service. It's a whole process that ultimately must become part of your culture, not just a program."

About his career, Wilcox said he remembers always seeking new opportunities to expand his skills. "I really never had a job I didn't like. I was always trying to be the best at whatever I chose to do at the time, and then I wanted to move on to the next opportunity."

He attended Marshall University in Huntington, W. Va., from 1967-1971. Although he enjoyed it, he couldn't see the connection between classes and a career. "I was bored with the classroom end of it. I started out in math and then moved to accounting. I kept changing my major—seven times in four years."

As part of his six-year obligation to the National Guard, Wilcox completed his active-duty requirement at Fort Knox. "I had one more semester left when I came back to Marshall, but it was the middle of the semester." Always one to stay busy, Wilcox used the time to help a friend with a marketing business in Columbus. The opportunity didn't work out, but Wilcox had another plan. A friend worked at Xerox and had challenged Wilcox to get a job there, too. So he did.

"I applied and ended up getting a job offer I wasn't sure I really wanted. My goal was just to prove I could get hired. Luckily, I accepted the position," he said.

For most of the next 10 years, Wilcox was the top salesperson in the office. "I'd been promoted to sales manager, and a guy came by one day and suggested I get myself one of those new PCs to help manage my sales staff."

That day would change his life. Wilcox remembers his experiences trying to purchase a PC. The three stores he visited that sold them at the time either didn't have the right equipment or the sales staff weren't properly trained. "I remember thinking to myself, 'This is too hard—no one's doing it right.' I was never very technical, but I understood sales and customer service."

The experience prompted him to quit his 10-year career at Xerox and buy his own PC franchise, which he opened in a local shopping mall in 1983. "It was the wrong franchise. They knew how to sell more franchises but not computers," Wilcox said. The store also struggled, because it didn't sell "big" names like IBM or Apple.

However, Wilcox didn't give up. In 1985 he bought an Inacomp franchise which proved to be a much better decision. With help from the new franchise, he gained an IBM distributorship and things took off. "We got out of retail and started selling direct to large companies," said Wilcox. He started the company with four employees; and at its peak, it employed nearly 3,000 people in 26 locations.

He believes his success is all due to customer service. Wilcox explained, "Like nearly all other businesses today, the technology business was very competitive. Everyone sold the same product at the same price. The only way we were able to differentiate ourselves was by taking better care of our customers than anyone else in the business."

Today SARCOM still takes its customer-centric philosophy to heart, even when it comes to hiring employees. During the interview process, the company looks for people who want to serve others. "Selecting and supporting the right people is the key," Wilcox said.

Wilcox instituted and conducted a mandatory customer-satisfaction meeting every month in each location so all of his employees could openly review their customer surveys ratings. "If there was a bad survey, the manager had 24 hours to make it right, and figure out how to prevent that particular thing from happening again in the future."

"Over the years, we saw many other organizations greatly improve their customer service by adopting our process into their culture. And that really got me excited," he said.

From his point of view, success is about being the best at whatever you do. "A lot of people sit around thinking and never try. The difference about successful people is that they try. Things may not work out, but they'll just try something else. If they are willing to admit it, most successful people have had one or more significant failures."

Always into something new, Wilcox stays busy exploring, planning and challenging himself with new opportunities, such as developing real estate and helping start a community bank. "I can't wait to get up every day and see what the day will bring. Every decade has been better than the last."

CHERYL KRUEGER

PRESIDENT AND CEO, CHERYL & CO.

Words to live by:
"Don't ever take a job for money. Take a job for passion."

Hometown: Bellevue, Ohio
First job: ticket taker at Cedar Point
Hobbies: flower gardening, walking, traveling
Favorite book: "Good to Great," Jim Collins
Favorite movie: "The English Patient"
I am: "Humble."

Cheryl Krueger has never forgotten her roots. She grew up on a dairy farm in northern Ohio where her social structure centered on church and farming. Today she uses her moral beliefs as her barometer in business.

"I'm very religious, and I'm proud of it," Krueger said. "I don't believe for a moment that I'm in control of my own destiny. I think God has plans for all of us. He also gave us all talents; how you leverage them is key."

Krueger has indeed made the most of her own talents. Using her grandmother's old-fashioned cookie recipe, she opened Cheryl's Cookies out of her kitchen in 1981. The company changed its name to Cheryl & Co. in 1988 to reflect an expanded product line that included gourmet baked goods and specialty gift items. 1-800-FLOWERS.com bought the company in 2005 for $40 million. Krueger has stayed on as president.

The sale of her company was one of Krueger's happiest moments. Up to that point, she had wondered whether her company's success would be equally valued by others. "It was great to see there was a lot of value in the eyes of other people. I've had the good fortune of still being able to work here without as much risk," she said. An even happier moment was having her son, Cavin, whom she describes as "the center of her life."

Krueger's love for retail sales began at Bowling Green State University in Ohio. She was studying teaching, her "lifelong ambition," when she accepted a summer job at the late Caryl Crane's clothing shop in Sandusky, Ohio. Crane was impressed with Krueger and asked her to come along on a buying trip to New York City. "She saw in me what I didn't realize, which was a real knack for retail. And I loved it. I changed my major to business," Krueger said.

Krane opened many retailing doors for Krueger. After early executive-level jobs in New York's retail industry, Krueger worked at The Limited in Columbus, Ohio. There she met businessman and developer Leslie Wexner, whom she still admires today. "He took fundraising and philanthropy to a new level. I learned a lot from him from a risk-taking standpoint," she said.

Krueger's grandmother also provided ample inspiration. "She was a phenomenal baker. She had a real keen sense of hard work, fairness and great moral fiber. And yet she had an incredibly compassionate side. She was very philanthropic. I learned the joy of giving from her," Krueger said

The moral fortitude she learned from her grandmother has shaped Krueger's leadership style. She describes herself as "very honest and trustworthy, inspiring and visionary." She believes others see her as humble and approachable. "It's important that you don't believe your own press," Krueger jokes.

She strives to be "the best but not the biggest. I think if you're going to choose to be the biggest in anything you want to do, there's a cost associated with that."

Krueger's view of success has changed over time. "Success when I started out was getting a well-paying job. Today my version of success is finding inner peace and happiness in what I'm doing, surrounding myself with people who have the same core values that I enjoy, and finding a balance in life."

However, success hasn't come without pain for Krueger. She talks openly about the untimely death of her business partner and her divorce from her first husband, both extremely painful experiences. "The hardest things for me have been the personal losses and deaths," she said.

Today Krueger stays motivated by her intense customer focus. "When you get it right, it's a rush. They vote every day with their money. When we win the vote, it's exciting," she explained. She is also heavily involved with many philanthropic programs. For example, Cheryl & Co. gives over two million cookies each year to local food banks, and their "Cookies for As" program allows students to bring their reports cards into the company's retail stores to receive a cookie for every "A" earned.

"I hope my legacy is that the business will do really well after I'm gone. And that it will live well beyond me," Krueger said.

David Meuse

Principal, Stonehenge Partners

Words to live by:
"Know who you are. Be willing to take risks, and understand that struggles will help build resiliency."

Hometown: Cairo, Ill.
First job: paper carrier
Hobbies: mountain climbing, exercising, horseback riding
Favorite book: "The Great Gatsby," F. Scott Fitzgerald
Favorite movie: "Zorba the Greek"
I am: "Empathetic."

David Meuse is motivated by creating things. "Implementing ideas is exciting. I enjoy seeing the connections and understanding how they fit. I admire excited, enthusiastic people who care about making an impact."

As for his own impact, he makes it quietly—by listening to others. "We don't spend enough time just being quiet and listening to someone else. I've never thought I was brilliant, but I also never thought my point of view was the only one." Meuse believes these listening skills, along with his ability to relate to others and willingness to take risks, are the strengths of his leadership.

His spirituality also guides the way. "Without it, it would be very hard to have peace of mind and understand where I fit in the scheme of things," he said.

Meuse is a principal in Stonehenge Partners, a private equity firm investing primarily in the Midwest, which started in August 1999 as a spin-off of Banc One Capital Holdings Corporation. Meuse and his partners manage $475 million in investments.

"Having my partners know I care about them is a very strong value. There's a saying that goes, 'Strength without gentleness is brutality, but gentleness without strength is sentimentality.' Both strength and caring are needed to make a good partnership," Meuse said.

Resiliency is another value that came in handy for Meuse. He, his three sisters and mother had the opportunity to live in many cities throughout the country. "I learned to adapt and work hard. My dad expected a lot, which in turn resulted in my good work ethic. I worked in manufacturing and roofing, caddied, and worked in a pro shop. I also serviced grocery stores for Beechnut Baby Food and sold insurance."

Despite his various jobs, Meuse didn't have any mentors until college. "I think it's really important for younger people to have mentors. It's important for them to learn, but it's also important for the older person to stay connected," he said.

After graduating from high school, Meuse entered John Carroll University in Cleveland and earned a bachelor's degree in political science. He also attended the Cleveland Marshall College of Law and the Securities Industry Institute at the Wharton Business School. Meuse thought he might go into politics, but a Jesuit priest who taught corporate finance instead led him into a career in the investment banking field.

Meuse began his investment banking career at Ball, Burge & Kraus in Cleveland, where he became partner at age 26. He later joined McDonald & Company Securities, Inc. as a full partner. Meuse founded Meuse, Rinker, Chapman, Endres & Brooks, a regional investment banking firm, in Columbus in 1981. He served as chairman and CEO.

In 1989 the firm was sold to Bank One Capital Holdings Corporation. Meuse then became chairman and CEO of the new corporation, which served as the holding company for the investment banking, merchant banking, securities brokerage, investment advisory and insurance activities of Bank One Corporation.

Meuse explains: "In the 10 years we were with Bank One, we built a 50-person firm into a 170-person firm. Bank One acquired our firm to consolidate and manage its investment banking and capital market units. In addition, we started a private equity and mezzanine business, ultimately making proprietary investments in excess of $1.5 billion. Our success in these areas prompted John B. McCoy, chairman of Bank One, to ask us to lead all non-bank investment-related business, including trust, insurance and retail brokerage activities.

"Those were the Camelot years for us. We always tried to make money for everyone, which we did."

In addition to his daily responsibilities at Stonehenge, Meuse serves as non-executive chairman of the board of Diamond Hill Investment Group, Inc., which has over $3 billion in assets. He also serves as vice-chairman of The Columbus Foundation, and on the boards of Kenyon College and State Auto Insurance, among others. He is also past-chairman of United Way of Franklin County and the Columbus Association for the Performing Arts.

"I've always been active in the community. I just want to make an impact. I enjoy creating an environment for people to reach their potential. I hope my legacy is that I brought entrepreneurial people into the nonprofit world, and they provided valuable mentoring," Meuse said.

Although his commitments are many, his energy remains high. "The question I have to answer is, 'How can I continue to increase my energy but not wear myself out?' When I was in my 30s I worked very hard and I wasn't detached enough to achieve true balance in my personal life. My worst times have always been when I've gone to excess in any single part of my life," Meuse said.

"Originally, success was about fear—I was afraid not to do well. Today success is about balance—balancing work, family, exercising, spirituality and reflection. I want to have enough balance so that I can continue to be energetic and close to my family—Mo, my loving wife of 37 years, my three children, their spouses and my grandchildren."

"I don't look back too much, but I do wish I would have had the wisdom I have today throughout my career."

Tammy Troilo-Krings

Chairman and CEO, Travel Solutions

Words to live by:
"Be persistent."

Hometown: Columbus, Ohio
First job: York Steak House
Hobbies: traveling, photography and doing arts/crafts with her children
Favorite books: anything by James Patterson
Favorite movies: "Braveheart," "Highlander"
I am: "Approachable."

Travel has been in Tammy Troilo-Krings' system since her childhood when she moved all around the world as an "Army brat" and dreamed of becoming an astronaut.

She considered joining the U.S. Air Force to fulfill her dream, but the former requirement for perfect eyesight prevented her from doing so. Instead, she earned an aeronautical engineering degree from The Ohio State University and helped build the B-1 bomber.

Troilo-Krings let her dreams take flight at the Columbus, Ohio, division of Rockwell North American Aviation Operations, where she worked on the space shuttle as well. "My experiences there taught me that I wanted to interact with people and solve problems. I have a knack for collaborating to figure things out."

During her five years at Rockwell, Troilo-Krings honed her collaborative skills by volunteering for a special project to solve production and budget issues relating to the B-1 Bomber. To meet the challenge, she formed a team representing the manufacturer's union, Rockwell management and the Air Force. The team consisted of 13 men, including a four-star general. Troilo-Krings, the only female member, was in her early 20s at the time.

"I volunteered out of complete, naïve ignorance," she laughs. "My boss hated me, and I was sure he was setting me up to fail. But it turned out to be a great opportunity because I learned to express my opinion and back it up."

Her segue into the travel industry began when she volunteered to leave Rockwell during layoffs. They didn't want her to leave. "I was ready for a change," she said. After taking the summer off, Troilo-Krings answered a newspaper ad for an account manager at a local travel agency. She got the job—and due to her operations expertise, wound up revising their entire reservation system to make it run more efficiently. "This helped me build credibility in a field where I was inexperienced," she said.

Troilo-Krings gained even more experience working at Wagonlit, American Express and Thomas Cook—all the while with her 3-year-old son in tow. "I was divorced, and as a single mom, I took my son everywhere. I commuted between Columbus, Manhattan and Boston for several years. So, I would strap him and his teddy bear on my suitcase and just roll him right along," she laughs.

She opened her own travel consulting firm, Troilo and Associates, in 1995. "It was a great time to start a business because the industry was turned upside down, and that was a compelling reason to listen to us. Corporate America had to decide the value of a travel agency."

A true entrepreneur, Troilo-Krings made her mark by developing a custom, menu-based model for corporate clients who wanted to outsource travel arrangements they couldn't make for themselves. She wanted to sell the model to local agencies, but they didn't appreciate her savvy.

"They thought I was trying to eliminate them, but I was trying to help them," she said. Undaunted, she opened a corporate travel agency of her own, Travel Solutions, in 1996. Troilo and Associates still operated as a separate consulting arm of the business. Today half her clients use full-service and half use the menu-based model. Central Ohio clients include American Electric Power and Huntington Bank.

Troilo-Krings remains motivated by the changing nature of the travel industry. "Change brings opportunity. I'm good at sorting out what new opportunities exist and how I can leverage them," she said.

The next opportunity arrived in May 2001 when Troilo-Krings launched her own crisis-management plan. It enabled her agents to locate and bring home travelers who become stranded in a foreign country. When Sept. 11 occurred, she shared the plan for free with many local agencies and corporations. "My primary guideline is to never compromise on ethics, and it's guided me well."

Troilo-Krings believes having a sense of humility, sharing responsibility for everyone's successes and failures, and being sensitive to others' feelings are her key strengths. "People here would tell you that I don't judge—that's part of our culture," she said.

Today the 40-employee, $100-million company is the nation's seventh-largest corporate travel agency. However, Troilo-Krings doesn't define herself strictly by the numbers. "I used to define success by money and what it buys. But now success is about balance, and realizing that I can be comfortable and not work myself to death."

Cameron Mitchell

President, Cameron Mitchell Restaurants

Words to live by:
"If it were easy, everybody would do it. Integrity takes years to build and days to ruin. Listen to your elders. Be driven by your values and principles."

Hometown: Cleveland, Ohio
Hobbies: golfing, traveling with family
Favorite book: "Good to Great," Jim Collins
Favorite movies: "Memphis Belle," "The Hunt for Red October," "Saving Private Ryan"
I am: "Enthusiastic."

Life took a wrong turn for 9-year-old Cameron Mitchell when his father left the family—Mitchell, his mother and two older brothers. Angry with his parents, Mitchell rebelled and started smoking in the seventh grade, advancing to drugs and alcohol by high school. In the tenth grade, he dropped out of school and ran away from home.

Barefoot and penniless, Mitchell returned home for his junior year of high school, stopped using drugs and found a job washing dishes at a local restaurant. "I had the 'can do' but not the 'will do' in me at that point," he explained. He was elected president of his senior class, but finished last in his class, attending summer school to graduate. "I was last there, too, but there was only one place to go from there."

After high school graduation in 1981, 93 percent of Mitchell's class went on to college. Mitchell took a $4.50/hour job as a cook for Max & Erma's restaurant in his hometown of Columbus, Ohio. "I was lazy; I cut corners. I was the worst guy in the kitchen at that point," Mitchell recalled. While on probation for tardiness in 1982, Mitchell experienced an epiphany in the kitchen during the pandemonium of a Friday shift.

"I looked down the line, and time froze. I knew I wanted to be in the restaurant business the rest of my life," he said.

Late that night after his double shift ended, Mitchell went home and wrote down his life's goals: to attend the Culinary Institute of America in Hyde Park, N.Y., and become an executive chef by age 23, a general manager by 24, a regional manager by 26, a vice president of operations by 30, and president of a restaurant company by 35.

"I woke my mom to share the goals with her. She looked relieved," Mitchell said. The next day, his work showed an immediate turnaround. "I went from working for beer money to working for a career. The 'will do' switch got turned on."

Mitchell accomplished all of his goals, after first being rejected by the Culinary Institute for his poor grades. He reapplied and was finally accepted because he took some college courses and earned straight A's. Today he serves on the school's board of trustees where he chairs its alumni committee. He's also the school's largest alumni donor.

A second epiphany launched Mitchell's drive to start his own restaurant company. Because he was unhappy with the management style and owners of the restaurant group he was then working for in Columbus, Mitchell sought investors for his dream. A first attempt failed when the location fell through, but Mitchell rallied. He raised $400,000 in the eleventh hour and started his business. All told, it took 14 months after Mitchell left his job before his first restaurant opened its doors.

"I knew I just needed that start," he said.

Today, Cameron Mitchell Restaurants is a $110 million company, with 2,500 employees in nine states. The company has 10 concept restaurants, a catering operation and a traditional Italian trattoria wine bar slated to open in spring 2007.

Success to Mitchell "is happiness—a great family and friends. It's a journey. It's also having a huge funeral." To ensure his company's success, Mitchell said, he focuses on his visionary skills and leadership ability. "I'm a very dynamic driver of the bus," he said. "We manage by committee, but there's no doubt in anyone's mind that I'm the commander in chief. I drive people nearly to the brink of exhaustion, but they know I care deeply about them and their success."

Mitchell does indeed prioritize his employees' needs through the company's culture and philosophy. One of the company's core values is that "associates come first." Mitchell explains: "We don't think we have a direct relationship with our guests. We believe that if we take care of our people, they take care of our guests, and our guests take care of our company. That's very, very different than most restaurant companies."

This restaurateur has few regrets, except that he wishes he'd attended a four-year college and enjoyed the camaraderie of fraternity life. Though he says he's still motivated by fear and the need to provide for his family, he describes himself as "a 'good-time Charlie.' Everyone who knows me knows I look at the bright side of life."

In addition to growing his business and enjoying his family, Mitchell has big dreams for his legacy. "Maybe one day we'll put the 'Cameron Mitchell School of Hospitality Management' next to the Fisher College of Business at Ohio State University."

Mary Margaret Leavitt

"The Flag Lady," The Flag Lady's Flag Store

Words to live by:
"Don't forget those who pulled up beside you and helped you dig your well."

Hometown: Columbus, Ohio
First job: 13 years old, janitor at R&S Dime Store
Hobbies: anything related to "God and country," spending time with family, keeping up with politics
Favorite book: Bible
Favorite movie: "My Fair Lady"
I am: "Patriotic."

Patriotic roots run deep in Mary Leavitt's family. "It's in my blood!" she proclaims. She'll proudly tell you of relatives who served in the Revolutionary War, the Civil War and World War II, including her "beloved brother Bobby," who was 16 years older.

Growing up, she thought everyone flew the flag. "We took the train every Friday to Indianapolis to visit the family. I saw the white-haired ladies give their seats to the servicemen. I remember walking across the park, from one grandparents' home to the other grandparents' home, and seeing the band marching by, with men in uniforms carrying the flag, and everybody stopping to put their hands over their hearts. The men took off their hats and placed them over their hearts."

Today, Leavitt always gives 4"x6" U.S.A. flags away because her "Grandma

Haley" always carried a flag in her purse. She recalled, "One day I asked her, 'Grandma Haley, why do you always carry that flag in your purse?' She replied, 'Who knows, I may get a chance to wave it today.'"

In high school, Leavitt portrayed the Statue of Liberty in a play. She listened to nearly all of President Franklin Roosevelt's "fireside chats." She led the Pledge of Allegiance at the 1996 Republican National Convention. Many neighborhood civic groups bear her name on their founders' list, and she lobbies for small-business issues.

Her flag-waving turned into flag-selling in 1978, while living in Libertyville, Ill. One of Leavitt's sons was serving in the U.S. Navy during the Iranian crisis, and she tried to buy a flag to fly in his honor and in remembrance of the American hostages. Finding no flags for sale locally, she convinced a wholesaler to sell to her as a retail customer—and her spur-of-the-moment decision to ask for 12 more launched her business. She must have appeared earnest. The vice president let her take the flags on just her promise to return with the money the following week—she'd left home that day with no cash and no checks.

Not long after that first flag purchase, the *Chicago Sun Times* wrote a story about Leavitt who was selling U.S. flags out of the trunk of her car. The headline dubbed her "The Flag Lady," which she embodies today.

On the surface, Leavitt's story holds the best of the "American dream." Dig a little deeper, and Leavitt reveals a life challenged by poverty, hard times and an unyielding mother—yet uplifted by a loving father, his two sisters and faith.

Born in 1936 to her German mother and Irish, railroader father, Leavitt grew up north of "Flytown," a poor, culturally diverse neighborhood in Columbus, Ohio. Her doting father called her "Spud" because she loved potatoes. He died of cancer when she was just 13 years old, which forced the young Leavitt to find work to support the family.

The pressure was immense; her mother also wanted her to quit school just as she had also done, at the same age, when her own father had died. "I wanted to honor my father and the commitment I'd made to him that I'd finish high school. And I also wanted to honor my mother by working to support the family."

Leavitt honored both by convincing her mother that she could work three jobs and go to Columbus North High School, a college-preparatory high school, promising she would "never cause her any trouble." The young Leavitt was already demonstrating perseverance, determination and advocacy—her lifelong leadership qualities.

Many people "stepped up beside me," she says. In high school, a teacher helped her get a job with Hugh Huntington, a prominent attorney, which led to a 30-year career as a legal secretary, ending up as administrative assistant to Arthur Vorys, grandson of the founder of a renowned law firm.

After high school, Leavitt (whose maiden name was Haley) married classmate Tom Leavitt, with whom she had three children. The family moved to Illinois, returning to Columbus after "the Flag Lady" was born. Leavitt again worked for Vorys, but not for long. At the time, the local Veterans' Memorial facility was about to christen a new wing—but no money had been set aside for flags. Convinced she could find a sponsor, Leavitt called on Chrysler dealer Bob Caldwell, one of Vorys' friends.

Caldwell agreed to foot the bill for 8'x12' flags. When Leavitt arrived for payment, Caldwell asked her why she wasn't selling flags. She quickly listed her obstacles: no money for an office or inventory, and no car to drive to make sales calls. In response, Caldwell offered her an office beside his own, a business loan and the use of a car.

Two weeks later, she opened for business, working out of her new car and her basement. When her home became overrun with flags and supplies, her husband said, "I think you need a storefront." As the company grew, Leavitt hired her own seamstresses to produce custom flags and banners.

Now 70 and a widow, Leavitt strives to keep the meaning of the flag alive and to achieve her vision of promoting "God and country." She enjoys a lively relationship with her seven grandchildren and chuckles when she tells how her granddaughter introduces herself as "The Flag Lady, Jr."

"I thank God I was born in the United States of America," Leavitt says. "I can't think of a better gift."

Mike Rosati

President, Rosati Windows

Words to live by:
"It's always about customer service."

Hometown: Columbus, Ohio
First job: 7 years old, in his grandfather's grocery store
Hobbies: golfing, practicing martial arts
Favorite book: "The Art of Zen," Stephen Addiss
Favorite movie: "Dr. Strangelove"
I am: "Passionate."

Walk into Rosati Windows' new 52,000-square-foot headquarters, and you can't miss the huge scrapbooks displayed in the lobby. They're packed with thank-you letters from happy, satisfied customers—ample evidence that the guiding principles of customer care and service listed on the Rosati Windows' Web site aren't just empty promises.

"I live, eat and breathe customer service. And if we make a mistake, I will do everything I can to fix it," said Mike Rosati, the company's president. What's the source of his personal mission for customer service? "The whole way we do business today comes from my grandfather."

The elder Rosati came alone to America when he was just 13, an escapee from a prisoner-of-war camp during Dictator Benito Mussolini's infamous "Reign of Terror." Rosati eventually founded the Rosati grocery store chain in Columbus.

The store had an auspicious beginning. "My father and his sister were playing with matches in the house and burned it down. My grandfather used the insurance money to buy his first grocery store—it had an apartment on top." Rosati explained, "My grandfather built a business out of nothing. He was my greatest influence."

Young Rosati started working with his grandparents at age 7, "standing on a Pepsi crate and working the cash register." Seven years later, he became a butcher, a job he quickly grew tired of. "I'd had enough. When you cut meat, you smell like meat, you look like meat. You're covered in blood."

When he turned 19, Rosati decided to join his father in the real estate development business. But after the energy crisis hit in the 1970s, he left the field to sell windows. He was recruited by The Window Factory, which he ran for 15 years before founding Rosati Windows in 2001.

"The best time of my life was the day I turned the key and walked into my new place. Even now, when I'm feeling blue, I get up and walk out to the plant, and I think, 'This is pretty cool.' And I haven't lost that feeling," Rosati said.

In addition to customer service, taking care of his employees is Rosati's other priority. "They're the reason I get out of bed in the morning. I've watched them grow up, get married and have kids. We don't have turnover, so I think they feel that my leadership style is something they haven't seen before. I'm very honest, very sincere and very passionate."

Rosati's definition of success revolves around the happiness he gets watching his company "run like a smooth machine," and in knowing his employees are happy. "We have a lot of respect for one another," he said.

Emphasizing customer service and employee satisfaction has been a powerful combination when it comes to the company's success. In just six years, the company exceeded $14 million in sales in its custom replacement-window division. A subsidiary of Rosati Windows, Rooms of Distinction, opened for business in 2004 with just 10 people and has already surpassed $1 million in sales. To further enhance customer service, in 2006 Rosati Windows acquired The Fix-It Crew, a two-year-old company that provides a wide variety of commercial and home repair services.

Rosati's accomplishments helped him earn the Columbus Chamber of Commerce Small Business Leader Award in November 2005. It was a bittersweet moment for Rosati. "My dad was a proud papa. He went to all of my award events, except the last one. He was gone." He credits his father for helping him along the way to his current success.

His father's death in November 2005 has proven to be Rosati's most difficult time. "I'm not sure that I've overcome it, or that I ever will. But I've learned not to take life for granted. I take life more seriously now. Since I was 7 years old, I've never taken Saturdays off from work. But I did for the first time in May," he added.

Although he wouldn't change anything about his own personal or professional life, Rosati said, "I have a real issue with how businesses treat their customers. Customer service is in the toilet. I wish people would wake up and go back to doing business how it used to be done. You can be honest and still be profitable."

Nick Soulas

President, Jolly Pirate Donuts

Words to live by:
"For any field you enter or job you take, make sure you enjoy at least 50 percent of it. You've got to eat—that's the other half. If you're not happy with the first half, pick something else or you will be unhappy."

Hometown: a village near Sparta, Greece
First job: working in a pharmacy
Hobbies: gathering with friends, often to eat and play cards
Favorite "read": trade magazines, Kiplinger letter
I am: "Genuine."

"You have to taste the bitterness to appreciate the sweetness," says Nick Soulas, founder and president of Jolly Pirate Donuts. His philosophical advice is punctuated and authenticated in some way by his Greek accent—and, of course, by the image of his company's tasty treats.

Now 72, Soulas grew up in the 1930s and 1940s with two sisters and two brothers in a rural village about 40 kilometers from Sparta, Greece (one sister and one brother now live in Columbus, Ohio, near Soulas). Their father transported oil and traded it for any commodity they needed. "Of course," Soulas noted, "you could also find anything at a price in the black market."

Soulas remembers tending sheep once in his village and admiring a new highway installed by the government in place of a path—"It wasn't even a road before." He was fascinated with it, wondering where it led, who had built it and how it was designed. "In a small village, you didn't see much," he said. He dreamed of becoming an engineer or an architect.

Education was also a dream for Soulas. "I was hungry to learn anything I could." He completed a sixth-grade education in his village, but his family couldn't afford to send him to the high school in Sparta. Instead, his father sent the 12-year-old Soulas to Tripoli to live and work with a friend who was a pharmacist. "I was chosen to leave, and I wanted to leave," he said. "In those days, it was legal for the pharmacists to do everything—give first aid, prescribe medicine, give shots, pump stomachs. I learned to do it all."

"I sort of grew up in that field," said Soulas. However, without an education he couldn't be licensed to work on his own. So, after five years in Tripoli, he decided to immigrate to the United States; jobs in Greece were scarce due to the impact of the German/Italian occupation during World War II and the Greek civil war. Soulas' aunt in Boston petitioned for him to join her and her family; he arrived in New York on September 23, 1952.

Once in Boston, Soulas found a manufacturing job that paid 75 cents an hour. In the afternoons he'd use his bicycle to deliver Greek newspapers shipped from New York, which eventually earned him more money. Manufacturing layoffs found Soulas standing one day in a "mile-long unemployment line, from morning until afternoon." Once he reached the front of the line, he decided not to accept unemployment but to find another job instead.

Fate, perhaps, led him to a friend who was working in a Dunkin' Donuts store. The manager hired Soulas for $1 per hour as a porter to clean up and mop the floor. He started on April 15, 1954—Easter Sunday. "I thought it wasn't a good thing to work on Easter, but I had a job to start, so I did."

Still hungry for knowledge, Soulas stayed after his shifts to help the bakers make the donuts. When a baking position opened up, Soulas said, "I was given a chance. The elderly manager took me under his wing. I was willing to do anything." He did, and he learned how the business operated, too. In 1957, Smith Management Corporation in Chicago recruited Soulas and his manager to open a new donut shop in Detroit. Next, Soulas went to Chicago and opened 17 more, then traveled the country as 'troubleshooter' for various companies.

"I didn't grow up with children my own age. I grew up with people who were 30, 40, 50—even 60 years older than me. I listened to their stories and accomplishments, and I learned from them as great mentors. I developed a life with good ethics. I suppose I had a good manner about me," Soulas said, recognizing that his abilities to work well with all people, be honest and develop lasting relationships are skills that led to his success.

That's why, in 1961, having had enough of traveling, Soulas opened his own donut business in the Columbus neighborhood of Whitehall. Within nine years, he wanted to expand his company, then called Jolly Rogers. First, he had to choose a new name because Jolly Rogers Steakhouse in California had registered the title. Thus, Jolly Pirate Donuts was born.

"Though I've had some success in business, my biggest success was my marriage," said Soulas. When he first met his wife, she was a bridesmaid in his sister's wedding in Montreal. A matchmaking uncle lied to both of them about the other's age (he was 10 years older) until Soulas proposed. "I became a family man with three children, and now I have eight grandchildren. I fed my children; my wife raised them. I told them, 'Anything you are, you owe to your mother. You never went hungry—you owe that to me.' My children respect me."

Success, to Soulas, "is in the eye of the beholder. If I have one donut and one cup of coffee today, and tomorrow I have two donuts and two cups of coffee, then maybe that's success."

"I'm not a materialistic individual," he continued. "I don't need a fancy car. If it has four wheels, I turn the key and it starts, and it stops when I press on the brake, then that's OK. If I see something that bothers me, I will step in and try to do something." That's why he ran for mayor of the city of Whitehall in 2003. "I lost, but I was hoping to win because I thought I had something to contribute."

One thing that Soulas gives, and expects in return, is loyalty. In 1964, his store was on a city road slated to be widened from two to four lanes. Expecting business to drop off, Soulas asked his vendors to help by extending his credit to get through the tough period. "All but one creditor helped me," Soulas proudly recalled. "The one who didn't came asking for money after agreeing to help. I paid the $50 or so to settle the account and asked them to come get their equipment. I thought it was best to part ways."

Overcoming challenges and giving back to those around him have created what Soulas sees as his legacy: a great family, work in the Greek community (including taking the lead on designing the new Greek Orthodox Church in Columbus) and activity in many clubs. Still going strong, he says, "The best time is now!"

Charles Penzone

President, Charles Penzone Inc.

Words to live by:
"Don't ever do it for the money. Do it because you love it."

Hometown: Grandview Heights, Ohio
First job: neighborhood grocery store
Hobbies: wine, food, traveling, photography
Favorite book: "Atlas Shrugged," Ayn Rand
Favorite movies: "Raging Bull," "The Usual Suspects"
I am: "Intense."

Charles Penzone has been in the beauty business for 43 years, 37 of which have been spent as a business owner. It's been a labor of love. Penzone said, "Growing a company is very close to child rearing. It's very dear to your heart. My motivation is to protect, embellish and enrich the brand."

Indeed, Penzone is passionate about his namesake company. "I can't say enough about the brand, which is 37 years old. It's taken that long to make it what it is. And I intend to protect it in any way, shape or form."

Penzone, who owns some of the world's largest salons and day spas, knew by the time he was 16 what his career would be. "It wasn't uncommon for a second-generation Italian-American male to go into barbering or beauty, or the restaurant or construction business," Penzone said.

At the time, several of Penzone's relatives already had their own salons and barber shops. "I looked at them and thought 'I can do that. And I can do a couple of things that no one else is doing.'" He started cosmetology school one week after graduating from Grandview High School in 1963. He attended Otterbein

College in Westerville. Penzone opened his first business, Charles Penzone Incorporated, in 1969.

During those early years in business, Penzone said he was self-motivated. While he didn't really have a mentor, he's quick to credit those who've helped him along the way. "I've been blessed to surround myself with incredible, talented people. Plus, I'm not afraid to ask questions," he added.

He continued, "I think I've put together an organization that is good for those who embrace it. Our people understand that there are great benefits to being a part of this brand."

By 1991, Penzone had consolidated five of his nine Columbus locations to open the first Grand Salon in Dublin—18,000 square feet of hair-styling and manicure stations, spa treatment rooms, a training room, and a private garden. The second Grand Salon, at 20,000 square feet, opened in Gahanna in 1996 and was the largest of its kind in the world.

The company has since expanded to include MAX The Salon (two locations), Q Salon & Day Spa, and The Studio by Charles Penzone. Combined, the Penzone salons serve more than 500,000 clients each year.

How does Penzone define his incredible success? "My success was due to the great people who I surrounded myself with, who were smarter and more creative than I was. After that, success is predicated upon a wife and children, and friends and co-workers. But after the coffers are full, it comes down to how you're thought of," he said.

Success didn't come without its share of hard times, however. Penzone said, "I nearly lost everything in 1989. Not because the brand had failed in anyway, but because I had failed as a manager. I took things for granted. But we overcame a difficult time due to an incredible brand and even more incredible associates and professionals who rallied behind the brand." Perhaps this struggle is why, looking back on his career, he said the one thing he would change is he "would have managed things better. There's room to improve on how you manage day-to-day life, and you keep working at it. I still keep working at it to this day."

He credits his brand with saving the company. "The brand was so strong it was able to withstand the pressure," Penzone said. "I learned that a great brand and good people can overcome certain obstacles in business."

Penzone himself undeniably had something to do with the turnaround. He said he's "honest, fair and brutally protective of the brand." How would others describe him? "I hope my friends would say, 'he's a loyal and trusted friend.' I hope my enemies would say, 'he's a nightmare.'"

As for a legacy, Penzone says, "The last phrase in our mission statement is 'And it will last for at least 100 years.' My leadership legacy will be the perpetuation of this company. We're 37 percent of the way to 100 years. The foundation is laid to be able to do that."

Still, the best time of Penzone's life is now. He said, "I'm blessed to have an incredible relationship with my wife and children. It's something I cherish. In addition to my family, my joy comes from this company and the people in it. I don't have a problem with Monday mornings at all. Coming to work is incredible."

Larry Clark

CEO and President, Made From Scratch

Words to live by:
"Be passionate about what you do. When you love what you do, it's not work anymore."

Hometown: Bay Village, Ohio
First job: 12 years old, selling his artwork
Hobbies: searching eBay for deals, playing "Call of Duty" online
Favorite movie: "Tommy Boy"
I am: "Passionate."

When he moved to Columbus, Ohio, 7-year-old Larry Clark envisioned becoming an artist who expressed himself through many mediums. In fact, he was selling his own artwork by age 12. Two years later he sold art on consignment, using his welding skills to create statues from a huge assortment of his father's nuts and bolts. One of Clark's dog statues sold for $20 in the first five minutes at a local art show. When he reproduced it at home later, he cried because he realized his creative process would have to become a manufacturing one if he were to make any money. He knew then he'd never become an artist. "That was a huge disappointment for a 14-year-old," he said.

As luck would have it, Clark discovered his passion for the art of food preparation just two years later. He was 16 and looking for a summer job in retail, with no luck. At the end of a long day spent knocking on doors and pounding the pavement, he decided to apply at a local restaurant, thinking his family's experience in the food business was enough to prepare him for a job. Unbeknownst to Clark, the chef with whom he interviewed knew his father and decided to hire Clark.

"It turns out I didn't know a thing then," Clark laughed, recalling how he slipped around the kitchen that night because he was still wearing the smooth-soled dress shoes from his job hunt.

The best coincidence of the day was yet to come. Clark's parents arrived at the restaurant for dinner and were highly surprised to learn from the chef about their son's new job. "Up to that point I'd shown an avid interest in eating, not cooking," he quipped.

Clark could have claimed he inherited his desire to work in the food business. His mother was a dietician who ran the test kitchen for Worthington Foods and later ran the tasting lab at Ross Laboratories, both in Columbus. Her father was a German chef who trained in Hamburg in the early 1900s and cooked for the ship he took to immigrate to America. Clark's father earned a master's degree in food technology, and his grandmother ran the kitchen for the United Methodist Church in Lima and produced many cookbooks.

Nonetheless, it was that summer job that convinced Clark he'd be in the food business for life. "It was an all-absorbing, driving passion," he said. His boss, the chef who hired him, mentored Clark and suggested he should either attend the Culinary Institute of America in Hyde Park, N.Y., or seek a variety of jobs that would teach him the same skills while he was getting paid. Clark followed the second option.

At 17, Clark was promoted to night sous chef at the restaurant. "I had to grow a moustache to appear older and have more clout with older staff who reported to me." He was an executive chef at 19 and studied classical French cooking techniques at Columbus restaurants in his 20s.

By the early 1980s, Clark was looking for a new direction in his career and considered heading to Colorado. Fate stepped in again. At the time, Clark's father and a partner operated a food service business for a country club. The duo also ran a catering business, called Made From Scratch, on the side. Business lagged, and Clark's father was ready to sell.

Clark bought the business, seeing opportunities for growth in both the banquet and catering sides of the business. "I never believed in reinventing the wheel," he said, so he toured an established catering company in the Washington, D.C., area for ideas on how to model his new company.

The rest is history. Today Made From Scratch Events is a full-service catering and event-planning company that occupies 56,000 square feet in four buildings in

Dublin, Ohio. Its in-house divisions handle every detail from food to flowers, entertainment, linens, equipment and the facility itself. "We produce everything customized to our customers' wants and needs. We're also expanding our range of event planning services to include everything related to the event plan, its execution and its marketing," Clark said. He plans to rebrand the new venture as MFS (Made From Scratch) Events.

Creativity, passion and "great beginner's luck," Clark says, helped him accomplish his dreams. "It doesn't hurt to have a deep voice, too," he joked. Though others may see him as very aggressive, Clark says, "That's a problem because I embody the classic passive-aggressive temperament of an artist."

He strives to act within his personal guidelines for business and life: "Lead by example. Apply yourself vigorously at all times. Anything worth doing is worth doing well."

Clark takes a philosophical look at his life. "I started out as an artist, emoting through many mediums. Then I discovered food arts and the art of business. Now I realize that my life is my art, and it's an ongoing project."

Jim Hopkins

Co-owner and CEO, Hopkins Printing

Words to live by:
"Do unto others as you would have them do unto you."

Hometown: Boissevain, Va.
First job: paper carrier
Hobbies: reading, boating at Buckeye Lake, spending time with his grandchildren
Favorite book: Bible
Favorite movie: "Gone With the Wind"
I am: "Pragmatic."

Jim Hopkins started his first print shop in his garage in 1974 with a $2,000 bank loan and a $1,000 gift from his mother. Two years later he opened Hop-To Printing, a small printing business in German Village. The company has grown from those humble beginnings 30 years ago to become one of the leading printing companies in Central Ohio, with over $16 million in annual sales.

The path to a printing career wasn't apparent early in Hopkins' life. Growing up in Pittsburgh, Hopkins held a variety of jobs, including running a paper stand, setting pins in a bowling alley and counseling at the YMCA. "I learned something from every job I had. But I didn't really know what I wanted to be," he said.

"When I was in high school I read some career counseling material that said a good field was aviation. My family didn't necessarily see the long-term value of education, and I was a product of my family. So I went into the military. I benefited greatly from the structured environment, but I didn't end up in aviation. So as it turned out, I spent four years in the military without furthering my career path."

There was one other important benefit: While stationed in Canada, Hopkins met and married his wife, Arnie. Newly married, Hopkins worked at Columbus Stove before taking a job at Timken Roller Bearing Company, where he worked for 12 years. Hopkins said, "I realized I was in the wrong area if I ever wanted to be more than just a cog in the wheel. I had actually tried to escape the manufacturing arena when I went to a drafting school a year earlier, but I wasn't able to make as much money per hour as I did at my factory job."

Hopkins started each day at Timken and after work each afternoon went door-to-door selling Fuller Brushes. He said, "I learned sales from the school of hard knocks. I learned how to give presentations, handle rejections and work with customers."

Besides drafting, Hopkins was interested in photography and printing. He had met someone at Timken who had a small newsletter and photography business and printed his own copies from a mimeograph machine. The process intrigued Hopkins. He said, "I had training as a draftsman. The core of printing is photography, and I knew that process from having my own dark room and producing both film and pictures. And I also had a fair mechanical ability. What I really had was the core skill set for the printing industry."

Hopkins bought a small press and started printing for his church and some local business clients in his garage at night. He had a friend who was the chairman of the Metallurgical Association who allowed Hopkins to print their monthly newsletter. This was a great start for the small business.

When it came time to take the print shop out of the garage, Hopkins purchased a quick-copy camera and opened Hop-To Printing just south of downtown Columbus. He continued working at Timken for the first year. During the day, Jim's wife, Arnie, took walk-in orders, which he continued to print at night. Sleep must have been hard to come by in those days, but Hopkins chalks it up to "doing what had to be done" to support his family and invest some extra money into his business.

Hopkins credits one of his first customers, Jim Bannister, with helping him further his career and making his shop successful. Bannister was not only a source of work, but a great business role model, who was willing to teach and guide Hopkins with his new printing business.

Hopkins said, "Success is when a person has adequate material things to sustain a lifestyle that makes them happy. You don't have to be wealthy to do that; I think that if a person can be at peace with themselves and their family and friends, then that person is successful. I really believe that if you do the things you should do today, then tomorrow will take care of itself. If you can string enough winning days together, in the end you'll win."

He also credits his wife of 43 years for his success. "I'd go back and do it all over again just to meet her. She's a wonderful person," he said. "Like so many marriages, in many ways we're opposites, but we've found a way to make a whole. She's always been there, from Day One, to do whatever was helpful."

Hopkins said his organizational skills, personal discipline, vision and goal-orientation are his strongest leadership skills. He believes his employees would describe him as "disciplined, a good negotiator and fairly easy to work with."

Overall, Hopkins said, "I would change very few things about my life. I wouldn't want to take any chances and mess up what I have today. I'd be willing to go down this road again."

When asked what his legacy will be, Hopkins says, "What I've done, although it wasn't my intention, was to live the American dream. I started a business in a garage that's become a successful, multi-million dollar company. Not too many people have been fortunate enough to have done that. Things have worked in my favor."

ARTIE ISAAC

CHAIRMAN, YOUNG ISAAC, INC.

Words to live by (from Chaim Potok): "Choose a friend; acquire a teacher."

Hometown: Columbus, Ohio
First job: paper carrier
Hobbies: writing, public speaking, serving on community boards
Favorite book: Bible
Favorite movie: "Words That Hurt, Words That Heal: How to Choose Words Wisely and Well," Rabbi Joseph Telushkin
I am: "Curious."

Artie Isaac, president of Columbus advertising agency Young Isaac, Inc., is on a quest for self-discovery. "At 46, I have not figured out what my contribution's going to be. And I'm only now starting to say if I'm going to have one, I'd better figure it out. I'm happy to be a late bloomer."

Isaac grew up in Bexley, Ohio, and graduated from The Columbus Academy, a country day-school. He studied teaching and earned an English degree from Yale. Isaac headed next to New York "for a weekend, but I stayed for eight years." During those years, he earned an MBA in marketing from Columbia University and worked for two New York City advertising agencies. He returned to Columbus in 1990 to join a management buy-out of an advertising business, which was reflagged "Young Isaac." Five years later, he bought out the founder, Brooks Young.

During Isaac's first 15 years at Young Isaac, the agency was often short on cash and long on credit. "The business was not performing. We produced moments of brilliance for our clients, but the financial results were unimpressive. After 15 years, I thought, 'I'm not earning enough for the aggravation. I'm going to quit and go home.'" A long-time silent partner, Henry Hauser, dissuaded him from leaving. "He told me, 'You own the company. If you don't like the people, change them. If you don't like what you do, do something else. But you can't run away. You are Young Isaac.' It had never occurred to me that I had so much authority over the company. I had graduated from business school, but missed the class where they told us, 'Do something about it.'"

Isaac stayed at Young Isaac. He decided to refine his management skills through some career coaching, but he soon realized that he was no manager. "I found out very quickly that I like having objectives, but I don't like enforcing them on others," Isaac admits.

Though career counselors at Jewish Family Services first encouraged him to work on his weaknesses, Isaac said no. "I was finished working on my weaknesses. I thought it was unlikely that, after 15 years, I'd suddenly become a superior manager." He hired a CEO, Mary Kall, to manage the agency, and he shifted his focus. "I'm working on my strengths," he says. "Now I'm getting in touch with my emotional core: how I feel about things, what's important to me, do I like what I'm doing—things I've never asked myself. I'm working harder than ever and am much more valuable to Young Isaac and its clients."

In addition to his duties at Young Isaac, Isaac is committed to "helping others to discover their own essence." He teaches ethics to seventh graders at Temple Israel and creativity to MBA candidates at The Ohio State University. He is heavily involved with "helping others find creative solutions to life's problems" at Jewish Family Services, where he is chairman of the board—as well as a grateful client.

Whether at his agency or at JFS, Isaac believes his humility, humor and a "desire to debate and question what I'm hearing" are his three strongest leadership qualities. Strong ethics are another guiding force.

"We are a weird ad agency in that we work only for principled clients who are selling important things—like health care, financial services, education—to people who are afraid to buy them because they don't know how," Isaac said.

On creativity, Isaac shares, "So many people have creativity beaten out of them. The whole essence of it is redeveloping in ourselves the freedom to be wrong." This can often be what he describes as an emotional and messy process that poses its own problems. "In our current culture, we reward creativity but we punish a lack of control. And because we punish this lack of control, it's very difficult to get people back to an emotional, creative approach." In his own life, Isaac seems willing to embrace the risk.

When asked about his personal guidelines, Isaac is quick to remove a laminated card from his wallet. It's his copy of the Isaac family's mission statement, first crafted in 2004 by Isaac, his wife and two children. "It has a picture of a panda bear, because our daughter liked it. Our mission is to continue to strengthen our minds, our bodies, our spirits, our family and our friendships through cooperative, vigorous living in our home, schools, work and community. Our vision is to create rich, creative, Jewish lives in a peaceful home. Creativity begins at home. After all, we've 'made' people!"

NANCY KRAMER

FOUNDER AND CEO, RESOURCE INTERACTIVE

Words to live by:
"Find the time and a peaceful place to block out the noise that sidetracks you and listen to your inner voice. Have the courage to trust your gut."

Hometown: Columbus, Ohio
First job: cashier at Kroger
Hobbies: watching her children's sports, reading, working out, eating healthfully
Favorite books: "Growing a Business," Paul Hawken, "Built to Last," "Good to Great," Jim Collins, "The World Is Flat," Thomas L. Friedman
Favorite movies: "Sound of Music," "Out of Africa"
I am: "Courageous."

When she was a young girl, Nancy Kramer's father sold Keebler cookies, and he often took her along as he stocked orders in local grocery stores. "He taught me that Nabisco was the 'evil empire' and that Oreo cookies were poison!" she laughs. "I'd poke holes in the Nabisco bags to try to help my dad sell more Keebler cookies. I still feel guilty about doing that. I didn't eat an Oreo until I was out of college."

Today Kramer knows more sophisticated ways of promoting her favorite products. She's the founding and driving force behind Resource Interactive, a multi-million-dollar, international marketing powerhouse in Columbus, Ohio. The company's clients are among the most well known in the world: Apple, Procter & Gamble, Hewlett-Packard, Shaw Industries, Victoria's Secret, Wal-Mart and Coca-Cola, to name a few. You may even be familiar with her work, since Resource created Super Bowl commercials for Victoria's Secret and CompuServe.

Kramer started her career by studying journalism and then working in co-op advertising for a Columbus radio station, following in her older brother's footsteps. "I probably should have considered other fields that I was interested in, like veterinary medicine or education, but I stayed with what was in front of me."

It was a good choice. Within a few years, two manufacturing representatives noted her successful co-op work and recruited her to help them create a new company that would market products for a then-three-year-old company—Apple Computer. "At that time Apple was very technical and not very promotional," said Kramer, reflecting on how her skills would affect the new company.

However, before accepting the offer, the 26-year-old Kramer had interviewed for the first sales position with another start-up company—MTV. "I thought it was one of the dumbest ideas I'd ever heard. Who'd ever want to watch music on TV?" she laughed. "When people tell me I have great vision, I have to laugh and say, 'Let me tell you about the vision I didn't have!'"

Working with Apple, she said, "was a really great opportunity"—to say the least. The company agreed to pilot her co-op advertising efforts for a year in five states. Within nine months, impressive results prompted Apple to ask her to expand the program for the entire country. She did it for 17 years, helping Apple and its retailers launch every new product, including the Macintosh. In 1984, Apple brought its sales in-house, eliminating reps like Kramer's partners. The next year, she bought them out, becoming the sole owner of Resource Interactive. She then moved on to her next advertising coup, which was creating Apple's strategy for selling desktop publishing and the new concept of laser printers.

"The reason I love what I do is that I love the folks here in the business. I learn something new from them every day. I am so blessed to have a terrific group of people," Kramer said. "I love seeing people grow and change and meet their own definition of success. It's a never-ending continuum."

She continued: "Personally and professionally, success to me is being able to have my values and life in alignment. It sounds simple, but it's hard to calibrate. I work hard at this—it doesn't come naturally. When I was younger, my dad really built me up, but my mom and brother used to tease me about being a 'dumb blonde.' I'm highly sensitive, and I took them literally. It dragged me down. I was in my 40s before I could look in the mirror and overcome it. That was a really big accomplishment."

Also, she said, after her divorce, "I learned to really listen to the voice inside of me and trust my gut, though I wouldn't wish divorce upon anyone."

Kramer grew up in Columbus and attended Eastmoor High School, part of the city school system, whose student body was one-third Jewish, one-third African-American and one-third "everything else—including me." Racial tension occasionally erupted; Kramer herself was twice "jumped and beaten up." On the flip side, Ohio State University football legend Archie Griffin and his brother, Ray, led her school's football team to glory. "All in all, it was a great foundation. It gave me a broad understanding of all types of people," she said.

Back then, Kramer spent many summer days in the library because her home was not air-conditioned. She focused on books about Africa: "It was the farthest place I could think of from Columbus, and I was fascinated by the people and the culture. I knew I would go there someday." After college, she did. She studied Swahili as a foreign language, saved her money and went to Africa on her own. Photo-journalism classes helped her capture quality images of her trip, which hang in her office space today.

"My dad helped me believe I was capable of doing whatever I decided to do," Kramer said. Other inspiring individuals in her life were scientist Jane Goodall, whose biographies she studied, Apple Computer founder Steve Jobs, with whom she worked and who *Inc.* magazine in 1980 described as the man who "changed business forever," and popular business author Jim Collins, with whom she corresponds.

"I like people who live by their own set of values, whether it's popular or not. People who aren't afraid to express their point of view around values and be definitive about it," says Kramer. Her personal guideline is that "anything is possible." Describing herself as curious, Kramer also says, "I work for my people. I believe in demonstrating in meaningful ways the company's values, even when it may not be in the best interest of the business financially."

One thing Kramer values is people who admit their mistakes. "I make a lot of mistakes every day. We fundamentally value taking risks over maintaining the status quo. No one gets fired for taking risks." This focus on values extends to her three children, now ages 17, 15 and 13. "They're my legacy—nothing else matters as much."

DWIGHT SMITH

FOUNDER AND CEO, SOPHISTICATED SYSTEMS

Words to live by:
"Be thankful for the blessings you receive each day, and always appreciate people."

Hometown: Springfield, Ohio
First job: busboy at Derr Road Inn
Hobbies: exercising, traveling, spending time with his wife
Favorite book: any business book by John Maxwell
Favorite movies: "Remember the Titans," "Miracles," "Glory Road"
I am: "Blessed."

He practically bursts with joy. Dwight Smith appreciates his life. He loves the Lord, his wife and his mother. Smith lives his life according to a very specific guiding principle—"to serve the Lord. I'm very religious. That's no secret."

He also just happens to be the founder of one of the most successful software integration and consulting firms in Central Ohio. His customers include a variety of Fortune 500 companies, small and medium firms in the private sector, and many state and local public sector entities.

Smith started his company, Sophisticated Systems, in 1990, using a business plan he wrote on his dining room table. "That table will always have a place at the company. But nobody wants it! It keeps landing back in my office," Smith laughs. Today Sophisticated Systems employs 100 people including subcontractors. Company revenues are projected to be $20 million in 2006, with significant growth projected in the future.

As a leader, Smith believes, "When times are really good, leaders ought to be invisible. And when times are bad, a leader needs to stand up and take responsibility."

He knows what he's talking about. Sophisticated Systems recorded a profit every year except one. The company was $2 million in debt and had broken the covenants on its line of credit. Smith reflects: "I would wake up in the night, sweating. I learned you don't wait until times are tough to get down on your knees and pray."

Smith guided his company back into profitability, paying off the debt within two years. Today the company remains debt-free. He defines success as understanding what "servant leadership" is all about. "It's going to bed every night feeling great about what you did that day—doing the right thing and appreciating things in your life."

This dynamic leader credits his success to the support of his close friends and family, especially his mother. "She worked hard and raised four kids by herself. We always had what we needed—she always sacrificed," Smith said. "That's why I give back now—there was always someone there along the way for me.

"My mother taught me a quote from the Bible that says, 'To whom much is given, much is required,'" Smith said. Early on, he was challenged by how to apply that lesson as his success became well known. He would receive requests from people who wanted to meet with him to share their ideas for new businesses that they wanted Smith to fund.

"One man told me, 'I was praying to the Lord, and he told me you'd give me $10,000 to start my business.'" Smith honored several such requests, until one time he realized an investment was used for a personal vacation instead of a business venture.

Thereafter, Smith began following a friend's advice and asked callers to complete a questionnaire about the proposed business for Smith to review. To date, he's never gotten a completed form back. "You've got to have a plan," Smith says.

Smith's life plan specifically outlines time for his personal life. In fact, he recently resigned from several community boards to have more personal time. He schedules a week each quarter to vacation with his wife, Renee. He also walks many miles in Sharon Woods Metro Park while connecting with friends. "It is so very easy to mix your personal identity with that of your company. I have to remind myself daily that the company is what I do, it's not who I am," he said.

JOE CHYLIK

PRINCIPAL OWNER, PROMEDIA OF OHIO

Words to live by:
"Don't look back. You can always second-guess yourself, but don't have any regrets."

Hometown: Cleveland, Ohio
First job: paper carrier
Hobbies: golfing, skiing, listening to music
Favorite book: "Good to Great," Jim Collins
Favorite movie: "Shawshank Redemption"
I am: "Driven."

Joe Chylik thrives on the challenge of buying unprofitable businesses and turning them around. "I've always bought struggling companies," he said. "I don't have this desire to have a giant media empire, but it's like I almost get bored.

"Every business can't be a $10 million or $15 million or even a $1 million company. I enjoy taking something and making it happen. Success is making something viable and providing a livelihood for people I work with," Chylik said.

In 2000, Chylik purchased Promedia, a Columbus-based, multi-media company that provides corporate video and audio production, interactive authoring, Web development and 3-D animation. A recent purchase of Grove City-based VDS (Video Duplication Services) has expanded Promedia's portfolio to include complementary services such as CD and DVD duplication, screen printing, direct mail and custom packaging.

Chylik is adept at blending the culture of his new company with Promedia's. Although proscribing accolades to himself doesn't come easily, Chylik believes he provides good vision and motivation. "I think I'm also a really good coach. The feedback is that I'm pretty direct, very honest and fair."

He also seems to have a knack for building teams. "As a leader, I make sure everyone's a part of the team. I close the deals, but I can't edit, I can't shoot. I'm worthless. As a team, though, we're incredibly effective."

The seed of Chylik's entrepreneurial spirit was planted at St. Ignatius High School in Cleveland. "It had the greatest impact on my discipline. I chose a lot of classics. I took Latin and Greek." Chylik thought he'd be a doctor, but an organic chemistry class changed his mind. "I had no science aptitude," he said.

What he did have was an aptitude for sales and marketing, two professions not highly thought of by his father, whom Chylik describes as an "extremely disciplined" chemical engineer. His father was a big influence in his life, and Chylik's career choice initially disappointed him since "he didn't view sales as a profession. However, my father continued to take an interest in my pursuits. To this day, I turn to him for advice or support."

After graduating from Miami University in Ohio, Chylik worked in sales at large corporations before going out on his own to buy his first company from an acquaintance. The experience was the worst of his career. He didn't discover until afterward that the company had been overvalued.

"I went into it from a pretty nice job. And suddenly my whole plan was in disarray. But it was a great character builder because up to that point, life had been pretty good. It was a humbling experience. It couldn't have come at a better time because I thought I was infallible," Chylik said.

Today Chylik's motivation comes not only from his restless spirit, but from his drive to excel. "I just don't want to fail," he admits. "But it's more about the enjoyment of it. No one needs to tell me to get up in the morning."

"If you're going to do something, give it everything you have and follow through. I really enjoy the end result and seeing people pull together," Chylik said.

However, "We don't want our people to simply be workaholics. We're not going to keep that type of person long-term, because they're going to burn out and go somewhere else. A culture that fosters not only hard work, but an enjoyable work environment, is one of the keys to retaining and attracting great people."

"Business is important. We're committed and intense, but we want our employees to balance their professional and their personal lives."

Paula Inniss

Founder and President, Ohio Full Court Press

Words to live by:
"Understand that work itself is subordinate to some higher purpose. You don't have to choose between your values and success."

Hometown: Columbus, Ohio
First job: 15 years old, wrapping holiday packages for a jeweler; was paid 50 cents for a month's work
Hobbies: golfing, water and snow skiing, exercising, performing ministry
Favorite book: "How To Meet Your Life Goals," Peter J. Daniels
Favorite movies: "The Color Purple," "The Wizard of Oz," "What Lies Beneath"
I am: "Passionate."

If you'd known Paula Inniss as a child, she would have told you, emphatically, that she was going to be a veterinarian when she grew up. She rescued hurt animals from the woods and creek near her home, nursed them to health if possible, and if not, held a funeral service with neighborhood children in attendance. "Without a doubt, I loved animals. I was really adventurous as a child," Inniss said.

Today Inniss is president of the award-winning company she founded in 1995, Ohio Full Court Press. It's a technology-based, document-management company that offers on-demand products. She's not saving any wildlife, but she is rescuing many companies from the task of filing and storing documents and providing them with high-quality, on-demand publications.

"Call me crazy for having entered this business on my own. But after I wrote my business plan, it was compelling enough for me to leave my job and start my own company," Inniss said

Before OFCP, Inniss was an up-and-coming manager for Xerox Corporation. In 1994 she was pursuing business from Craig Taylor, one of her clients, who promised to buy equipment from her if she could prove to him that ink, paper and digital processing could work together. Once convinced, Taylor agreed to the purchase—if Inniss would quit her job and work for him. She counter-proposed that he become her "angel investor" and finance her own start-up company. Taylor agreed to the proposal.

"I totally didn't mean it, and he totally did," Inniss laughed. "At the time, I was a single mom with three teenagers. I'd been with Xerox for 14 years and was making a nice salary. Planning the new venture was nine months of agony."

Inniss' entrepreneurial spirit reflects her upbringing by two like-minded parents. Her father owned and operated a carryout and a Laundromat. Her mother, who never finished high school, was an Avon manager.

"My childhood was perfect. We had everything we thought we needed. Of course, you didn't know what you didn't have," Inniss reflected. She realized later in life how hard her parents struggled to provide opportunities for her and her two older sisters to dance, act, model and play in the orchestra. "We didn't miss a beat."

Perhaps that's why Inniss admires people who start their own businesses and run them successfully. "It's so difficult. There's nothing easy about running your own business." That's why she offers a business-cultivator class at her church—to teach others how to start and run a business, and to make the path easier for them.

"I want others, especially young people, to see what's possible—especially because I'm an African-American female from the inner city."

Inniss describes two sides to her leadership—she can be democratic, getting people involved and believing in the vision, and autocratic, being directive without soliciting buy-in. She respects people who engage in "direct, healthy confrontation." And she's motivated by her pride in her company and her sense of responsibility for her staff.

Success to Inniss equals having an inner peace and a relationship with God, knowing "I did the right thing" at the end of the day, and understanding what really makes her happy. The best times in her life were happy events, including marrying her husband, Malcolm, and watching her children graduate from college. "Because I was a single parent for a while, I couldn't have been more proud."

This entrepreneur jokes that she wishes she could be "much more successful now so I could retire!" But, she said, "Hard work builds character, and I'm not sorry for it."

Her spiritual character will be reflected in a book she's writing, "Who Are We, Really?" It explores where we start in life, where we end up, and why we do the things we do along the way, often trying to impress others instead of fulfilling our own desires. "If only my kids and grandkids read it, then I'm OK!" That, she says, would be a legacy fulfilled.

Ron Pizzuti

Chairman and CEO, The Pizzuti Companies

Words to live by:
"Always take the high road—
it may sometimes be painful,
but in the end it's always beneficial."

Hometown: Kent, Ohio
First job: in grade school, cleaning a restaurant, mowing lawns
Hobbies: collecting contemporary art, traveling
Favorite book: "Fountainhead," Ayn Rand
Favorite movie: "Shawshank Redemption"
I am: "Compassionate."

Ron Pizzuti thought he was going to be an architect when he grew up, but that didn't last long. "Although I didn't envision myself at that time in real estate, I always thought I'd be successful. I was always entrepreneurial," Pizzuti says. "In college, I was a bartender, managed a clothing store and was a cigarette representative on campus. I made more money working those jobs than I did working a full-time position out of college with two degrees," he said.

Pizzuti was raised in humble beginnings. His father, an immigrant from Calabria, Italy, worked in a factory during the day and developed apartments at night; his mother was a homemaker. "We lived in an immaculate 800-square-foot house, and I guess we were poor, although we didn't see it that way then."

If there's one thing he could change, Pizzuti said he would have pursued athletics when he was younger. "Because my dad worked afternoons at the factory, my brother, sister and I went straight home after school to do chores. We learned how to remodel apartments, and we did everything. To this day, I still don't like to paint," he said.

Pizzuti earned two bachelor's degrees from Kent State University in 1962: one in marketing and one in economics. He then moved to Columbus to work at Lazarus Department Store for $87 a week—about $200 less per month than he made doing odd jobs during his senior year at Kent State. "My dad was ready to kick me out of the house when he heard that I took that job instead of the one at Goodyear," Pizzuti laughed.

He credits the Lazarus management for helping him form his own leadership philosophy. "To this day, that's still the best job I've ever had. At the time, positions at Lazarus were highly coveted. They had terrific leadership and great community involvement. They also had a wonderful training program and a strict 'promote-from-within' policy. When we can, we embrace those same practices at Pizzuti."

After some time working as an executive in retail sales with Les Wexner at The Limited, whom he credits as "the most visionary person I know," Pizzuti decided to branch out on his own. He and his wife, Ann, started The Pizzuti Companies in 1976.

With operations in Columbus, Chicago, Indianapolis, Jacksonville and Orlando, The Pizzuti Companies have developed more than 35 million square feet of Class A office, retail, residential and institutional-quality industrial development facilities throughout the Midwest and Southeast regions of the United States. Pizzuti has completed office, institutional, residential, mixed-use, municipal and build-to-suit projects in Florida, Illinois, Indiana, Kentucky, Nebraska, Ohio, Oklahoma, Pennsylvania, South Carolina and Texas. Additionally, the company has speculative construction projects in each of their major markets where Pizzuti has extensive land holdings. Pizzuti is known as a major player in the industrial development field across the nation.

Locally, the company developed Miranova, a luxury office and residential mixed-use development located just west of the new Franklin County Courthouse site within the RiverSouth District.

"We saw the need for luxury living in downtown Columbus. And it was virtually impossible to do any type of feasibility study because there was nothing like it in existence," Pizzuti says. "It was a gutsy move on our part."

Pizzuti saw opportunity and potential in a piece of brownfield property. Located at the south end of downtown Columbus on the Scioto River, the land's proximity to and view of downtown held great promise.

"In July 1987 we started looking at the property, which had been an industrial site with some contamination," Pizzuti says.

Developing the property would entail a great deal of work and require spearheading brownfield legislation and other government concessions. The Pizzuti Companies decided both they and the city of Columbus would benefit from the development of Miranova.

Working with the city, Pizzuti gained Tax Increment Financing (TIF) and special permitting. Additionally, Pizzuti worked closely with then-Gov. George Voinovich on creating legislation to encourage brownfield development. The site was cleaned under brownfield legislation administered through the Ohio Environmental Protection Agency. The result is a standout, urban mixed-use project, which includes a 112-unit high-rise condominium landmark (One Miranova Place) and a 240,000-square-foot high-rise office tower and parking garage (Two Miranova Place). Both feature unmatched amenities and an uncompromising view of the city. The successful completion of Miranova has spurred a downtown housing revival with numerous loft housing projects finished or under construction, and established Pizzuti as an experienced leader in public/private development.

Despite his many successes, Pizzuti steps away from giving accolades to himself. He prefers crediting his associates. "We've developed a culture where we hire really smart people—we're very selective. Even if they're not from our industry, we know they work hard and that they can achieve anything they envision. We're successful because our people are successful."

About his leadership skills, Pizzuti says, "I'm a good listener and I like to think I lead by example. I think people here would say that I have a hands-on, compassionate and strong leadership style. I think you have to look at your mission and ask yourself, 'Is what I'm doing getting me closer to my goal?'"

His wife of 38 years is a true partner in his business. "Ann's always been a devil's advocate for me. I don't make a major decision without consulting her. I admire her and value her opinion."

Pizzuti is equally proud of his three children, who have served in various positions within the company. In fact, his son was named president of Pizzuti earlier this year. "I didn't let the kids work in the business immediately out of college. I wanted them to gain some experience on the outside so they could bring more to the table," Pizzuti said.

Today, although he admits a component of success is financial, he's "not as motivated to earn the next dollar as I was when I was younger. Today success means knowing that my wife and I have raised three successful, well-balanced and highly educated children."

"I hope people say, 'He was honest and fair, and he contributed to society as well as business.'"

ROBERT DAVIS

PRESIDENT, DAVIS WINCE LTD. ARCHITECTURE

Words to live by:
"Find something you enjoy doing."

Hometown: Columbus, Ohio
First job: paper carrier
Hobbies: golfing, traveling, playing piano
Favorite book: anything by Tom Peters
Favorite movie: "The High and the Mighty"
I am: "Complex."

Many Ohio buildings bear the mark of architect Robert Davis: in Columbus, the Columbus College of Art and Design, the Rhodes State Office Tower, Columbus Public School buildings, two downtown Hyatt hotels, and buildings on The Ohio State University campus; in Athens, buildings on the Ohio University campus; and in Cleveland, the Cuyahoga Justice Center—just to name a few.

In 1995, Davis took 20-plus years of success, combined them with leadership skills he learned in the Army, and incorporated his own firm. According to him, "Success is having a passion for your work and enjoying what you're doing."

Davis credits his parents for instilling his values and good work ethic. "My dad instilled in me an entrepreneurial spirit, and my mother taught me the importance of making good life choices," he said.

After graduating from North High School in Columbus, Ohio, Davis earned a bachelor's degree in architecture from OSU in 1964. At the time, the architecture program had an aggressive "weeding out" policy. Davis explained, "We graduated only 14 of the original 100 students that started the program. I was good in math and physics, and that helped me overcome the adjustment into architecture." During his second year at OSU, he met Professor George Tilley. "He took an interest in me and got me focused," Davis said.

Like many young men during the pre-Vietnam era, Davis joined the Ohio National Guard after earning his degree in lieu of being drafted. He entered Officers Candidate School at Ft. Hayes in Columbus, Ohio, becoming Second Lieutenant in 1966. "Serving as an officer for six years was my graduate program," he said. He said that a particular manual, called "F.M. 22-7," taught him the leadership principles he's used throughout his career.

He believes integrity and understanding mark his leadership. "I was very intense in the past, but now I've mellowed out. Although I still have a somewhat low tolerance for errors, I've become a much better leader in the last 15 years. I'm motivated by bringing people together to accomplish something they think they can't do," he said.

He began implementing his design and creative know-how as a first-year architect for Design Associates Architects, a small Columbus architecture firm. From there he joined the Columbus Public Schools as a staff architect, but after two years, was laid off because Columbus could not pass bond issues. During that same time, the state of Ohio was building the Rhodes State Office Tower as a joint venture between two architecture firms. The joint venture hired Davis for a temporary six-month assignment to help detail the exterior of the 42-story tower in downtown Columbus. "I developed a really good dialogue with the chief designer. His job was to be creative, and mine was to get things done."

When the initial six months was over, Davis was asked to stay with the joint venture, partially at the encouragement of Turner Construction, the construction manager, to help complete the building. "That became my responsibility for the next four years," Davis said.

After the Rhodes Tower was completed in 1974, the construction manager advised Davis to speak with the Cleveland branch of Turner Construction about the possibility of working on the Cuyahoga County Justice Center. "This was a $125 million project in 1970 dollars, and it had so many problems." Davis was hired to coordinate all of the architectural responsibilities until the project was completed in 1976.

"My leadership style was somewhat unique for a project architect at that time. Getting everyone on the same page was my biggest initiative. I told the senior partner that, 'My job is to get you out of Cleveland without being sued.' And we did just that. I was in over my head, but I figured I still had more knowledge than anyone else involved," Davis recalled.

About the Rhodes Tower and the Justice Center, Davis said, "These two projects were incredible learning experiences that gave me a base of knowledge that was more valuable than any college degree could possibly have been."

After the Justice Center was completed, Davis acted as the project architect on the two Hyatt hotels in downtown Columbus. Once these hotels were completed, "I traveled three months for Hyatt and researched a new type of hotel they wanted to build—a modified suite hotel. I managed all the design and construction for four mini-suite Hyatt hotels built in the Washington, D.C. and Chicago areas," he said.

Now 65, Davis has no intentions of slowing down. His 11-year-old firm is doing well, and, he said, "I love what I do. I recently read where 'the new 65 is the old 40.' I take things day by day, and think ahead as much as possible. I want to stay flexible. Plus, I want to see my employees succeed."

Edward James "Jeg" Coughlin

Retired owner, Jegs Automotive/JEGS Mail Order

Words to live by:
"Be a good listener. Learn how to filter the good ideas from the bad ideas."

Hometown: Columbus, Ohio
First job: railroad head braker
Hobbies: wine collecting, car racing, sailing
I am: "Fun."

Jeg Coughlin is enjoying life. These days he's busy spending time with his five children and 10 grandchildren at his 65-acre home, aptly named "C'est La Vie." He's retired from racing and the daily rigors of running Jegs Mail Order, a business he built out of a small shop 46 years ago into one of the nation's largest retail and mail-order high-performance businesses.

He's earned the right to relax. His accomplishments in racing and business are many. In 2002 he received the Ernst & Young Entrepreneur of the Year award for his business savvy. His racing record reflects 11 major racing wins in Top Fuel, Pro Comp and Super Eliminator in the 1980 Division Three Top Fuel stockcar racing championship.

Coughlin recalls always loving to fix things, an ability that he didn't inherit. His father, who worked at Lazarus Department Store, was a "great merchant but not interested in mechanical things," Coughlin said. Regarding his own abilities, he explained, "It just happened that way. Maybe being an only child I didn't have a lot to do so I just fixed stuff." At 12 years old, Coughlin built a Heathkit stereo and assembled and repaired Little Wizard motorbikes.

He also loved cars and by age 16 was racing his own hot rod. "People would come to me and say, 'I want you to make my car go fast,'" he said. His work became so popular that three years later, in 1960, he opened Jegs Automotive Inc., a small car-repair and parts business he ran out of his parents' garage. The shop was directly under his parents' bedroom; eventually they had enough of the noise and issued an ultimatum to move the shop.

"I found a building that was 40' x 40', and I rented it. I tried it. I did very well," he said. His mother also worked with him. He credits her with giving him the idea to diversify his business. "My mother motivated me a lot, too. She was in the office, and every morning she'd say, 'Jeg, we don't have any money. We're broke.' I thought that was an interesting comment, because if we didn't have any money, then I needed to get into some other situations. That's what really made me learn to live on my earned income," Coughlin said.

Coughlin's business endeavors along the way included llama and lobster farming. In the 1980s he bought a 59-foot Hinckley sailboat that he (the "captain") and wife, Susie (the "mate"), chartered for wealthy clients wishing to sail in style in the Caribbean. Unlike other chartering services that hire out their captains, the Coughlins often sailed the boat themselves so they, too, could join the adventure.

Coughlin is remarkably humble about his success. "Success is happiness. You measure success by saying, 'I'm going to get up this morning and go to work and I'm really happy with that.' Work is not work. Work is just a place I go where I'm really enjoying myself," he said.

"I think the key to success, if you want to be anything in life, is to listen. Listen to people. Work with a person and listen to them. The next thing you need to do is ask 'Why? Why do we want to go in this direction?' You have to replace the word 'OK' with 'Why.' Surround yourself with good people and I think you'll do really well. And that's my theory."

His employees seem to agree with these theories. Coughlin said that 35 percent of his employees have been with the company for 30 years, and two employees have been there 40 years. "Whatever we've done has worked very well. I think they would say I listen and I reason with them." He continues, "If we do something in the company that works well, you guys did it. If we do something that doesn't work well, I did it. Let's just have this philosophy for life."

According to Coughlin, "Motivation and attitude are the majority of success. Motivation is easy," he said. He describes his attitude this way. "I can take any problem anybody has, and I can work it around to where it will be fun for them."

"It's just been fun. Businesses have a lot of problems. But you fix them. Fix the little problems all the time. Maybe that's why I don't have any big problems."

As for quality, Coughlin believes, "If you're going to sell an item, you want to be the best you can be in that particular business and don't deviate from that business. I believe if you keep working at a project that is working and just fine-tune it, that's a much better idea."

Coughlin describes his best time in life as when his five children reached their teenage years. "The most fun I had was when the kids were between 14 and 20. It was so much fun raising them because they were being molded into something at that age. I could talk with them and reason with them."

He laughed, "My rule was the first car had to be 4-cylinder, no turbo, no tint."

Damon Canfield

President and CEO, New Product Innovations, Inc.

Words to live by:
"Life is full of second chances."

Hometown: Aurora, Ohio
First job: night shift at a corrugated box factory
Hobbies: golfing, enjoying food and wine, working outside around the house
Favorite book: "The World Is Flat," Thomas Friedman
Favorite movie: "Top Gun"
I am: "Insatiable."

Damon Canfield describes his childhood in the 1960s as "adventuresome and not very constrained. I was on a path of exploring life in all its fullness and not really excelling in school. My legacy at high school was that of a troublemaker." He also admits to being somewhat of a "hippie," adding "the times, they were a'changin'."

Canfield said his "newly discovered thoughts and beliefs were shaken pretty hard" when three weeks out of high school, he found himself newly married with a baby on the way. Determined to support his family, Canfield worked the night shift in a local corrugated box factory. "There had to be something better," he said. Canfield moved the family to Bloomington, Ind., where he and his wife attended Indiana University.

He credits his family with helping him along the way. "My parents didn't put me through college but were very supportive." Canfield also worked as a custodian and trash hauler. "I just did what I had to do," he said.

Four-and-a-half years later, armed with degrees in chemistry and business, Canfield found work in Goodyear's chemical division. A year later, he took a job in sales with General Electric. According to Canfield, "I never considered myself the outgoing type. But for whatever reason, GE hired me. And the world just kind of took off."

Canfield rose steadily in the ranks of GE's plastic division. He spent more than 20 years at GE with key roles in sales, marketing, product development and business management.

The most difficult time in Canfield's professional life followed in 2001, after he left GE to start a new venture between GE Plastics and two partners from FITCH, one of the world's largest retail design and branding companies. He was president of the new venture. "Strangely enough, we had been growing this new company pretty nicely for a couple of years. Then we bought it, and within six months, we almost went out of business," Canfield said.

"This was a very hard time," he continued. "We were an ideal company for all the 'dot com' startups. We validated our business model this way. So after the startup boom petered out, we had to work hard to keep people here. We asked them to make sacrifices. This really tested our mettle, but it galvanized us, and we've been strong ever since."

The joint venture eventually evolved into New Product Innovations, a unique, new-product introduction company that offers research, design and manufacturing as a single process. Some of their customers include Motorola, Sunbeam, Georgia Pacific, TimberTech, Maytag, Jenn-Air and more.

How does Canfield define success now? "Life changes a lot when you get out of that (corporate) craziness and you decide to do your own thing. Now our definition of success is satisfying a customer by delivering and launching a successful product; and having that product and the entire experience be so good that the client wants to work with us again."

Canfield said that one of his company's most memorable experiences occurred with client Procter & Gamble. "Our collaborative business process proved so successful that P&G asked us to continue the relationship by working on another project."

When asked about his leadership style, Canfield says, "We're big on collaboration. Plus, being able to keep the fire lit, and being able to communicate where you're going and why you're going there are very important." In this vein he hopes that his legacy at NPI is that employees know he "really cares about people and collaboration. Our people are so important. It's our little family."

Canfield said he remembers telling his partners on the day they started the business, "'I'm ready to do this if we don't screw up the culture.' We had people who believed in the idea and it felt really good. I didn't want to mess it up."

In addition to his passion for his employees, Canfield is also motivated by integrity, honesty, diversity, humility and personal satisfaction—his company's core values. "If I can do this, then it's pretty motivating. There's a family here and I play a role. I can't let them down."

Tim Newcome

President, Newcome Electronic Systems

Words to live by:
"Never do things the way you've always done them."

Hometown: Dayton, Ohio
First job: emptying the dishwasher at home
Hobbies: worldwide mountain climbing, bicycling, reading, skiing
Favorite book: "The Hidden Role of Chance in Life and the Markets," Nassim Nicholas Taleb
Favorite movies: "Ferris Bueller's Day Off," "Glory"
I am: "Curious."

It's not often that you hear a mentor described as a cigar-chewing bootlegger from the Prohibition Era. But this colorful character provided the spark that flamed Tim Newcome's growing love for electronics.

Newcome laughs as he recalls his childhood mentor, Ora Clay Feeback. Newcome was 12 years old when Feeback offered him his first paid job removing parts from salvaged televisions for repair jobs.

"A guy could walk up to me on the street right now, offer me a million dollars in cash, and it would not be more exciting than getting that job," he said. "I learned a lot from Clay. I learned electronics…and patience."

However, by the time Newcome met Feeback, his curiosity for electronics was already well established. Newcome's father was an engineer, and clearly influenced his son. As a 10-year-old, he helped his father install a new heating and air-conditioning unit and water heater in the family's home. "I did the electronics, and Dad did all the rest," he said. He remembers being fascinated with how things worked. "I was always building stuff," he said.

Knowing he had always wanted a career in electronics, Newcome enrolled at The Ohio State University to study the field. He soon became bored with academic life, so he opened a small repair shop in his dorm room. Newcome also worked at a campus nightclub, building and running sound systems for incoming rock bands such as The Doobie Brothers and the J. Geils Band.

In 1978, Newcome earned his degree and, with a partner, formed Newcome Sound. The business was incorporated in 1979. "I didn't start out to 'be successful.' I started out pursuing what I loved to do. Any business success I had was completely accidental."

"At that time, my friends were getting jobs at General Electric, buying Oldsmobiles and getting married. I just couldn't do that," Newcome said.

He remembers that in the late 1970s, most people thought entrepreneurs were "on the lunatic fringe. There was no social, academic or business support back then. You were a weirdo."

Newcome said he really didn't have anyone to help him out during those early years in business. His father and Feeback had both since passed away. "My partner and I carved the business out of granite. We were just inventing stuff as we went along. It was like being lost on a mountaintop and having to find your own way."

Newcome Electronics has grown to include a New Jersey branch as well as its Columbus office. The company provides world-class voice, data and audio/video communication systems to primarily Fortune 100 clients in all 50 states as well as Canada, Puerto Rico, Mexico, Brazil, France and Belgium.

Today Newcome stays motivated by figuring out how to "simplify the complex." What else makes him a good leader? "I require everyone to be curious. It's a career-limiting move here to answer the question 'why?' with 'because we've always done it that way.'"

"I'm very focused on customer needs. I'm also the person who's speaking about the direction we're going. People here would probably say, 'Tim pushes us,'" Newcome said.

The worst time in Newcome's career came in the late 1980s when he started a new side business in electronic networking. All his partners had previously worked in big business, and Newcome felt his experience in small business was lacking by comparison. "I tended to undervalue my experience. I thought I was second rate." He got out of the business, a decision he refers to as "the worst business move of my life."

As for what he would change, Newcome said, "I would be more deliberate and reflective. As you age, there are a lot of things you do and you don't understand why. If I could rewind, I would be more conscious of what I'm doing."

On that note, Newcome says he hopes he'll be remembered for encouraging people to "take the adventure of finding out why you're doing what you're doing. Be curious and explore."

Stampp Corbin

Retired CEO and President, RetroBox, LLC

Words to live by:
"Whatever you do, do it with passion."

Hometown: Chicago, Ill.
First job: IBM
Hobbies: traveling
Favorite book: anything by Patricia Cornwell
Favorite movie: "Song of Bernadette"
I am: "Driven."

Stampp Corbin isn't modest about his success. And you won't hear him apologize for it either. He was an extremely gifted child who remembers how his older brother, Michael, would "test" him on subjects he was taking in college. Corbin, who was 5 years old at the time, relished the challenge. "I was always the star of the family. I was the one who wanted to be very successful," he said.

Now 45, Corbin has already reached his lifetime goal of financial independence. His company RetroBox merged with Intechra Holding Corp. in January 2006 to become the largest full-service information technology disposition company in the country, with $40 million in annual revenues. Corbin stayed on for four months after the merger but has since left the company. "I've led a very charmed life. To know I don't have to worry about money, that is really freedom," he said.

Corbin reflected on his success: "After college graduation, success was making my age in salary. In my 30s, success was about building something that would endure. Now it's about impact. Then it works into how I can help nonprofit organizations that don't have people like me. I bring a lot of value by helping them in the financial arena," Corbin said.

Corbin grew up in Chicago with a strong mother who wanted him to have every advantage academically. She removed him from traditional public school during his sophomore year to attend Whitney Young, a prestigious, "selectively public" preparatory school. Corbin's stepfather was a private investigator who introduced Corbin to many of the city's renowned attorneys. Not surprisingly, when he entered Stanford University, Corbin wanted to become a lawyer. But he changed his mind once he got a taste of the research involved. "This was before LexisNexis," he remembers. He graduated with degrees in economics and French.

Next, although Corbin applied and was accepted to the Harvard Business School, he deferred to stay in California and work in sales at IBM, a job which Corbin said groomed him for his future by instilling strong leadership skills.

He returned to Harvard two years later and earned his MBA. He still recalls being impressed by a speech given there by Mary Kay Ash, founder of Mary Kay Cosmetics, Inc. "She said, 'Nothing happens until somebody sells something.' If you forget that, then all is for naught, because you won't have the revenues to support and grow your organization," he said.

He used Ash's philosophy, along with his Harvard MBA, as a foundation to continue his career in Boston at Honeywell Bull. At 28, he became their youngest executive. "I did extremely well. I developed a program for upgrades within my own territory that the company took national. It was the most successful program that they had ever had," Corbin said.

Not everything Corbin tried turned to gold, however. One of his most difficult experiences was a failed investment in a Boston dry-cleaning business. "You can't trust people to do the right thing all the time. This early business failure took away my naiveté," Corbin remembers.

Corbin left Boston for a sales job at a small West Coast software company. He made two large sales to Rockwell International and American Express, which amounted to 50 percent of the company's annual volume. He left California again in 1992 to take the head position at Resource One, a $4 million, computer consulting company in Columbus, Ohio. Four years later, under Corbin's leadership, the company had grown to $25 million.

Nonetheless, Corbin still wasn't satisfied and had already moved on to his next idea. He added another company, RetroBox, LLC to Resource One. The addition meant his product mix now included the remarketing and recycling of desktop computers and servers.

"I made IT disposal a national issue," he said. "I invented the industry. I made it what is it today. Had I known better, I would have patented my concept. RetroBox became 'the' national firm to go to for information-technology disposition."

Corbin is very serious about his role as a leader and believes he excelled in creating a vision and instilling loyalty and trust in others. He thinks others would describe him as "tough but fair." "Leadership in a small company is sometimes like being president of the United States. There is always an opposing view but you must build consensus for your company to succeed," he said.

Despite his accomplishments, he's already wondering what's next. Corbin said his leadership legacy is his passion. "It's all about the vision of what we're doing," he said. "I have come to realize that I'm all about ideas. Employees refer to them as 'pearls' that come out of my mouth. When I talk about the future, my employees believe my vision is what's going to happen."

Tom Augustine

President, Minds On Marketing, Inc. and Lacelet, LLC

Words to live by:
"Passion drives success and no more 'what ifs.'"

Hometown: Vermilion, Ohio
First job: bag boy at a grocery chain
Hobbies: fly fishing, golfing, watching movies, playing board games with his family, inventing
Favorite book: "The Purple Cow," Seth Godin
Favorite movies: the "Star Wars" trilogy
I am: "Passionate."

Inventor, designer, entrepreneur and parent Tom Augustine's true leadership abilities were put to the test when his then-5-year-old daughter Alainna was diagnosed with type 1 diabetes in January 2003.

New routines, countless shots, finger pokes and calculated meals had put their family on an emotional roller coaster. Augustine decided to take all the shock, fear and worries he was experiencing and turn them into something positive.

That "something" is the "Within Reach" Lacelet, a fashionable shoelace accessory that displays messages in practical, versatile and fun ways. Augustine created the "Within Reach" Lacelet to raise awareness and bring a community together for one purpose: making a cure for diabetes within reach. "I never dreamed that a little piece of plastic could do some much to help others. It's a way for people to instantly connect with others who have the same trials and tribulations that our family has had with diabetes," said Augustine.

Currently, 150,000 people in the United States and New Zealand are wearing Lacelets. They have also become New Zealand's official diabetes awareness tool. Lacelets are sold online at www.lacelet.com.

Growing up in Vermilion, Ohio, Augustine was surrounded by a large, loving Italian family. His father, a steel worker, taught him the value of hard work and business loyalty. His mother, a teacher, taught him people skills and the value of relationships. He believes these traits have molded him into the person he is today.

"I was an average student in high school who grew up with a passion for drawing. I always knew that my career would involve creativity." In 1988, Augustine graduated with a degree in industrial design from The Ohio State University.

Out of college, Augustine entered the corporate world as a graphic designer at the Dublin, Ohio, headquarters of Sterling Commerce. The company offers multi-enterprise, collaborative technology solutions throughout its offices in the United States and abroad.

Little did he know that he would help lead this Fortune 500 company into the Internet age. "It was 1994, and the Web was just starting to hit corporate America. I saw the potential and the power of the Internet early, and I took the initiative to develop a Web site for a division of Sterling. I also created a plan on how we could leverage the Internet as a marketing, sales and customer-service tool."

These efforts earned him an executive-level position, a large staff and a multi-million dollar budget to manage. "Before we knew it, we were creating Web sites globally for Sterling—we were cutting-edge and forward-thinking. We were all on a cloud," Augustine said. "I had the invaluable experience of learning the business at the highest level and being a corporate entrepreneur."

"This is where I got the entrepreneurial bug," he said.

By early 2003, Augustine was planning to leave corporate life to start his own business. As fate would have it, his daughter's diabetes diagnosis came at the same time. This led to second thoughts about leaving a secure corporate job. "Here I was, stressing about my decision to completely start over, and then I saw Alainna having her whole world turned upside down, without one complaint. She changed me forever—I learned that life is too precious and short to give up on your dreams."

Augustine followed his dream and with his business partners formed Minds On, Inc., a marketing and Web development agency in Lewis Center, Ohio. Today the company employs eight people who provide services to help grow companies like Donato's Pizza, Dominion Homes, Adexis Storage and Intellinetics.

His partners support him 100 percent when it comes to his obvious passion for diabetes awareness and education. Together with Kroger, they've raised over $40,000 selling Lacelets. In 2005, they were asked to sponsor the "Walk for a Cure," an annual fund-raising event hosted by the Central Ohio chapter of the Juvenile Diabetes Research Foundation. "Usually it's 'the big guys' who sponsor something of this magnitude. It was a real honor for us."

"Before Alainna's diagnosis, I defined success as how fast I could move up the corporate ladder and how much money I could make. It was after Alainna's diagnosis that I realized I was out of balance. I was spending too much time with work. Now, success is more about bringing balance to work and family and how I can give back," Augustine said.

He believes his passion, ability to execute and willingness to accept change are his top leadership skills. "I believe that true leaders never give up on their dream."

Creating a business foundation that allows people to learn, grow and prosper is Augustine's business legacy. However, he hopes his personal legacy will be that he put his heart and soul into the search for a cure for type 1 diabetes. "I want people to know that even the 'little guy' can make big things happen," he said.

To that end, he and his partners are busy growing Minds On, Inc., and are currently working on a new venture, a Web site that will provide positive and inspirational messages for those living with type 1 diabetes. The site will also include news about advancements in treatment. They also plan to expand Lacelets into a complete accessory line.

"Out of all the things I've done—including bringing a Fortune 500 company into the Internet era and starting my own business—raising awareness for type 1 diabetes through Lacelets will be my most important legacy."

George McCloy

President, McCloy Financial Services

Words to live by:
"Figure out what you need to do, break it up in small pieces, and stick to it."

Hometown: Cleveland, Ohio
First job: mowing lawns
Hobbies: swimming, golfing, boating
I am: "Enthusiastic."

George McCloy remembers his first "lesson" in doing his best as if it were yesterday. It came in the form of a challenge from a high school chemistry teacher at Bexley High School in Columbus, Ohio. "I was flunking chemistry, and the teacher told me, 'I'll stand on my head in class, in front of all the students, if you get an A for the semester.' I got an A—and he stood on his head. He showed me that I could do whatever I wanted to do once I put my mind to it."

Success, according to McCloy, is "accomplishing what you set out to do," and step by step, he's done just that. He and a friend began selling insurance over 40 years ago as students at The Ohio State University. "We answered a blind ad that read, 'Make over $250 a week,' which was more than I was making selling clothes at The Union. So we got our license and started selling insurance. It wasn't a bad job, so I stayed."

Today he owns McCloy Financial Services in Columbus, a division of New England Financial that specializes in investment, annuity and insurance products.

McCloy is also a lifetime member of the industry's distinguished Million-Dollar Round Table.

McCloy established his own agency in 1968 and was affiliated with Penn Mutual Life Insurance Company.

In addition to being "stubbornly determined," McCloy names his ability to motivate people and to finish projects as his top leadership skills. As for his style, McCloy thinks others would describe him as fun. "I try and add fun to whatever I do. I like to work hard and play hard."

Even while growing up in Bexley, Ohio, "fun" dominated McCloy's agenda. "I had no concept of what I wanted to be when I grew up. I was more concerned with what I was going to do on the weekend or what kind of car I'd drive," he admits.

He performed well in athletics, and in high school he became captain of the swim team. McCloy laughs as he explains, "I chose swimming because I'd rather be in water in the middle of August than running on a hot football field." However, he didn't do as well in academics. "I was a terrible student and graduated close to the bottom of my class," he said.

Despite his poor academic record, McCloy wanted a college education and was accepted to OSU. "They let me in despite my bad grades, and I was a mediocre student there, too. Lucky for me, my degree doesn't list my grade-point average," he said.

Although he didn't have many childhood mentors, McCloy remembers attending an insurance seminar at OSU and being mesmerized by the speaker, New York Life agent Ben Feldman. "He had $100 million a year in sales and was the number-one insurance salesman in the entire world at that time. He wasn't dynamic—he was short, overweight and spoke with a lisp—and he was very humble, despite his success. I didn't take a single note, but I listened to every word he said," McCloy said.

McCloy has used the simple guideline of "do what you say you will do" to build his own success. "In the field of life insurance, our company's name has endured through the years. People who come here want to be affiliated with us," he said.

Looking back on his life, McCloy reflects, "I don't have many regrets. My worst times, however, were finding out my son had juvenile diabetes, and then finding out my 5-year-old granddaughter had rheumatoid arthritis and juvenile diabetes. And I had a heart attack at 40."

Despite his personal hardships, McCloy remains positive. "I have a great family—two grown children and six grandchildren. And I've been married to a former Miss Ohio for the past 40 years. And that's not too bad!" he laughs.

MICHAEL MATRKA

PRESIDENT AND FOUNDER, MICHAEL MATRKA INC.

Words to live by:
"It's OK to be afraid, but don't let it stop you. Love is freeing. Follow your heart and never give up."

Hometown: Columbus, Ohio
First job: cutting grass
Hobbies: reading, playing tennis, traveling, riding his mountain bike and road bike, skiing
Favorite book: "Raising the Bar: Integrity and Passion in Life and in Business," Gary Erickson
Favorite movies: "Walk the Line," "The English Patient"
I am: "Persistent."

Mike Matrka thinks he was born with a natural inclination to take things apart and find out how they work. "When I was in nursery school, my mom would get calls asking her to return all the doorknobs I had removed with a knife and spoon," he remembers. On special occasions when the family, including his sister and four brothers, went out to eat, he said, "I would be the one underneath the table, figuring out how it was put together."

In eighth grade, Matrka designed and built the deck on his parent's first house; at 13, he helped his father, a medical doctor, remodel his first office. "I was self-employed most of my life. In seventh grade I wanted to take flying lessons, so I painted my neighbor's house to get the money."

The family tree included a long line of carpenters. In fact, Matrka still has his mother's great-great-grandfather's tool chest from the 1860s. Still, it wasn't a career choice that was necessarily encouraged at home. His grandfather was a carpenter in Cleveland, and Matrka would often visit and help out on jobsites. "He thought he would teach me a lesson and encourage me to get good grades so I wouldn't have to do this type of work when I got older. But it didn't matter—it was in my blood and I loved it," Matrka said.

Matrka credits his parents with helping him develop a strong work ethic, and recalls having long talks about how important it was to work hard and always do your best. "It's important to find something you enjoy. Then the work will be fun," he said.

Matrka continued his knack for always finding work, taking on one project after another for neighbors and friends until a small business began to grow up around him. He founded his home remodeling and renovation company in 1981. Now the team of 20 at Michael Matrka Inc. considers themselves master renovators and builders.

Their Web site says, "When you invite Michael Matrka into your home, you get more than a team of master craftspeople who specialize in quality renovations and restorations. You get a group of experts who believe that what they do is an expression of who they are."

This certainly tracks with Matrka's background and life experiences. He believes that being passionate, authentic and focused on learning and personal growth are his key leadership qualities, which he gladly shares with his team of craftsmen. He challenges them to "stretch, explore and not be afraid to do more than you think you can."

However, defining his own success has been a bit more difficult. Matrka explains: "I don't like the word 'success.' It means you've arrived, and I think it is much more of a journey. For me, life is about having a blast along the way and continually learning and improving. I want to be the best—and I'm curious and I like learning and growing. Sometimes people worry about making mistakes, but my attitude is, 'Let's try and see what happens.'"

"I want to live my life as big as I can and then it'll be up to someone else to decide if I was successful," Matrka said.

The most difficult time for Matrka was his divorce in 1992. "I was very anxious about others controlling my life. However, I got some help and finally learned there is always a choice. I learned that I control myself, and this freed me to continue on my life journey."

Matrka said his life's mantra comes from the words of Francoise Chateaubriand. "If you understand this quote, you understand me: 'A master in the art of living draws no sharp distinction between his work and his play; his labor and his leisure; his mind and his body; his education and his recreation. He hardly knows which is which. He simply pursues his vision of excellence through whatever he is doing, and leaves others to determine whether he is working or playing. To himself, he always appears to be doing both.'"

Bret Adams

Partner, Adams, Babner & Gitlitz LLC

First job: 13 years old, detassling corn

Hobbies: working his farm, bow hunting, motorcycle riding

Favorite book: "A Sorrow in Our Heart: The Life of Tecumseh," Allan Eckert

Favorite movie: "And Justice for All"

I am: "Passionate."

Bret Adams always knew he would be a lawyer, not the sports agent he is today. However, he says, "being a sports agent has enabled me to afford to work on my real passion—to change the legal system. I perceived early that life wasn't fair, and I wanted to change things." To that end, he sued the Ohio Supreme Court in 2004—and won—arguing that a state rule that prevented lawyers from running advertisements with client testimonials was unconstitutional.

"My main passion is to make the law available and advantageous to the average person so they can control the legal system—not the lawyers and not the judges."

He remembers a time during his freshman year at Ohio University in Athens, Ohio, when his father tried to purchase a gas station. "The seller pulled the rug out from under him and changed the agreement. My dad decided to sue and found an attorney who would represent him for free. He won the case because of his lawyer. It was an eye-opening experience for me and drove my passion to try and make a difference."

As the oldest of six brothers and sisters who grew up in a "house on wheels" in Circleville, Ohio, Adams knows the value of hard work. His father was a diesel mechanic who moved the family around southeastern Ohio as he found work. "I knew that no one worked harder than my dad to take care of his family. It's amazing that my parents managed to raise six kids on the money he made," he said.

That's probably why today he says, "I'm for the underdog—that's where I came from. I relate to the person who has been slapped down and comes back. I really admire politician John Edwards, who stole my line, 'I'll never forget from where I came.'"

Although he wasn't surrounded by a host of role models growing up, Adams credits Bill Gardner, former owner of Distribution Properties in Columbus, Ohio, as a mentor. "He gave me a sign for my desk I still have that reads, 'Face the issue.'" Adams has adopted that sign into a personal guideline to "hit challenges head on, and realize in any negotiation that you have to respect the other party. It's all about credibility and your word. Unfortunately in the legal profession, you can't say that about everyone."

After earning his law degree in 1984 from Capital University, Adams started earning his own reputation by working felony cases for $20 an hour. A judge asked him to accept the cases because no other attorneys would work for that rate. Adams represented primarily African-American defendants in Columbus and Circleville with all-white juries. "I couldn't win them, but it was great experience," he said.

He realized he had been representing athletes from The Ohio State University who had gotten into legal trouble. "That's how I became a sports agent. I did a good job and built my reputation." His first well-known professional sports client was NFL player Byron Lee. "He told me, 'I know you have no idea what you're doing but I trust you.'" At one point, Adams also represented Daryl Strawberry. "It was happenstance. Suddenly, I was on the map by representing two highly recognized players." As for his current clients, Adams says, "They have no pretentiousness. I'm very lucky that I represent good people, and I don't have to represent jerks to make a living."

Today his client list reads like a "Who's Who" of the country's best athletes and coaches: former OSU football players Chris Spielman and Clark Kellogg, both of whom Adams describes as "good guys who give back;" George Karl, one of the NBA's highest-paid coaches; Boston Celtic basketball head coach Dennis Johnson; and Katie Smith, formerly of Logan, Ohio, now a professional basketball player for the Detroit Shock in the WNBA.

Success is "how I'm perceived by others. This is a very tough business, and I want to be known for my integrity. Having it enables me to represent quality people," Adams said. He believes that trust, integrity and a willingness to work hard are his top leadership skills, saying, "I can't be outworked, something I learned from my dad."

This small-town boy hasn't lost his appreciation for the best things in his life, which he says are riding his Harley-Davidson motorcycle and driving his tractor around his farm. A near-fatal motorcycle accident in 2005 has helped Adams to keep this perspective and has created an even stronger bond with his wife, Diane, and their three children.

"When you grow up checking to see if you have lunch money when you get on the bus, you're motivated by money. Material things certainly had an effect on me earlier, but now that I'm older, it's not about the money. I've been in the same house since 1991, and I don't need to have the biggest one on the block. I drive a nice car but I bought it at auction.

"My motivation now is to be happy and to be accepted by my family and friends and to have a good reputation. If people say, 'We always respected his opinion and approach even if we didn't agree,' then I've done a good job."

Ray Giesse

President, American Whistle Corporation

Words to live by:
"People are what matter. Surround yourself with the right people, and you'll do well."

Hometown: Mayfield Heights, Ohio
First job: cutting lawns
Hobbies: traveling, golfing, reading
Favorite movie: "Caddyshack"
I am: "Open-Minded."

Ray Giesse uses a rephrased Charles Dickens quote to describe the experience of owning American Whistle Corporation: "It's been the best of times and the worst of times. If everyone owned their own business for at least six months, the world would be a better place," he observed.

Giesse bought his pain and pride, American Whistle Corporation, in March 1987. The Columbus, Ohio, company, founded as Colstoff Manufacturing in 1956, was failing. Giesse acquired it from the founder's son-in-law by negotiating a deal based on market research, which indicated a promising market niche.

"I went into it with a certain amount of money that I was willing to lose. If the business didn't do well, I would just walk away. Then Wal-Mart and Kmart came to town, and I wanted to get their business," he said.

Giesse describes his most difficult time: "It took a year for Kmart to sign its first purchase order. And then when we finally did get the business, we discovered we couldn't meet the demand. Our manufacturing process was too labor-intensive. So we stopped selling to them, and we dug ourselves into a huge hole."

The debt weighed heavily on Giesse's mind. "I spent a couple of years not sleeping much. But I was too stubborn to quit. We came through it by hard work and focus—and we had great employees who helped turn it around," he said.

Today American Whistle Corporation is the only manufacturer of metal whistles in the United States. With safety and sports customers all over the country, its specialty is providing whistles customized by die-striking a company's logo on top.

Giesse's wife of 35 years, Diane Serraglio, and nine employees help him run the business. "So many people have helped make this company successful. My parents were very influential, and my wife is my true partner in business and in life. We work with great people—they are our assets."

Other leadership assets are Giesse's strong work ethic, marketing expertise and an ability to lead by example. "I think people here would say I'm open-minded and that I treat them fairly. I'm very people-oriented," he said. "It's all about teamwork—we motivate each other."

Giesse grew up in the suburbs of Cleveland wanting to be a veterinarian—in high school, he worked for three local vets. He entered Kent State University in 1969 and was on campus during the infamous Kent State shootings in May 1970. "They forever changed my thinking about politics and the media. The event was so sad and polarizing," he said.

After two years, Giesse dropped out of Kent State and got married. The couple came to Columbus so he could enter The Ohio State University's veterinary program. "I had a young child to support by then, and I figured vet medicine was too long a road. I switched my major to business."

While at OSU, Giesse worked any odd job he could to support his family, including driving a taxi during the holidays and managing apartments for a professor. By the time he graduated with a bachelor's degree in business administration at age 23, he was running his professor's real estate management company. "I was buying and managing real estate all over town. At that time, I had no intention of staying in Columbus, but my work locked us in," Giesse said.

Giesse left the real estate field to work for a national trucking company, where he was promoted to sales before quitting. "I was ready to do something on my own." He worked as an independent broker for another year as he looked for a business of his own to purchase. That's when he bought American Whistle, which he's owned for 20 years. "We meet a wide range of people in our business.

I love it—it's really fun."

In fact, Giesse's living the best time of his life right now. "We have a small but successful company. One of the beauties of getting older is that life becomes clearer. When you're younger, you're more focused on money. Success for me today isn't financial, but it's about my family—people are the most important thing. I believe you change the world by changing the people around you."

Part III
Corporate Movers & Shakers

PHIL URBAN

PRESIDENT AND CEO, GRANGE MUTUAL CASUALTY COMPANY

Words to live by:
"There's no straight path. Be willing to work hard and recognize your mistakes early."

Hometown: Dayton, Ohio
First job: lifeguard
Hobbies: reading, spending time with family, golfing
Favorite book: "High Output Management," Andrew Grove
Favorite movies: "Uncle Buck," "Airplane"
I am: "Introspective."

Even as a kid growing up in Dayton, Ohio, Phil Urban always ended up the leader. "I never set out to be in charge, but it just ended up that way."

The son of a medical doctor, Urban always thought he, too, would go into medicine. Participating in a Junior Achievement program his sophomore year in high school planted another seed. Urban and a friend, with the support of their JA-sponsored company, built their own business by taking junk manufacturing parts and making hurricane lamps.

"We sold them door-to-door, traded stocks and learned how to run a company. When I was a junior, we were named 'company of the year.' And I thought, 'This is pretty cool.' In retrospect, there was a message here that I didn't fully appreciate for many years," Urban said.

In addition to his early business acumen, Urban was a very good high school swimmer and was ranked fifth in the country in his event. Oddly enough, neither his coaches nor parents pushed him to go further with his swimming.

"I was very self-directed. Here I was winning state records and was good enough to have really done a lot. But no one was pushing me that way.

"Today I believe in a saying that goes, 'You are today all that has come before you.' If you're happy with where you are, don't be unhappy with the pathway," Urban said.

Urban bypassed a swimming career to enter the pre-med program at Miami University in Miami, Ohio. "I hated it. So I jumped onto a more productive path and switched majors to psychology because I thought it was fun. I had no idea what I would do with it. Along the way, though, I took a couple of business classes and became interested in how much psychology meshed with marketing," he said.

Urban graduated early with a psychology degree. He then took additional business classes before entering The Ohio State University, where he earned an MBA.

"It was common in those days for fresh MBAs to go to companies with revolving management programs like RCA or an investment bank. But I was a nonconformist. I graduated from college as a flower child, as part of the anti-war generation. As a result, I've always had this strong, altruistic compass."

Urban followed his compass and purposely accepted a job as marketing director for an international trade association in Washington, D.C. "I had a ball. I was 24 years old and teaching them about marketing strategy and research."

"Getting into insurance was completely happenstance," he said. Urban had moved to Florida after his Washington, D.C., job in order to start his own marketing business. "It was doing OK, but one day my dad suggested I put my education to better use," he explained. So Urban answered a blind ad in a St. Petersburg, Fla., newspaper and remembers how his heart sank when he called the recruiter and discovered the job was actually an insurance position in the Cleveland branch of Progressive Insurance.

Despite his initial disappointment, Urban withstood a four-hour-long interview and was offered the job. He accepted, and spent eight years with Progressive, accepting promotions throughout the country. "I've clocked in at all four time zones," he said.

Urban admits he made his first career mistake when he left Progressive for Berkshire Hathaway in Los Angeles. "I didn't like the city or the job. It wasn't a good situation for me and my family." Urban left nine months later for a position with Great American Insurance in Cincinnati. He stayed there six years before taking over as CEO for Guaranty National in Denver.

"I've learned from every situation, both good and bad. I once had this very intense job and worked for an extremely demanding, mean-spirited mentor. But it was terrific. It taught me that being mercurial is not a good thing," Urban said.

He explains how he landed at Grange Insurance in 1999: "It was an accident of fate. One day the phone rang, and it was a recruiter who wanted me to interview at a mutual company in Columbus, Ohio. I accepted their offer."

Urban thrives on creating new strategies for Grange to impact the insurance industry. "I'm passionate about strategic planning," he said. "I also think a lot about what others in the organization think. I want us to have a very noisy, open culture," he said.

He believes the hallmarks of his leadership are integrity and an ability to connect disparate dots into new approaches. "I think others would say that I'm a high-energy person who is always looking over the horizon and spends no time pointing fingers," he said.

Urban is modest about his success. "I think what an individual aspires to do changes over time. You move through life stages. Today I think that success is self-actualization and using your skills to make an impact."

"My experiences have taught me that life isn't all about work." Today Urban enjoys spending time with his wife, Kathy, and two children, ages 20 and 17. "My wife is the best partner I could ever have had. And our two kids still want to spend time with us. You've got to smell the roses. It's all about life balance."

DONNA JAMES

MANAGING DIRECTOR, LARDON & ASSOCIATES

Words to live by:
"You can recover from any mistake, except from the one that takes your life."

Hometown: Greensboro, N.C.
First job: working at a drycleaners
Hobbies: writing a book
Favorite book: anything by John Frey
Favorite movie: "Crash"
I am: "Growing."

Recounting her childhood, Donna James says, "I was a strange animal. I was bound and determined not to let people try and push me aside, to discount me." She overcame tremendous obstacles—such as growing up in the segregated South and being a teenage mother—to become one of the country's highest-ranking African-American female executives.

In March 2006, James retired as president of Columbus-based Nationwide Strategic Investments, a division of Nationwide Insurance Co., a $157 billion, Fortune 100 insurance and financial-services company. She directed the management of several Nationwide affiliates, including GatesMcDonald, Nationwide Advantage Company, Nationwide Health Plans, Nationwide Global Holdings, and the Nationwide Strategic Investment Fund LLC. Together, these subsidiaries generated about $650 million in annual revenues. She also created a new company, Nationwide Better Health.

Growing up in Greensboro, N.C., James was an excellent student who had big dreams for her future. In addition to becoming a scientist or an actress, she also wanted to be President of the United States. "My aspirations were all over the place," she laughed.

Much to her family's surprise, James became pregnant when she was 16. "No one ever thought this could ever happen to me. My mom was terribly disappointed, but she supported me through everything. She really inspired me."

After graduating from high school, and despite having no money and a new baby, James set her sights on attending college. "It amazes me now that I wasn't deterred." After receiving a $1,000 scholarship from the African-American sorority Delta Sigma Theta, she entered North Carolina A and T State University. She earned a bachelor's degree in accounting in 1979 and later passed the CPA exam.

James went to Detroit for a summer internship. Next, she accepted an audit position at Coopers & Lybrand (now PricewaterhouseCoopers). Her goal there was to become partner; however, after two years working a primarily nonprofit portfolio, she became restless. "The nonprofits were challenging and interesting, but that wasn't the track to a partnership."

Fate stepped in when Nationwide recruited James in 1981. "I started an accounting department from scratch, and it was a great learning experience," she said. She advanced through roles including investment products administration, vice president and assistant to the chairman and CEO, senior vice president of human resources, and executive vice president and CAO for U.S. and global operations. James was the company's first African-American senior executive.

At Nationwide, James credits Michael Bleiweiss, who hired her, for teaching her "how to listen and pay attention to things." She also learned along the way, "from someone else, who was brilliant, but a jerk," how to "continue to manage and not become derailed from my goals. I learned what to emulate and not to emulate."

James says her integrity and the ability to stay focused and solve problems are her key leadership strengths. "I'm very good at coaching because I know how to touch people, how to mentor them. People would say that I'm impatient but very determined."

In December 2005, James announced she would retire in March 2006. Nationwide CEO Jerry Jurgensen tried to convince her to stay. However, after 25 years, James was ready to begin the next part of her life. "I still see myself as CEO of my own company," she said.

Suffering a stroke in January 2006 "was a wake-up call in a major way. I didn't have any previous medical problems that would have indicated this, and it was very troublesome not knowing why it happened. The hardest part of making this decision was getting over my own ego, too. I remember being on the cover of *Black Enterprise* around the same time I was in the hospital, and calling up my mom to say, 'Hey, I'm in the same group as Oprah Winfrey!'"

These days, James is reflecting on the rest of her life. "I'm in transition now. I have a unique opportunity right now to really focus on what I'm interested in doing, rather than what someone else says I should be interested in. I was out of balance, and now I'm taking time to think about that. Today I want to experience those things that I love."

Success, in James' mind, is "being comfortable and happy about your life. It's also about being in a position to make a difference for other people." She's inspired by "people who have passion and can articulate what they feel. I admire people who are real and deal with important issues that affect the quality of life for others."

Today James is helping others through her firm, Lardon & Associates, which opened soon after her retirement from Nationwide. The firm specializes in business and executive advisory services. She also sits on the boards of Limited Brands, Inc. and Coca-Cola Enterprises.

James and her husband, Columbus attorney Larry James, enjoy collecting African art and spending time with their family, which includes two grown sons, their wives and five grandchildren. She says, "All my best things are around my family. I haven't figured out my legacy yet, but I think I've touched others and helped them better themselves. I wouldn't change anything."

Tom Hoaglin

CEO, Huntington Bancshares

Words to live by:
"Keep focused on the destination, but stay flexible and open to change. There will always be ups and downs. Seek help—you don't have to do things on your own."

Hometown: South Charleston, W. Va.
First job: paper carrier
Hobbies: golfing, reading
Favorite books: classics
I am: "Tall but also Balanced."

Tom Hoaglin's early jobs provided a sneak peek at the skills he would later develop to become a respected CEO. As a paper carrier, he enjoyed distributing papers and talking with customers, but, he laughed, "I hated collecting—ironic for a future banker!" During summers off from college, Hoaglin installed equipment for Western Electric. "I was lousy at my job. I'm not a very handy person, and I really didn't understand what I was doing. What I was good at was being reliable and dependable," he said.

Customer service, product delivery, reliability and dependability are hallmarks of Hoaglin's leadership at Huntington Bancshares. He entered banking in 1973, after earning an MBA from Stanford University and a degree in economics from Denison University in Granville, Ohio. While at Stanford, Hoaglin was recruited to work for City National Bank (the forerunner of Bank One) in Columbus, Ohio, by John B. McCoy, son of the bank's founder.

"I accepted John's offer because it wasn't limiting. He offered to give me a wide range of experiences in a short time and to let me decide what interested me most," Hoaglin said. "Also, my dad had recently retired, and I wanted to be close to home."

Home was South Charleston, W. Va., a suburb of Charleston, the state capitol. There he grew up with an older brother and loving parents who instilled strong values in their sons. "My dad was a Ph.D. chemist at Union Carbide, and he was very research-oriented. My brother got 100 percent of that, and I got zero. My dad also loved sports and business. I got 100 percent of that, and my brother got none," Hoaglin explained.

Growing up, Hoaglin set his sights on excelling in school. "I remember my seventh-grade science teacher asking me, 'Are you going to be as good a student as your older brother?' He was a straight-A student. I decided that I would be, too." Hoaglin complemented his academic efforts with leadership roles, becoming captain of the tennis team and president of both the junior class and the student council.

Hoaglin may have been motivated to meet his brother's performance, but it was his father's reputation that made a long-lasting impression. "I didn't really understand what my dad did, but I saw a guy who worked hard every day, who was admired by his peers, respected, and had a great work ethic. He was a wonderful role model," he said.

Obviously, Hoaglin exhibited similar qualities early in his tenure at Bank One. Within four years, McCoy senior asked Hoaglin to run a bank in Wooster, Ohio, with about $40 million in assets. Hoaglin, who was 28 at the time, said, "I had no idea how to run a bank then." He learned, and he performed so well that he was promoted to run larger banks throughout Ohio.

When Bank One bought a failed bank in Dallas in 1989, McCoy again asked Hoaglin to relocate, this time to revive a $10 billion bank. "It was very intense professionally. John knew I was smart enough to call for help if I needed it," Hoaglin said. "I admire both McCoys for putting people in places that forced them to grow."

Bank One continued to offer Hoaglin opportunities for growth and change. In 1992, he returned to Ohio to direct banking operations in Ohio and West Virginia. In 1995, McCoy decided to change Bank One's business model from decentralized to centralized operations. "I found myself at a decision point. I loved the old model and had thrived with it. I chose to stay, and I volunteered to head the transformation," Hoaglin said.

In Columbus in 1998, Hoaglin oversaw Bank One's merger with First Chicago MBD. When the merger was completed in March 1999, Hoaglin was 50 years old and had celebrated his 25th wedding anniversary with his wife, Ann. "We decided to take time off and play," Hoaglin said. "We loved being with each other, but by the end of the year I was feeling a little bit of a professional itch."

Hoaglin wanted a CEO role, but opportunities were few. Instead, Hoaglin accepted a number-two role at AmSouth Bank in Birmingham, Ala. "It didn't work out. The job wasn't what I understood it to be," he said. On the day the moving truck arrived at his Birmingham home, Hoaglin received a call from Frank Wobst, retiring CEO at Huntington Bancshares, to see if Hoaglin were interested in his position back in Columbus.

Newly arrived at Huntington, Hoaglin faced a sense of urgency from shareholders, skepticism from employees about the "new guy" who came from their rival, and soon thereafter, an investigation by the Securities and Exchange Commission, a "dark moment" for Hoaglin. "I thought it was unfair, but it was there." His early tenure was difficult, "yet stimulating in a professional sense. I feel we emerged successful," Hoaglin said.

Now he's motivated to "convince naysayers that a well-run bank in the Midwest can succeed financially and deliver results. Most investment-community people aren't impressed with Midwest banks because there are no high-growth markets here."

Hoaglin thrives on developing a game plan and strategy, implementing it, watching the organization change and seeing results. Fairness and respect are also high on his agenda. He relies on his abilities to connect well with associates, be approachable, communicate effectively and judge talent well.

"Today success means better financial performance for my company, better customer service, and enabling a team to feel pride again. It's not about 'what's in it for me?' It's about contributing to the larger community," he said.

He wants his leadership legacy to prove you don't have to be autocratic—that you can trust and rely on others—to achieve results. "And, like my Huntington forefathers, I want this organization to continue to be a corporate leader in the community."

DONAL MALENICK

CEO AND CHAIRMAN, COLUMBUS STEEL CASTINGS

Hometown: Ingram Branch, W.Va

First job: 9 years old, working as the elementary school janitor

Hobbies: golfing, horseback riding, bird hunting

Favorite movie: "The Jerk"

I am: "Honest."

Donal Malenick was enjoying retirement from his job as president of Worthington Industries—a position he held from 1976 until his retirement in 1999—when he was presented with an opportunity he just couldn't refuse. He was asked to rescue a bankrupt steel company in Columbus, Ohio, that was led from 1908-28 by President George H. Bush's great-grandfather, Samuel Prescott Bush.

"I could have just stayed in retirement, and the company would have been liquidated. But I wanted to save the jobs. There were 1,000 workers there," Malenick said.

Reorganized by Malenick and a group of investors, Columbus Steel Castings today is the largest single-site steel foundry in the world, covering over 80 acres, 22 of which are under one roof. It manufactures steel castings for freight and passenger cars, locomotives, earth moving equipment, steel rolling mills, dams, bridges and more.

"I've tried to set up a business that will still be around in 100 years. I've made decisions that will be good long-term for the company and not just make money in the short-term. I will not make a decision simply to boost my own ego," Malenick said.

He learned his progressive attitude during his childhood in West Virginia. Malenick was the third oldest of seven children; his mother took care of the home and the children, and his father worked in a local coal mine. "We were very poor, but I didn't know it. The company owned everything—we had a company house, used company coal and shopped at the company store. I realized at a very young age that if I wanted things, I'd have to work for my own money."

This realization prompted the 9-year-old Malenick to work as the janitor of his elementary school for $14 a month. "I shared it with my brothers and sisters, and my dad insisted that I save some of it, too," he remembers.

He credits his father with teaching him his work ethic. "With seven kids around, there were a lot of chores. My dad demanded you do it right. I knew that if I did them right the first time, I'd have more time to play," he laughs. "And if we didn't do it right the first time, we did it until he said it was OK."

Malenick continues, "I learned my definition of success back in my childhood, that a person is successful when they enjoy their work and can provide a comfortable lifestyle, no matter how much money they make."

While at Oak Hill High School in the mid-1950s, Malenick made $1.25 an hour working evenings and Saturdays at a local grocery store. "I was completely self-supporting by the time I was 16. My dad never gave me any money after that. After graduating from high school, I was working 60 hours a week. I knew I didn't want to spend the rest of my life making just $1.25 an hour, so I left for Chicago."

He spent a year there working in a steel mill, then left for Columbus in 1959 to work for Worthington Steel for $1.66 an hour. Except for one summer working in construction, he never left. About his career there he said: "I started as a laborer, then I was promoted to a machine operator, then a supervisor. Along the way, I always wanted to do more each day than what I was paid for. I always had the desire to work hard."

"I always felt that as long as I worked hard, John McConnell (the owner of Worthington Steel) would give me a chance to be whatever I wanted to be. He was my role model. I don't think he realizes how many people he's touched," Malenick added.

Malenick had been retired for three years when the opportunity to reorganize Columbus Steel Castings came about in 2002. Located on Columbus' south side, CSC had its roots as Murray-Hayden Foundry, a small iron foundry that served the local agricultural community starting in 1881. Ten years later it began making iron couplers for the relatively new railroad industry. As the railroad expanded and the demand for stronger steel couplers increased, the company grew. By 1902 the company had changed its process to steelmaking and changed its name to Buckeye Steel Castings.

Worthington Industries had acquired Buckeye Steel's flagship, Buckeye International, in 1980, in a stock-for-stock merger. However, by 1999, Buckeye International was sold to Key Equity Capital in a leveraged buy-out and functioned as a stand-alone company for the next four years. A weak rail market in 2000 and then the effects of Sept. 11 decimated the company. By 2002, the company was bankrupt and out of business.

Malenick and his investors renamed the company CSC, and instituted a "pro-employee," union-free philosophy, designed to reward employees when the company makes a profit. Malenick has made his mark by instituting profit sharing, flexible job assignments and "pay-for-performance" compensation.

"My strongest leadership quality is that I'm a people-person. You get results from people. I've always believed in being fair but firm. I ask their input, but then when I make a decision, I expect them to support it."

"I've learned to have a sense of humor about myself, too," he adds.

About his management style, Malenick said, "I think the workers trust and respect me. I never bluff them—if I don't have the answer to a question, I say so."

It's hard for Malenick to pinpoint the single-best time of his life, saying, "I've had a great life. So many good things have happened to me along the way, and much of it's been because I've been in the right place at the right time."

He reflects, "I really believe that people make things too complicated today. I believe in keeping it simple—that's worked for me. As long as people understand what they're supposed to do, that's what counts."

Brian Ellis

President and COO, Nationwide Realty Investors

Words to live by:
"Treat people like you want to be treated."

Hometown: Youngstown, Ohio
First job: IBM
Hobbies: spending time with family, golfing
Favorite book: "The DaVinci Code," Dan Brown
I am: "Family-Oriented."

Brian Ellis, president and COO of Nationwide Realty Investors, describes his leadership style as "action-oriented, I try to see the big picture, and despite some ambiguity, still move forward decisively."

A few months after he was made president of NRI, these skills were put to their strongest test. On May 5, 1997, a city sales-tax levy that would have provided public funding for a national hockey arena in downtown Columbus failed.

It was a pivotal moment for the newly formed company. Ellis explains, "The next day we were given what became the largest 'other duties' as assigned projects of all times: to determine whether or not a privately funded arena was feasible and, if so, build it.

"One of the reasons the tax levy failed was because many thought Columbus had a 'plan B.' But there was no 'plan B.' The day after the levy failed, the National Hockey League assured us they really wanted to be in Columbus. If we could build a suitable facility, then we would be selected as an NHL franchise. With a number of other interested cities waiting, they told us, 'You have 30 days.'"

Undaunted by the deadline, Ellis and Nationwide's chief investment officer, Bob Woodward, started from ground zero to come up with a plan. The plan was strongly supported by then-Nationwide CEO Dimon McFerson and the Nationwide board. "On June 2, we announced that Nationwide would build the arena. But we also had the vision to build a district," Ellis said. "The Arena District isn't the only project we've done, but it certainly has shaped our future."

In 1989, when Ellis was 27, he began to run what was informally known as Nationwide's "Partnership Portfolio." In this role, he managed commercial real estate ventures with third parties. This assignment came at a time when Nationwide had become less involved in real estate development after a more active period in the 1960s and 1970s.

"I had a good variety of opportunities when I started with Nationwide," Ellis said. "People didn't think I would stay this long, but it always remained interesting and challenging."

Ellis did his job so well that in 1996, he was given another opportunity. "Bob Woodward asked me to determine how Nationwide could become 100 percent engaged in the real estate development business and act as an opportunistic investor in equity real estate. I made a recommendation to create a separate, distinct affiliate with streamlined approval processes and an entrepreneurial culture." On January 1, 1997, NRI was formed and Ellis was elected president and COO.

Today NRI is the real estate development affiliate of Nationwide, a Columbus-based Fortune 100 company. It is one of the country's largest diversified insurance and financial services organizations, with more than $157 billion in assets.

It would be easy for a man in Ellis' position to describe success by the numbers, but he explains, "You have to start out with what's important to you. Establish your goals and dreams, define what you want to be, and make a 100 percent effort toward those goals."

Ellis feels strongly that a critical component to success is a willingness to compete —continuously striving to be your very best.

"I've been fortunate to work with and for great people. I've always been supported by the leadership at Nationwide," he said. He gives credit to Bob Woodward, who hired him as vice president of real estate investments; McFerson; and current CEO Jerry Jurgensen.

Ellis summarizes his style this way: "I think people see me as pretty aggressive leader who is fairly direct. I don't leave a lot to the imagination; I let people know how I feel about things. I try to treat people how I'd like to be treated."

Alan Hoover

President and CEO, Kahiki Foods

Words to live by:
"Do your very best every day and the 'scoreboard' will take care of itself."

Hometown: Charlotte, N.C.
First job: mowing grass, washing cars
Hobbies: reading, bicycling, weight-lifting, exercising
Favorite movies: "Field of Dreams, "Bull Durham," "Out of Africa"
I am: "Hard-Working."

Say "Kahiki" to many Central Ohioans, and the word evokes memories of a Polynesian restaurant on Columbus' east side. With giant tikis flanking oversized wooden doors, the building looked like a tropical oasis and offered diners a taste of one as well. Though the landmark restaurant closed in 2000, the Kahiki brand flourishes today in the frozen-food market as a $25-million company, shipping to locations throughout the United States and Canada.

To gain insight from the company's leader, however, you need to trade the image of a grass skirt for a grassy playing field, because President Alan Hoover credits his sports experiences with teaching him how to succeed.

As a baseball and basketball player during his undergraduate years at Clemson University, Hoover says, "I learned what it takes to be successful: hard work, sacrifice, dedication, balance and consistency." He relied on these ideals as he helped build Kahiki into a high-growth business, prompting the company to relocate into a new 119,000-square-foot facility and introduce an array of new products.

Hoover knows how to "step up to the plate" when times demand it. Having begun his career at Kahiki in 1999 as vice president of sales and marketing, in 2005 Hoover succeeded Kahiki's founder and president, Michael Tsao, who died unexpectedly of complications from diabetes. Hoover aims not only to carry on Tsao's desire for Kahiki, which was to "step it up, and take it to another level," but also to strengthen the company's finances, build teamwork and make the highest-quality Asian foods in the market.

In business, keeping score means tracking the bottom line and knowing what gains or losses are made every day. At Kahiki, the company had to overcome the loss of Tsao, significant and costly start-up problems in the new plant, and tight cash flow. Hoover kept the company afloat by relying on his "Four-Ds" game plan: discipline, dedication, determination and desire to achieve. "I've always worked hard for what I've gotten," he says.

Hoover also proudly coaches his international team at Kahiki. The company's 190 workers come from the United States, China, Mexico and Central America; and many of them are first-generation immigrants. Kahiki's managers hold "five-minute huddles" with staff to communicate the day's work plan. Hoover's goal is to put more accountability and responsibility at the team and group-leader level. This coach even uses actual scoreboards to provide quick, visual feedback of operational processes.

"I'm a stickler for details," Hoover notes, which is why he invests time in fine-tuning the fundamentals. "I want to see our people doing the 'right things right' every day."

Although Hoover didn't achieve his dream of becoming a professional athlete, having quickly realized "the pros are really good," he loves what he's doing. Along with the Chinese saying that "the journey is the reward," Hoover lives by the following advice: "Give it your very best, every single day, and I truly believe that good things will happen."

Gary Strapp

Senior Vice President of Aircraft Programs, NetJets

Words to live by:
"Really like what you're doing. Don't accept a job just for money, position or advancement—the satisfaction won't last long unless you like the work."

Hometown: Columbus, Ohio
First job: at a car wash/gas station with friends
Hobbies: golfing, playing basketball, enjoying his children's activities
Favorite movies: classics, anything by Alfred Hitchcock
I am: "Family-Oriented."

Many leaders struggle to balance work time and family time. NetJets senior vice president Gary Strapp keeps a tight handle on this challenge, always choosing work that enables him to prioritize his family.

This father of six daughters grew up in Columbus, Ohio, with two brothers and seven sisters of his own. "I tell people that I have one daughter turning 21 and one turning over," he laughed, describing the age range of his children. "My goal has been to be happy in my career so that it doesn't affect my home life. In fact, my personal guidelines are entrenched in my religion and my family. I want to be the same person at home and at work."

As a young boy, Strapp aspired to be a certified public accountant like one of his uncles, who also had a large family. "I thoroughly enjoyed growing up. I still have almost all the same friends," he said. Unique among many mobile executives,

Strapp has lived in one city his entire life, from birth through college and into his career. He met his wife of 24 years, Linda, in high school. He's played cards every month for 30 years with the same group. And he's golfed in a league with 30 friends for nearly as many years, too.

While staying connected to family and friends, Strapp earned his accounting degree from The Ohio State University. "As a boy, math was my best subject. I realized much later that there's not that much math in accounting," he said.

Strapp accepted his first job after college at a small, local firm. It soon merged with two national firms and became bureaucratic and "paper structured," prompting Strapp to take a new accounting job with Laventhal Horvath. There, he enjoyed his work and advancements until the firm suddenly halted all promotions, including the naming of new partners. Strapp again looked elsewhere for work, this time responding to a newspaper ad for a position at Executive Jet, the predecessor to NetJets.

It was a wise move. Within six months, Laventhal Horvath closed its doors. Strapp remains satisfied and challenged at NetJets, with 17 years under his belt. "I was intrigued by aviation—and it was just what I needed then because it fit in with my family lifestyle."

Fittingly, NetJets chairman and CEO Richard Santulli is also "adamant about family," said Strapp. "I have a passion for the company, and I enjoy coming to work every day." It's a place where he contributes "honesty, integrity and accuracy, both in numbers and what I say." He believes others in the company would echo this description by saying he "listens, analyzes and acts."

When Strapp joined NetJets, the company employed 150 and owned 14 aircraft. The company overcame financial troubles in the early 1990s and achieved explosive growth in the late 1990s. NetJets now employs over 4,500 and manages 450 aircraft, purchasing 50-60 new planes every year and disposing of them after approximately 10 years' use.

Founded in 1964, NetJets is the world's first, private business-jet-charter and aircraft-management company. In 1986, Santulli created a fractional-aircraft ownership program, which lets individuals and companies buy part of a private jet and guarantees availability all year with just hours' notice. Satisfied customer Warren Buffet, chairman and CEO of Berkshire Hathaway, acquired the company in 1998.

Strapp made his mark on NetJets initially by leading the financial department through dark hours in the early 1990s; now he runs the aircraft programs, relying on his long-term relationship-building skills to connect with manufacturers and vendors. Success, he says, is determined by others, but he hopes his legacy is that "people enjoyed working with me and for me. People won't recall the projects so much as the person."

If he could alter anything on his path, Strapp said, it wouldn't be the time he's spent with family. He's enjoyed the high points and suffered the tragedies, including the death of his 9-year-old brother when Strapp was in college and the deaths of his wife's parents within 30 days of each other.

However, if Strapp could change one element of his professional behavior, it would have been to interact more with the most senior leadership of the companies where he worked. Nonetheless, he reflected, "I'm not an aggressive person, and I'm not at a loss in my career for being that way."

Don DePerro

Publisher, Columbus Business First

Words to live by:
"Learn what you don't know as fast as you can."

Hometown: Buffalo, N.Y.
First job: 9 years old, paper carrier
Hobbies: running, working out, enjoying his children
Favorite book: "The Godfather," Mario Puzo
Favorite movie: "The Godfather"
I am: "Fun."

People who say they've gone through their lives with no regrets are just smart enough to have figured out how to forget the bad stuff. I'm the poster boy for learning from your own mistakes. I tell people I'm like the Irish Setter I had as a boy. I'm certainly not the brightest light in the room. I'm a slow learner. But typically once I learn, I don't forget."

Don DePerro may have made some mistakes along the way, but judging by his career path, they've never slowed him down. After he graduated from Buffalo State College with a journalism degree, DePerro landed his first reporting jobs in 1981 for The Buffalo News and the Niagara Gazette.

His journalism career began to take off when he accepted a job at the Buffalo edition of Business First, an affiliate of American City Business Journals. Within a few short years, he advanced within the company and moved south to Charlotte, N.C., where he held the positions of managing editor and then editor. Another promotion took him even further south to Jacksonville, Fla., to serve as publisher, a position he held for almost five years.

DePerro said his tenure at the Florida paper was the most difficult period in his life because the paper was in a turnaround situation. DePerro was the paper's seventh publisher in less than six years. "It was an incredibly overwhelming experience for me. I didn't sleep a lot." However, he describes the next few years after the paper's turnaround as wonderful, even the best time of his life.

DePerro became publisher of the Columbus, Ohio, edition 11 years ago. Reflecting on his career, he said, "What a great ride!" adding, "I could walk away from all this right now at the age of 48 and still be a happy man."

Growing up in Buffalo, DePerro dreamed he'd be a wide receiver for the Buffalo Bills professional football team. He remembers how he and his friends would paint a 100-yard football field on the street with some white paint and a yardstick. He also recalls how he always loved to write. "I was great in English. I wrote for our elementary school paper, The Marksman. I remember writing long stories when I was in fifth grade," he said.

DePerro entered the high school honors program at St. Joseph's Collegiate Institute. He remembers doing very well on his entrance exam, but math proved to be a struggle. "I was probably the only kid to flunk honors math, but I carried a high 90s average in English. So I was exempt from English finals but I had to go to summer school for geometry."

He credits his now 85-year-old father with teaching him his strong work ethic. "I remember hearing my dad clanking his spoon in his coffee every morning. He got up every day and drove his truck to make deliveries. He never called in sick, and Buffalo winters weren't easy."

DePerro also says that two of his college journalism teachers helped him early in his career. "I learned a lot from both of them." Rae Tyson, an environmental reporter at the Niagara Gazette, also influenced DePerro. "Ray taught me patience and persistence." Now he's motivated by his wife and three children.

DePerro said, "Success is in the eye of the beholder. Many millions of Americans work hard every day and go home to their families and have meaningful lives. Most of them believe in a higher being. They're all successful," he added.

If he could change one thing about his life, DePerro said, "I wish I hadn't been so naïve. Too many times I assumed people were telling me the truth." He hopes his leadership legacy will be that he left things in better shape than when he found them.

As for his own guiding principles, DePerro said, "I believe in really simple values...in fairness, hard work. I also try to laugh every day. I don't take myself too seriously." He believes he's a consensus-building leader. "I also care about my associates, and I'm a good judge of people. I make really good hires," he said. DePerro thinks his employees would describe him as fair and consistent.

DePerro reflected on his career: "I'm sensitive. I'd rather err on the side of being taken advantage of because I was a good guy. I've been a slow starter in every job I've had in my life. I've never been a fireball coming out of the chute. If I hadn't learned patience, I wouldn't have come as far as I have."

Wade Kozich

Managing Partner, GBQ Partners

Words to live by:
"Do something you're passionate about."

Hometown: Lorain, Ohio
First job: 9 years old, golf caddy
Hobbies: golfing, riding his bicycle, arts/theater
Favorite book: "Walden Pond," David Thoreau
Favorite movie: "Casablanca"
I am: "A friend."

Although Wade Kozich never had a particular childhood dream about what he wanted to be when he "grew up," perhaps accounting was in his blood all along. He recalls how, in the early 1970s, he hitchhiked from Ohio to California on a mere $6.

Kozich was 20 years old and back at home in Lorain, Ohio, after two years in the U.S. Naval Academy. "I had wanted to get away from home and try a new experience. I wanted something different and special." Kozich's experience at Annapolis "was excellent. They kicked my butt pretty good." Although he did well academically and athletically, he soon realized that a military career wasn't what he really wanted.

"I went home broke, but I didn't want to be a burden on my parents. My mother dropped me off at the Interstate with $40 in my pocket, and I hitchhiked to California. I spent $6 getting out there, including food," he explained.

He remembers being on his own for the very first time in San Francisco. "I was there in the 1970s, which was a pretty crazy time. I faced distractions, but I was always conscious of making good choices. I became my own person there. I learned self-reliance." Kozich completed college while out west. He left the West Coast two years later with a bachelor's degree, a car and "some money in my pocket."

Kozich returned to Ohio with the idea that he would attend law school in Columbus. Instead he took a job in 1976 at Groner, Boyle & Quillin and "really liked it." He's never left.

Kozich was chosen to take over as head of the company after one of its remaining founders retired in 1997. Since that time, GBQ has grown from 35 to over 100 employees and is now the largest locally owned accounting and consulting firm in Central Ohio. The firm has been named the last four out of five years as one of the "Best of the Best" firms in the country by *Inside Public Accounting* magazine.

"Life should be about constant improvement. I try and do things that will make me feel good about myself." He goes on to say this about success: "When I was younger, I would have said success is about making money. And now that I'm older, it's about trying to feel good about what I'm doing and knowing that I'm trying to do the right thing."

He describes his leadership style as "allowing people the freedom to perform. I try to bring vision, passion and courage." He admits that his staff would probably say he's great with ideas, but that he's "not as good with implementation." Kozich says that he treats people according to the "Golden Rule. It all starts and ends with people."

The young Kozich spent his summers playing sports from morning until dark. His father was an attorney; his mother stayed home with six children. "I grew up in the 'Ozzie and Harriet' era. I was very blessed as a child. I had good parents."

During that time, his teachers, coaches and parents were all influential. "I played sports pretty well; this was back in the Vince Lombardi days, when there was a high emphasis on winning. So I developed a winning attitude."

He remembers his father's law firm partner, Joe Ujhely, as someone he admired who was also influential. "Joe told me that even in your 'down times,' it's important to at least maintain where you're at and not go backwards."

Kozich has great admiration for "people who are faced with adversity and deal with it in a courageous manner. You can work through life's troubles. No one gets out of this life without pain. Just do your best and don't give up."

The best thing about his life, Kozich said, is that he's a "big believer in love. I value it tremendously." That's why, if he could change one thing in his life's journey, Kozich would "take more time off and spend it with my three great daughters. When I was younger, I worked too much."

His advice for others? "Life is what happens every day. Don't take it for granted."

Jim Hagedorn

President, CEO and Chairman, The Scotts Miracle-Gro Company

Words to live by:
"Believe in yourself."

Hometown: Sands Point, N.Y.
First job: at a pet store
Hobbies: flying; collecting cars, guns and homes; scuba diving; snow skiing
Favorite movie: "Pulp Fiction"
I am: "Happy."

Jim Hagedorn grew up as a free spirit. He ran away from home as a teenager, flew fighter jets after college and now commands the country's most famous lawn and garden company.

Born in Sands Point, N.Y., Hagedorn was one of six children, including two sisters (one a twin), and twin younger brothers. "When you have four kids in two years, you almost have a neighborhood," he said, remembering how they all enjoyed riding their Schwinn bicycles.

Despite close ties with his siblings, Hagedorn was often at odds with his father, Horace Hagedorn. "He was very focused and driven to grow his business," Hagedorn said. "We had our 'neighborhood,' and we didn't miss the 'sheriff.'"

Hagedorn knew he wanted to be an airline pilot when he grew up and assumed he'd enter the military. He built model airplanes and admired a neighbor who was a pilot. But true to his adventurous spirit, he left home at 15 to live in communes in Vermont. "It was the '70s. It was pretty much a good time," he said. Upon returning two years later, Hagedorn restarted his life and changed from being part of the "radical left" to working at a union print shop before entering college and then the U.S. Air Force.

"I'm not good at being in the middle of anything," he said. "I'm a very hungry guy when it comes to wanting more. More territory, more control, more space. I have this appetite for growth. I love to compete."

He earned a degree in aeronautical science from Embry-Riddle Aeronautical University in Daytona, Fla., and used his training to work seven years as a fighter pilot. Today, flying is Hagedorn's favorite hobby, something special he does for his own enjoyment, despite the company's reservations about his safety.

Between college and the Air Force, Hagedorn worked for six months with his father, who in 1951 co-founded the Miracle-Gro Company with Otto Stern. "It was like combat every day," Hagedorn learned. "In commercial combat, your 'territory' is market share. Even though nobody's leaving on a stretcher, it can be really ruthless in business."

When his Air Force service ended, Hagedorn wanted to return to Miracle-Gro. "I never intended for the military to be a career. So, I called up my dad and said, 'What do you think?' and he said, 'You can come interview with me.'" He aced the interview by honestly answering his father's question about what job he wanted with "your job." However, "I started in the basement" to learn the business."

Hagedorn calls his company a "giant among midgets" in their field. Under his leadership, the company has blossomed, growing from $30 million to $3 billion. "It has been a sheer pleasure creating the most powerful business of its kind in the world and watching a young team develop into leaders. I also got a lot of pleasure out of sharing the work for a couple years with my dad."

To create success, he said, "You've got to have innovative, out-of-the-box ideas, good judgment, not be too stupid, and believe in yourself. Fifty to 60 percent of my ideas are good ideas—which means that nearly half of my ideas aren't! That's why you must surround yourself with people to balance your strengths," he advised.

Others, he said, would describe him as "pretty crazy—and that was offensive at first. My style is a little unorthodox, but it works. I don't see people running out of here!"

"You can't do it by yourself," he continued. "You've got to get people to want to follow you. I have a somewhat New York view of the world—I use a lot of colorful language. It's high energy around me. You've got to have a thick skin." He runs his company like a night at the Hagedorn dinner table: He doesn't acknowledge hands held in the air—he prefers passionate people who have something to say and just say it.

Personal success to Hagedorn is "nebulous" but generally equates to happiness and doing what he wants. "Material success means squat if you're not happy." He's sharply critical of the country's focus on material things. "We're so material that people willingly choose to give up staying home with their kids because they want more stuff instead."

"At this point in my life, I'm not working for money. I enjoy leading, and I enjoy power." Being goal-oriented and working nonstop toward goals, Hagedorn doesn't understand why people give up so easily on their own desires.

At 20, Hagedorn set a personal goal when he first met his wife, Karli, then 16. He told his best friend at dinner the night after seeing her for the first time, "I'm marrying her." Six months later, they were engaged. The couple waited until after college to marry to satisfy her father's request. She's a key part of his success, raising their children (now 24, 21 and 15) and managing their home in Long Island, N.Y., for the past 12 years while Hagedorn commutes to Marysville, Ohio, for a five-day week at Scotts Miracle-Gro.

"My life is very narrow," he said, admitting that he's not social outside his family. That's counter to his leadership style, which he says is emotional and charismatic, embodying the ability to step out of the crowd and be unique. "I think leadership is genetic, not learned. I think a lot of people are smarter than I am, but they haven't done what I've done."

Hagedorn's legacy at his company, he said, would be that it lives beyond his leadership. His most important legacy, though, is in his children. "I think my kids are pretty cool."

STEWART ("STU") KEMPER

PRESIDENT, TIMBERTECH

Words to live by:
"Seek out people who know more than you do."

Hometown: Tallmadge, Ohio
First job: paper carrier
Hobbies: motorcycle riding, learning golf
Favorite books: "The Fountainhead," "Atlas Shrugged," Ayn Rand, "Good to Great," Jim Collins
Favorite movies: "Animal House," "Airplane"
I am: "Passionate."

Stu Kemper always thought he would be an attorney or an accountant because that's what he associated with being a successful professional. "I started out in accounting, and about half-way through my time at Ohio University I just knew it wasn't right for me. I switched to finance and management because I knew I wanted to run a business someday," he explained.

Inspired by Ronald Reagan—"because he had a vision and could execute big ideas"—Kemper also recalls being impressed by Lee Iacocca's strong personality when he led the Chrysler turnaround. "I also really admire my parents. My dad was a shoe buyer, and my mom retired from the Social Security Administration. They always encouraged me and my younger sister to do well in school, but they also let me satisfy my early hunger and aptitude for music." While in high school, Kemper played trombone in the jazz and marching bands and guitar in a rock band.

"Success is internally driven," Kemper said. "When I was younger, it was probably about money, power, prestige, fame and ego. But over the years I've learned that success is being comfortable with who you are, having a positive attitude and providing positive energy. It's about handling and facing challenges, whatever they may be, and being comfortable in your own shoes."

"Everyone has 'blessings and burdens' in their lives," he continued. "I like to look behind the scenes and see how people are really grinding it out every day. I continue to admire civil servants, for example, like policemen and firemen. I think they're often overworked and under-appreciated."

Kemper knows from personal experience about "grinding it out" through adversity. One of his twin sons is autistic, presenting many challenges for Kemper. "It's so frustrating that you can't fix or control the situation. It's been really tough on me, my marriage and our family, but we get through it one day at a time."

Along with Kemper's challenges are many blessings. In 1993 he joined Crane Plastics in Columbus, Ohio, to develop, launch and manage a variety of plastic-extrusion products. In 1995 and 1996, Kemper led the development of a new product using wood-composite technology in decking, dubbed TimberTech. He used this as the focus of his capstone project for his MBA at Capital University in Columbus.

TimberTech was so successful that the product was spun off into a stand-alone company in 1999, with Kemper named as president. "Tanny Crane and Chris Berger from Crane saw something in me and gave me an opportunity to run with it," Kemper said.

Today his company competes in a $4 billion market for deck and railing products; $750 million of the market comes from 80-plus composite competitors, with TimberTech producing more than $120 million last year. Recognizing his accomplishment, Ernst and Young selected Kemper as "Entrepreneur of the Year" in the Emerging Entrepreneur category for the Central Ohio Region in 2004.

Kemper is confident that his business acumen and his ability to build teams and instill confidence are what have enabled him to make TimberTech a leader in a fast-growing and highly competitive market. "My leadership style is hands-off. I like to delegate authority. I'll make a decision if necessary, but I believe my team should be making most of the decisions if things are running properly."

Quick to point out that he hasn't done it alone, Kemper said: "On the business side I still have a number of mentors with whom I try to visit as often as I can.

Looking back, if I could change one thing, I would have connected with and listened to mentors earlier in life. I didn't realize until later just how much that could've helped me."

Kemper believes people should choose mentors based on their ability to increase knowledge, not just to improve job opportunities. He says, "A mentor is someone who knows more than you on a particular subject. They could be older, younger, richer, poorer—it doesn't matter. They can still teach you something." In addition to his own mentors, in recent years Kemper has relied on TEC (The Executive Committee), a peer group of business leaders from about 15 companies that meets monthly to discuss common business issues and concerns.

Personally, Kemper relies on his family for balance. "Having kids, prioritizing life—it's all about them, though business is fun, too." He's also motivated to work hard to help his son overcome autism.

"I try to live a life of honesty and openness. My first priority is taking care of my family and living a balanced life. In business I like to be forward-leaning and help my team grow. I tend to be aggressive because I'm trying to make TimberTech the leader in our industry," said Kemper.

"I like building and guiding a company that will sustain over time—that will survive without me. I'm pretty sure TimberTech is a chapter in my book, not the book."

Steve Rasmussen

President and CEO, Property and Casualty Insurance Operations, Nationwide

Words to live by (a quote):
"Meaningful success comes to the aggressive with the love of mankind."

Hometown: Webster City, Iowa
First job: selling men's clothing in a department store
Hobbies: golfing, traveling
Favorite book: "Conspiracy of Fools," Kurt Eichenwald
Favorite movie: "Crash"
I am: "Determined."

Steve Rasmussen grew up in the small, quiet Iowa town of Webster City and led what he described as a typical childhood. He played several sports and earned a part in his high school play. "It was a musical. I don't remember what I played, but I was never one to get in front of the crowd, so I was probably doing something in the background," he said.

In addition to his love of sports, Rasmussen was fascinated with the thought of becoming an airline pilot. "I thought that would be kind of cool," he said. But his world changed when he entered The University of Iowa.

The Vietnam War was raging, and campus riots and political rallies began to alter his perceptions of the world. "It was an interesting time to grow up. You grew up with 'Ozzie and Harriet,' and then all of a sudden the '60s came along. You got involved with whatever your opinions were about the war," Rasmussen said.

Although he entered college to study accounting, he changed his mind after taking an insurance class led by a particularly inspiring professor. After earning a bachelor's degree in business administration, Rasmussen accepted a job in 1974 with Allied Insurance in Des Moines, Iowa (later acquired by Nationwide). He progressed from positions in underwriting, product management and sales, to eventually become president and chief operating officer.

Rasmussen remembers one of his bosses at Allied, Jim Kirkpatrick, as someone who helped him out along the way. "He taught me how to manage and understand people. He was an extremely effective leader," Rasmussen said. Now, he admires leaders such as Abraham Lincoln and Franklin Roosevelt. "I have a deep admiration for people who made a real effort at great personal cost to move the world forward."

His toughest challenge came early in his career in California when he had to shut down the local office. "The folks there had done absolutely nothing to deserve it. They had worked hard, but the company was having problems and needed to consolidate operations," Rasmussen said. "That had a huge influence on me. I decided from that point on, I was going to do everything I could to prevent bad things from happening to people who didn't deserve them."

Rasmussen was selected for his current position at Nationwide in 2003. He is responsible for the operations of Nationwide Insurance, Allied Insurance, Nationwide Agribusiness and Specialty Products. He describes his 32-year career as a "painting that's not quite finished. I look at the possibilities that exist for this company. That keeps me getting up every morning."

Rasmussen believes that his leadership style is defined by his determination and sense of competition. "I'm very determined. I also have the ability to set a vision and articulate it. And I have a relentless passion to get things done. I think others would describe me exactly the same way," he said.

"I'm a competitor. I'd just as soon we win as the competition."

It appears that Rasmussen has found the perfect marriage between his personal beliefs and work. "You have to build around your personal values, such as integrity. That's how you decide things. Nationwide is a strong, values-based company. Enron wouldn't happen here," he added.

Coming to terms with his success has been a long process for Rasmussen. He explained: "When you start out, it's about things or this 'north star' you're trying to get to. Then you recognize success involves what happens with a lot of other people and not just what happens with yourself. This has been a slow evolution for me, to determine where I'm taking people and the responsibility that brings with it."

Professional accomplishments aside, Rasmussen's best time has been his marriage and raising his three sons. Reflecting on his life, he said, "I wouldn't change a thing because then that would change a bunch of other things that matter."

"I hope that when I'm gone, the people at Nationwide can say I made a difference."

CARL KOHRT

PRESIDENT AND CEO, BATTELLE

Words to live by:
"Be intelligent, curious and passionate."

Hometown: Tuscola, Ill.
First job: cutting corn out of soybeans on local farms
Hobbies: freshwater fishing, anything on the water
Favorite book: "Team of Rivals: The Political Genius of Abraham Lincoln," Doris Kearns Goodwin
Favorite movie: "Star Wars"
I am: "Respectful."

Carl Kohrt was a small-town kid who always dreamed he'd be a science professor one day. He grew up surrounded by music and academics in Tuscola, Ill., the largest town in the county with only 1,800 residents. Kohrt spent summers working on area farms; during the school year he played football and basketball.

"I was the most athletic nerd the town had ever seen. I was a Sputnik kid. One of the reasons I was different from everyone else is that I read science fiction all the time when I was a kid," Kohrt said.

His mother was a fourth-grade teacher, and his aunt and uncle were college professors. All were very influential. "They just assumed I would be successful," Kohrt said. His father taught instrumental music and was the school's band director. In addition to athletics, Kohrt also learned to play most reed instruments, including oboe, clarinet and saxophone, whether he wanted to or not. "My dad would say, 'Someone's about to graduate, so you have about three months to learn this one.'"

It was Kohrt's athletic skills, however, that earned him a football scholarship to Furman University in Greenville, S.C. "I went to Furman for athletics but got my head turned by a chemistry professor. The school was kind enough to change my athletic scholarship to an academic one," he explained.

Kohrt's academic accomplishments are many. In addition to earning a bachelor's degree in chemistry from Furman, he received his doctorate in physical chemistry at The University of Chicago. He entered graduate school there as a National Science Foundation and Woodrow Wilson fellow.

"I was hoping for a faculty position at The University of Texas, but the funding ran out. They told me to wait a year. But my wife and I had two children by that time and she said, 'We have to do something about this.' So in 1971 I took a job with Eastman Kodak."

Twenty years later, academics beckoned once again. Kohrt left his job at Kodak for a year to enroll at the Massachusetts Institute of Technology (MIT) as a Sloan Fellow and earned a master's degree in management science.

Kohrt had intended to spend one year at Kodak but stayed 29 instead. "My career there was one-third management, one-third international business, and another third running a for-profit business."

During three of those years, Kohrt lived in China and established several factories and nearly 3,000 retail stores. "It was a life-altering, invaluable experience to live as a minority in another culture. Working there made me a better listener because I had to learn an entirely new approach to business."

"I learned there are a bunch of ways to do the same thing. It's a humbling experience, and if you can stay nonjudgmental, you can translate those skills to other cultures," Kohrt said.

After his success in China, Kohrt decided to retire from Kodak. Although he admits he isn't particularly introspective, he said this was his most difficult time. He moved back to South Carolina with the intention of teaching at a university, but Battelle had started recruiting him.

"I wasn't particularly interested until the CEO of Kodak encouraged me to talk to Battelle. He said he'd always thought I was a pretty smart guy, but if I didn't even talk to them, he'd have to reconsider. And I decided it was just too good an opportunity to make a difference," Kohrt said.

Battelle is a nonprofit, charitable trust formed in 1929. It now has 19,000 employees, $1.1 billion in assets and does $3.4 billion in research and development. Its principal businesses include fee-for-service contract research, laboratory operations, and commercial ventures with more than 5,000 projects for 1,500 industrial and governmental clients. Battelle scientists helped develop many popular products including the office copier machine and the optical-digital-recording technology that led to the compact disk. They also developed the diabetes insulin pen and recommended the bar-code symbol now used on grocery packaging.

Kohrt remains driven by his curiosity for the world around him. He's also fascinated by the idea of blending technical issues with business and admires others who have managed to do just that.

In turn, he strives to blend Battelle's academic, engineering and entrepreneurial cultures, which Kohrt describes as separate and distinct. "Sometimes getting them to cohabitate on the same planet can be a challenge," he said.

Integrity, respect for others and inclusiveness are the hallmarks of Kohrt's leadership. "You're successful if you're able to influence others in positive ways. For me, success has moved from being self-centric to organization-centric."

Decision-making is a collaborative process with Kohrt. "I start with the outcome and determine if it's worthy. I assume success and then I ask, 'Will anybody care?' Then I proceed through a collaborative process. I'm very horizontal. I'm able to look across and make connections with others."

However, he noted, "Sometimes people who aren't used to collaboration don't see this as a skill."

Kohrt added: "I have a strong philosophy I learned from my parents, that whatever you have, you share. Today I admire people who use those assets to help others. It doesn't have to be the Bill Gates of the world, but it can be the people who have little but give of themselves whom I admire most."

Robert Werth

Managing Partner, Vorys, Sater, Seymour and Pease LLP

Words to live by:
"Work hard, and treat your employees and clients with the utmost respect."

Hometown: Clyde, Ohio
First job: working on his father's farm
Hobbies: gardening, reading, watching sports
Favorite book: "John Adams," David McCullough
Favorite movie: "Major League"
I am: "Patient, Hard-Working."

Robert Werth has invested his entire professional career at Vorys, Sater, Seymour and Pease (Vorys). He took on the leadership role of managing partner in 1994. He says, "Quite frankly, I did not want this job. My predecessor talked to the other partners about choosing his successor, and they wanted me to be that person. The first time I was asked, I turned it down. Two years later, I said yes."

"I was never motivated to be the managing partner—I was motivated by wanting to be a good lawyer and serving our clients. My main motivation today is to make the 900 families who work here successful."

By all accounts, he has succeeded. Werth's 40 years' experience includes commercial, banking, savings and loan, real estate and bankruptcy law. He's been involved in several large workouts involving apartment projects, unimproved real estate, a marina and more. In 1998, Werth was the lead attorney in a $900 million-plus sale of a thrift institution to a bank.

Vorys offers litigation and business services in six major cities including Columbus, Ohio. It is one of 25 firms nationwide named as a "Cross-Practice Powerhouse Law Firm" by national clients surveyed by BTI Consulting Group. It also maintains a 97 percent client-satisfaction rating. Their clients range from some of the world's largest companies to individuals and small businesses.

"Success is working as hard as you can, in whatever you're doing, to try and achieve a maximum result. Of course, time and place are also important," Werth said.

Werth spent his youth in Clyde, Ohio, working hard on his father's fruit farm and playing high school sports. "There were 70 students in my high school class. The school was so small, I got to play football, basketball, baseball and track. There just wasn't much competition," he laughs.

Working on the farm was Werth's only job before entering college. "I knew I didn't want to become a farmer because I didn't want to depend on the weather for my success. And I didn't like getting up at 4:30 in the morning."

"My father always worked very hard, and my mother taught me how to study and to always do my best in school. Neither one had a college degree, but they worked hard and were successful. I admire anyone from a humble background who works hard to become successful."

To embark on his own successful path, Werth entered The Ohio State University's pre-med program. Late in his undergraduate work, he switched to social sciences because he decided he didn't like science and math. He earned a bachelor's degree in 1962.

Werth remembers his sophomore year at OSU as his most difficult time. "I left Ohio State for two quarters because my father died, and I had to go home and run the farm," he said. "Losing my dad was very difficult, as was managing our fruit and grain farm during the peak season. However, that experience taught me a great deal about management and dealing with people. I grew up in a hurry." Thereafter, he worked at a gas station to help pay for his education.

Undecided on what to do with his newly earned bachelor's degree, Werth decided at the last minute to enter law school. It was during this time that he met and married his wife of 41 years, Gloria. He earned a law degree from OSU in 1965 and graduated second in his class. Werth also clerked for Chief Justice Kingsley A. Taft of the Ohio Supreme Court for a year.

Before coming to Vorys, Werth had interviewed with another Columbus firm and had accepted an offer—only to have it withdrawn upon the loss of its biggest client. On advice from a friend, he interviewed with Vorys and started there as an associate in 1966.

Werth believes his leadership at Vorys is marked by hard work and fairness. "I work hard, which I think sets a good example. I listen, and I try to be fair. I think others would say that I do my best and I'm approachable. I hope my legacy will be that I took the leadership position of an excellent law firm in 1994 and was able to continue our tradition of excellence."

Part IV
All in the Family

Don Casto III

Partner, Casto Companies

Words to live by:
"Passion is the key to success. You should set 'stretch goals' for yourself and not be afraid to fail."

Hometown: Columbus, Ohio
First job: blacktop crew
Hobbies: anything outdoors—boating, hiking, mountain climbing
Favorite movie: "Blow - Up"
I am: "Persistent."

The Casto Companies have always had a reputation as innovators. In 1928, Casto, Sr., opened Grandview Avenue Shopping Center, the first shopping center built to serve customers beyond the immediate neighborhood. It was also the first to have more than one national grocery chain—namely, A&P, Kroger and Piggly-Wiggly. In 1949, Casto and his son, Casto II, opened Town and Country, the first regional shopping center in the nation, in the Columbus suburb of Whitehall.

Years later, in the early 1970s, Don Casto III answered the call to come home to Columbus and help his father. If he hadn't been a dutiful son, he'd probably still be practicing law in San Francisco instead of leading one of the country's most vibrant, full-service, real estate services firm.

Today the company's vast portfolio includes retail, residential, office, industrial, restaurant, hotel and mixed-use properties in eight states. Many of these projects and the company's expansion into other states would probably have never happened if Casto III hadn't returned to run the company when he did.

Born in Cincinnati and raised in Columbus, Casto describes living an "Ozzie and Harriet" family lifestyle. As a boy he dreamed of becoming a fireman or an astronaut; he certainly never envisioned being the third generation to run the family company.

Today Casto lives within 500 yards of where he grew up. After graduating from high school, he headed to San Francisco and Stanford University. "At the time it was as far as I could get from home, and I wanted a better climate," he explained. While at Stanford, Casto met and married his wife of 40 years, Ann. "We loved northern California. We'd both finished law school and were getting settled into our careers, living in a second-story walk-up on Telegraph Hill, not making any money but having a ball," Casto says. That's when he returned to Columbus to work with his father, uncle and cousin, Frank Benson.

Upon returning, Casto found that the city had matured in the 10 years since he'd left, and that perhaps he did have an interest and aptitude for the family business. Casto attributes his strong passion for the real estate business to his close relationships with his father, a World War II navy pilot, and his grandfather, whom he describes as an entrepreneur in the truest sense. Orphaned at a young age, his grandfather learned to survive by any means while growing up over a pool hall. After his death in 1963, radio commentator Paul Harvey described him as "the man who changed the shopping habits of the free world."

When Casto III took the helm of his grandfather's company, the stockholders were family members who weren't working in the business and weren't sure of the future without the elder Casto's leadership. "Probably most of them would've been just as happy to take their money and do something else," he says. Fortunately, with the help of his cousin Frank Benson, they survived the transition. Casto often thinks he may have been better prepared and things may have been a little easier if he had taken the opportunity to get his MBA the year after law school instead of starting his law practice.

Compounding these difficult times was the loss of Casto's father and mentor. Fortunately, Casto had a few other mentors to call on, including Wendy's founder Dave Thomas and John B. McCoy, son of Bank One founder John G. McCoy. "Thomas taught me to focus on the customer. McCoy taught me that, in order to grow a company, I needed to associate with and hire people smarter than me," he said.

Casto shared a close relationship with Thomas, who repeatedly encouraged him to become an early Wendy's franchisee. Not until Thomas offered him a franchise in his beloved San Francisco did Casto finally agree. Today he remains part owner in 20 Bay-area restaurants, which his brother runs.

The ability to build consensus, subordinate his ego, and embrace and celebrate failure are the key personal skills that enabled Casto to lead his company for the past 30 years.

His dream is to support and grow a respected firm in the real estate industry. "My partners and I have created a 'friendly-to-failure' organization—of course, we're not talking about laziness and ineptitude. It's a lot of fun to watch the next generation of young people in the organization take it to the next level. In recent years, with the help of my seven partners—most of whom aren't family—we've managed to grow and expand beyond a closely held family company to an organization that's not so reliant on me, or my cousin Frank, to succeed anymore."

Don't think he's going anywhere soon, though; he still loves the thrill of the chase and the details of putting each unique deal together. Here's his "three-Ps" advice for being successful in the real estate industry: "You must like puzzles, you must like people, and you must have patience."

JACK RUSCILLI

CEO, RUSCILLI CONSTRUCTION COMPANY

Words to live by:
"When you don't understand something, don't be afraid to ask a question."

Hometown: Columbus, Ohio
First job: paper carrier
Hobbies: golfing, collecting antique clocks, racing sports cars
Favorite book: "Built to Last," Jim Collins
Favorite movie: enjoys Hallmark-channel movies
I am: "Grateful."

Third-generation owner Jack Ruscilli is preparing to pass his 62-year-old company to the next generation by handing it over—gradually–to son Lou and nephew Tony Ruscilli. "My joy today is seeing the tremendous growth exhibited almost every day as Lou and Tony work together. Success for me is knowing they will each be better than I was at what they do. It's exciting and very satisfying."

Letting go has been difficult at times. "I have always given our management team authority to make decisions. If I see things aren't going right, I have been known to jump in. I'm doing my best, however, to allow Tony and Lou to make major company decisions now. And they're doing a great job," Ruscilli said.

Ruscilli started working for his father when he was 12 years old. "I made 50 cents an hour," he remembers. "I worked most summers for the company, and they gave me every dirty job there was. Dad would always say, 'This will teach you to go to school and get a good job.'"

As a youngster, Ruscilli was more interested in football than books. "To me, school was really about sports. I was an average student but played every sport I could." His skills earned him an athletic scholarship to attend St. Mary High School in Columbus, Ohio. He always planned to go into sales and eventually own his own business. "The Catholic school system trained me for sales because we were always selling either raffle tickets or baked goods," he laughed.

Ruscilli later earned a bachelor's degree in marketing from Findlay University in Findlay, Ohio. When he graduated and officially joined the family business in 1967, he set to work expanding the company's emphasis on general contracting and design-build services. These services now account for 80 percent of the company's volume. Ruscilli also founded Ruscilli Real Estate Services in 1978 and Ruscilli Development Company in 1995. Today he, Lou and Tony lead a $150 million company with nearly 200 associates.

"When I started, our volume was $650,000. I never thought about making a lot of money or becoming a large company. I just thought of reaching the next goal and enjoyed the challenge of meeting those goals," Ruscilli said.

He eventually focused his career on expanding both the top and bottom line and building on the company's solid reputation within the industry and Central Ohio. He believes integrity is his company's top quality.

"As the company grew and people were added, I realized there were individuals who didn't really understand our culture or what our company stood for. So I put together our core values and named it 'The Ruscilli Way.' We stand for safety, professionalism, quality, integrity, positive attitude, open communication, accountability, team management, and customer satisfaction.

"When we hire new associates, I expect them to be in agreement with our values and live them. We also post our values at all construction sites so our associates can see them and understand what is expected of us and how we are to treat one another. And, our values are emphasized during annual appraisals," Ruscilli adds.

In addition to mentoring his son and nephew, Ruscilli enjoys securing construction commitments for unique and challenging projects. This includes building his company's first downtown tower as well as Ohio's new Center of Science & Industry, constructing the mooring facility for Columbus' Santa Maria, and managing the expansion of Honda of America, as well as the construction of Ohio's largest high school. Most recently, the company managed construction for The Ohio State University's Scott Laboratory and several downtown condominium developments. "These landmark projects are gratifying and fun," he said.

As for the legacy he's handing down to the next generation, "I really feel that if we live by The Ruscilli Way, anything is possible. It doesn't matter how big we get, but it's important to enjoy what you do, create value for the customer and build character within your people."

Brian Giunta

Senior Vice President, Krema Nut Company

Words to live by:
"Do unto others as you would have others do unto you."

Hometown: Western Springs, Ill.
First job: paper carrier
Hobbies: golfing, traveling
Favorite book: "The 7 Habits of Highly Effective People," Stephen R. Covey
Favorite movie: "My Blue Heaven"
I am: "Passionate."

Brian Giunta is no stranger to hard work. He's proud of the fact that he's done a little of everything at Krema Nut Company, from cleaning the machines to hand-filling Internet orders and working in the factory's retail store. In college, he often worked 40 hours over a single weekend during the holidays, when filling orders often demanded that Krema employees work grueling 18-hour days. "In order to be successful in the food industry, you have to work long, physically demanding hours. Krema is no exception," he said.

Giunta credits his grandfather and father for his strong work ethic. The Giunta family has been in the food business for three generations, dating back to when his grandfather, Martin, and father, Mike, worked in Chicago's produce industry. "My dad used to get up at 2 in the morning to go to Chicago's big produce market—in a not-so-great part of town—to buy the products he would sell that day. Then he'd go back to his store and operate his retail hours, until six that evening. I never heard him complain. He was doing what he loved to do. I'm proud to be the third generation that follows this old-fashioned, hard-work ethic."

Even as an industrious fourth grader, Brian had a variety of odd jobs and remembers "having a knack with people." He continued, "Working the paper route and all the odd jobs taught me how to offer great products with a high level of service."

Krema Nut Company, located in Grandview, Ohio, was founded in 1898 and continues to be one of the oldest peanut-butter makers in the United States. Krema's products include their famous all-natural peanut butter, other nut butters and mixes, and their own chocolates and candies. The company has received national acclaim in *USA Today* and on CNBC and The Food Network.

Giunta said he's inspired today by his father, who bought Krema Nut Company in 1991. "My father has always treated his employees well—like family. He's made a point to be available to them, should they need help or advice. I still have so much to learn from him."

These values are evident as Giunta describes his three strongest leadership qualities as "leading by example—working side by side with employees. I'm also visible to everyone in the company, and I'm always busy. Plus, I try to be available to our employees for personal or business needs."

"Even though my grandfather died before I was born, my father has instilled in me what we call The Martin Giunta Creed. It's realizing that people aren't judged by their possessions but by their understanding, compassion, fairness, humility and kindness." Evidently, he's followed "the creed" successfully, because over 50 percent of Krema's 20-person staff has been with the company for at least 10 years.

When asked to define success, Giunta says: "Success is being passionate about what you do. Success is both personal and professional—personal because you must be happy with yourself and with others." His motivation for future success, he says, is "seeing our company grow. I enjoy playing a role in developing new products and then seeing those products become accepted and successful in the marketplace."

He talks about the success of the company's "Buckeye Crunch," a peanut-butter and chocolate-coated popcorn. "We were able to take this product and foster a partnership with the James Cancer Hospital to 'put the crunch on cancer.' We developed a system for retailers around the city to use their own labels to sell the popcorn at the retail level." A portion of the confection's profits then go to support the hospital.

When asked if there's anything he might have done differently, Giunta says he "wouldn't change anything." He continued, "I'm having an absolute blast! The best time of my life is today. All the hard work is paying off, and every day is a new adventure. I have balanced my working life and professional life. I've learned that I must always do my best and give 110 percent. It will always pay off."

W. GREGORY GUY

PRESIDENT, AIR FORCE ONE

Words to live by:
"Do unto others as you would have them do unto you" and "Make new friends but keep the old."

Hometown: Dublin, Ohio
First job: working 21, 11-hour days at the Ohio State Fair for $200
Hobbies: snow skiing, running, competing in triathlons
Favorite book: "1776," David McCullough
Favorite movie: "Caddyshack"
I am: "Considerate."

Greg Guy admits to being a Revolutionary War buff, having enjoyed many books on the topic, especially David McCullough's "1776." "I think the start of our country correlates well with starting a business," Guy said. "It's not easy, and you don't know that it's going to happen for sure."

In 1996 Guy joined his father, the founder of Air Force One and current CEO, as account manager. The heating/ventilation/air-conditioning company had just won Bank One (now J.P. Morgan Chase) business for Ohio, West Virginia and northern Kentucky. His challenge was to grow the business to support its new client.

"People love to be part of something growing and dynamic. If it's a sink-or-swim situation, people inevitably swim," Guy said. This positive expectation fueled the company's expansion, which resulted in a decentralized structure, with more decision-making happening at all levels of the company.

He continued: "Everything we do must ensure the best local service. I like to hire talented people and give them freedom to do their jobs." Guy believes in the "pyramid of strength" described by Jim Collins in "Good to Great"—that great organizations transcend the leader. "The best thing I could possibly do is work myself out of a job," Guy said. "I'm proud to say that 10 years later we still have all that business from Bank One."

Today Air Force One employs nearly 120 people who support the five core values Guy's father established when he started the company: integrity, commitment, loyalty, professionalism and quality performance. "We try to beat that drum all the time," Guy said. "I emphasize two more items that a service business like ours needs to be successful—an incredible sense of urgency and a high level of ownership for your actions."

Integrity, Guy says, goes right to your character and represents one of his strongest leadership skills. "I intentionally set people up for success. I try to run a very 'transparent' organization, with an open flow of information. That includes listening to criticism without getting defensive."

Before joining the family company, Guy earned a business degree from the College of Charleston in Charleston, S.C., in just three years. "I always knew I was coming back to work with my dad. We've always been very close," Guy said.

In 2002 Guy married one of his sister's friends, Lisa Ingram, vice president of operations for White Castle, her family's company. The two support each other personally and professionally. "Inevitably, she throws a wrinkle in my thought process, challenging me to be the bigger person and think from a long-term perspective," Guy said.

"I define success now as my ability to provide a stable environment for my wife, my children and my Air Force One associates. I strive to be a good person with a high level of integrity."

Joe Zanetos

President, Anthony-Thomas Candy Company

Words to live by:
"Use common sense; treat people the way you'd like to be treated."

Hometown: Columbus, Ohio
First job: making candy
Hobbies: traveling, flying his own plane, golfing
Favorite book: "The Founding Brothers," Joseph Ellis
Favorite movie: "Once Upon a Time in the West"
I am: "Driven."

Joe Zanetos is a third-generation candy man who started working in the family business for 25 cents an hour when he was 8 years old. Now he's in charge of Anthony-Thomas Candy Company, founded by his grandfather and father in 1952. "My goal is to have people all over the country know the Anthony-Thomas name," he said.

Zanetos explains the company's evolution: "My grandfather had emigrated from Greece in 1907 and started working as an apprentice to a local candy maker in 1916. Although he opened his first candy store in 1926, his real dream was to some day go into business with my father, Thomas. So my grandfather opened the Co-op Dairy in 1932. When my dad returned from service in World War II, he joined him in 1946 and changed the name to the Crystal Fountain."

However, the younger Zanetos had a few ideas of his own and convinced his father to offer ice cream, short-order food and candy. When the business was renamed the Crystal Fountain in 1947, it sold candy, ice cream and fountain drinks. Soon the word was out about the shop's candy—it couldn't be beat. In fact, it was so good that it outsold the ice cream. As a result, five years later the pair incorporated the Anthony-Thomas Candy Company.

Zanetos remembers that as he grew up, his father didn't give him an allowance but always provided plenty of money-making opportunities. "I was always dabbling with something. I took orders for Christmas cards. I even sold fruit off my grandparents' trees."

As he got older, Zanetos dreamed he'd be a lawyer or follow an uncle's footsteps and become an engineer. "But it always came back to candy," he said. Zanetos graduated from Pleasant View High School and attended The Ohio State University, but he dropped out and never went back, a decision he's always regretted. "I think now I would have gone ahead and finished my education," he said.

Instead, Zanetos got married and started working full-time for his father's company in 1966. He said, "Growing up in this business has given me many opportunities that I may not have otherwise had since I didn't finish college. I've tried to learn everything I can about the candy business. I feel fortunate that I'm doing something that I love doing. It's a fun business."

An admitted chocoholic who loves his business, Zanetos also stays motivated by using common sense to solve problems. Fairness, honesty and integrity have helped him to stay the course over the years. "In a family business, I do what needs to be done. I think I'm good at that. I think my employees would describe me as firm yet fair," he said.

Today Anthony-Thomas is a mid-sized candy company that employs 200 people who make 50,000 pounds of candy every day. "When we started, we were a small shop that wholesaled to other companies. In the 1960s and most of the '70s, wholesale and fundraising made up 50 percent and retailing the other half."

Under his leadership, the company expanded its manufacturing site in 1994 to meet the increased demand from its fundraising efforts. Zanetos said, "When we got into fundraising with schools, we had to automate the business. We also kept getting opportunities from other businesses, such as Nestle and Hershey, that wanted us to help them out, and we did. And we just kept expanding on the retail side, too. The goal was to stay diversified so we would never be in a position where one company could put us out of business."

By 2002, Anthony-Thomas was selling 12 million pounds of chocolate a year.

It has been a sweet ride for Zanetos, who remains humble about his success. “In your early years, it’s about how much money you can make and how big you can get. Today it’s having a successful business and a strong, close family. You don’t have to be a multi-millionaire to have success,” he said.

Zanetos provides more than just lip service to his beliefs. In 1993, a large national retailer offered to sell Anthony-Thomas chocolates in their stores, but under their own label. Although the deal would have made his company millions of dollars, Zanetos declined.

“I’m proud that Anthony-Thomas has a good reputation in Columbus and in the industry, both with the giants and the small companies. We take a lot of pride in that and in making the best candy we can. I want to leave behind a strong work ethic that shows you can accomplish anything if you put forth the effort.”

Chris Doerschlag

CEO and President, WD Partners

Words to live by:
"The harder you sweat, the luckier you get."

Hometown: Columbus, Ohio
First job: lawn mowing and working at his dad's business
Hobbies: paleontology and archaeology
Favorite book: "Now, Discover Your Strengths," Marcus Buckingham and Donald Clifton
Favorite movie: "The Aviator"
I am: "Lucky."

"Success for me has meant pursuing my passion. Some people search all their life and never find it. I simply can't imagine doing anything else. I'm motivated by delivering solutions. I've created my own personal brand—I'm that passionate about my work."

Chris Doerschlag admits, as do most entrepreneurs, he "lives, eats and breathes" his business. About his role as president of WD Partners, a Columbus, Ohio-based architecture and engineering firm, he said, "This work meets the needs of my soul, and I don't take it for granted. I spent my time growing up learning about this business from my dad, so I gained an owner's perspective early."

The company was started as a traditional architectural firm in 1968 by Doerschlag's father, Wolfgang, who emigrated from Austria at age 14. His mother came to the United States from Germany when she was 21 to visit relatives and never left.

Today WD Partners has evolved into a firm that provides integrated business solutions in engineering and architecture for national restaurants and retail companies. They complete more than 33 million square feet of space each year.

"I learned a strong, European work ethic growing up—to always do the right thing and to roll up your sleeves and work hard. My parents never restricted anything I did, so I learned a lot by trial and error. I always liked to build and create many different things," Doerschlag said.

He further built on these early influences by studying architecture at Kent State University, where he earned a bachelor's degree in architecture in 1988. Doerschlag then headed west and worked in San Francisco for the next four years. During that time, he met and married his wife, Suzanne, "We lived on bagels and bologna, but it was a lot of fun," he said.

Doerschlag returned to Ohio and joined the family business as vice president in 1993. He was promoted to CEO four years later. His brother, Martin, also worked at the company as CFO.

"I faced some tough issues working in the family business. My dad and I fought like cats and dogs. We both have a type-A personality. I thought I was going to die of stress." His father and brother have both since left the business, a transition he described as among the "most amicable I've ever seen."

Visionary, passionate and honest are the words Doerschlag believes his associates would use to describe his style. "I never fake anything. Leaders are leaders because other people choose to follow them," he said. The company's core values—profit with integrity, meaningful change, mutual respect and driven to be the best—are his personal measurements of success as well.

"I like to think even though I'm passionate, I can keep my ego in check. I really enjoy helping people be better leaders," Doerschlag said.

He credits his wife for keeping him grounded. "Suzanne helped me—she's always been supportive and understanding, even when we had to deal with family business issues that, at times, seemed to defy logic. I would have been a workaholic if she hadn't jerked me out of it."

In addition to his duties as president of his company, Doerschlag stays busy in his role as dad. He and Suzanne have seven children, all of whom are under the age of 12. He clearly remembers his most difficult time as when five of them were babies. "At one point, five of them were still in diapers—all at the same time—including our two sets of twins," he laughs.

People who have challenged conventional thinking gain his admiration. "I really admire people who have willpower and aren't willing to compromise anything for their dream."

Paul Greenland

President, Aetna Building Maintenance

Words to live by (from Zig Ziglar): "You can have everything you want in life by helping others get what they want."

Hometown: Springfield, Ohio
First job: the family's bookstore and cleaning company
Hobbies: golfing, traveling, eating, cooking
Favorite books: "Good to Great," Jim Collins, "Execution," Ram Charan
Favorite movie: anything with James Bond
I am: "Unsatisfied."

Paul Greenland always dreamed of becoming a professional baseball player when he grew up. "I was a pretty good Little League pitcher. I was the number-one pitcher on our team; and the kid who was number two was Dave Berba. He went on to play for the Cincinnati Reds. Obviously, he got better—and I didn't."

Maybe he didn't make it to the major leagues, but Greenland's entrepreneurial skills have helped lead his company to new heights. His late grandfather, David Greenland, founded Aetna Building Maintenance in 1936 as a one-man window-cleaning company in Cincinnati. The company has since grown to over 1,100 employees (600 in the Columbus area) with branches in Dayton, Newark and Cincinnati. The company also has two branches in West Virginia and three in Kentucky.

Greenland comes from a long line of family entrepreneurs, and he admires anyone who is self-made. His mother's family owned real estate, a restaurant and a chain of what he describes as "bookstore/carry-outs."

"The story was that my other grandfather was a magazine publisher in New York who bought a book distributorship in Springfield. At the time, distributors were beginning to open retail locations. So my grandfather opened a chain of six stores that sold magazines and books. A friend approached him about using some extra space he had in the store to open a pizza shop; and with the pizza came Hallmark cards and beer and wine. And that's how the business started," Greenland explained.

Greenland's parents provided the motivation and inspiration for his success. "They had a real drive for business and customer service." He explains that even though his parents made a great living with the cleaning company, the company didn't always make a profit because of their focus on customer service. However, things turned around for Aetna Building Maintenance in 1983 with the opening of the Ashland, Ky., branch. The company made a profit, and according to Greenland, "The business took off from there."

Greenland decided to join the family business after earning a business degree from Indiana University. His father taught him about the cleaning business by sending him to Kansas City for a year in 1987. Friends of the family there owned a much larger industrial cleaning company, which provided him with a solid industry foundation.

The toughest challenge in Greenland's career came when dealing with other family members in the business. "When family is involved, you always have a lot of issues. I'm a third-generation family business owner. My brothers used to be part of the business. My father is now semi-retired. The challenges of family dynamics are by far the most difficult thing I've had to overcome."

Would he do anything differently? Greenland says his father "was best at customer relations, and I wish he could have focused just on that. And I wish I could have focused on the other areas. The company would have been three times as big as it is today."

Greenland also experienced the best time of his life with family. In January 2006, he and his wife took a memorable vacation to Hawaii. "This was the first time in 17 years I had ever truly relaxed. When I came back, I was a better husband and father, and a better boss and service provider."

Success, he said, is "a journey, not a destination. You can't get there. If you think you're already there, you get lazy. Somebody comes along and 'eats your lunch.'

It's also important to define success as meeting goals along the way."

What continues to motivate his success? "Fear. Fear that tomorrow we could lose all our business—that the bank could call in our line of credit."

Greenland is also passionate about treating his employees well and providing opportunities for their advancement. "I want to challenge our employees to always do better and keep growing in the company. If they can't or won't improve, then there may be somewhere else they should be. But I don't micromanage. I hire the right people, pay them well and let them do their job." He continues, "I love taking somebody who's never achieved more than a minimum-wage job and helping them grow into something they never dreamed they could be. Everyone can achieve."

He must be doing something right because although the cleaning industry has an astronomically high employee turnover rate of 300 percent, Aetna's is a comparitively low 80 percent. "I do goal setting with employees so they know at each stage what they should be doing. My employees would probably say that I'm an eclectic leader—I like to focus on many things to make our customers happy."

Greenland quotes Zig Ziglar when he advises, "If you focus on *someone else's* success, you will be successful."

Mark Swepston

President and CEO, Atlas Butler Heating and Cooling

Words to live by:
"Never give up."

Hometown: Hilliard, Ohio
First job: stuffing envelopes for a mailing
Hobbies: watching his daughter's soccer games, jogging
Favorite book: "Straight from the Gut," Jack Welch
Favorite movie: "Close Encounters of the Third Kind"
I am: "Dedicated."

Atlas Butler was founded by McGee Swepston in 1921 with a commitment to community service. Mark Swepston has continued his grandfather's cause by volunteering at many Central Ohio organizations, including The Salvation Army, Mt. Carmel Health and the Downtown Kiwanis Club. "I spend anywhere from five to 20 hours a week volunteering," he said.

"I remember one line from the Jaycee Creed, that 'service to humanity is the best work in life.' If people remember me for that, then I'll be happy," Swepston said.

The company has evolved from its early days as a manufacturer of Butler furnaces into Atlas Butler, one of the largest heating, ventilating and air-conditioning companies in Ohio. Swepston's father, Dwight, a lawyer by training, also led the business for many years.

After graduating from The Ohio State University in 1976, Swepston enrolled in graduate school at Capital University to become a banker. During this time he went to work in his father's accounting department, "not thinking I would stay there, but I did." Swepston rose from the accounting department to management positions in sales and service before being promoted to the president's spot in 1986.

Swepston was heavily influenced throughout his career by his grandfather and father. Another business mentor, Nelson Evans, who Swepston described as "a little bit of a gruff type of person," taught him "how to be a problem solver. He taught me how to cut through the noise and get the facts that were important."

Today Swepston admires Columbus businessman Bob Walter. He said that not only does Walter have one of the largest companies in the world (Cardinal Health), but "he's also a very dedicated family person."

Swepston himself is a family man and, in fact, still lives just a few miles from where he grew up in Hilliard. He said the best time of his life has been watching his children go through high school. He defines success as "personal happiness." On the business side, he said that success is "putting together a winning team that can provide great service to people."

The most difficult time in Swepston's career came in 1989. Atlas Butler had just bought another company with the hopes of growing its commercial business. Swepston said, "At the time, the commercial real estate market was in turmoil. The company we bought had five key customers, and four of them went out of business because the market was so bad. It was challenging to keep everything together."

Internal problems surfaced as well, when Swepston discovered accounting discrepancies. "It was a very stressful time. We went from 86 to 45 employees through the shake-out," he said.

Just two years later, Swepston led his company to recovery. He said, "After we right-sized the company for what was going on at the time, we were able to focus on the profitable side of the business. And things went very well."

Swepston believes it's his dedication, honesty and equal treatment of employees that make him successful. His training as an accountant has also proved to be an asset. In fact, he admits that others would see him as a numbers fanatic. He explained he enjoys understanding measurements so he can direct his company's success.

If he could change one thing along the way, Swepston said it would be to "not to let so many things distract me." He continued, "A problem for anyone who's entrepreneurial is staying focused. I would try not to do too many things at once."

Rod Baesman

Executive Vice President, Baesman Printing Corporation

Words to live by:
"Treat your customers, employees and suppliers the way you would like to be treated and everything else will fall into place."

Hometown: Orient, Ohio
First job: working in the family print shop
Hobbies: wine enthusiast
Favorite book: "Angels and Demons," Dan Brown
Favorite movie: "Die Hard"
I am: "Focused."

Rod Baesman has spent his entire career working with family. "People are amazed when they hear this, because they think working with family would be almost impossible. It's worked well for us because everyone pulls their own weight and no one tries to ride the others' coattails. Plus, we work hard and trust each other implicitly."

Baesman Printing was founded in 1952 by Richard Baesman, Sr., with two small single-color presses. Today it's in its third generation: Baesman and his brother, Tyler, are in charge; their father, Richard F. Baesman, Jr., is chairman of the board. Since 1990, the trio has grown the company, which now employs 150 people working round-the-clock to offer commercial and digital printing, direct mail, retail and point-of-purchase marketing, and mailing fulfillment services.

Training for the family business started early for the two brothers. "Our dad did a great job of getting us involved early in our careers. When I was 23 years old, I attended meetings with our bankers, accountants and lawyers. Tyler and I were both added to the board in our 20s. Dad let us take initiative and calculated risks that gave us the experience we needed to grow the business," Baesman said.

Baesman graduated in 1987 from Miami University in Oxford, Ohio. He put his father's training to use at the company by working the next few years in sales. At that time, he was one of 20 employees. However, by the late 1990s, the company earned a "Fast 50" award from Business First for being among the fastest-growing companies in Columbus, Ohio.

The brothers took official ownership of the company in 2000. Then Sept. 11 occurred, and Baesman found himself in the unfamiliar role of leading the company's first significant sales decline. "This experience helped me realize I really could manage during a downturn," he said.

Managing through declining sales and a sluggish economy was a new experience for Baesman. Over the next 12 months, the company lost about 25 percent of its business. "One of my mantras has been to maintain a solid company financially so that we can weather the ups and downs. To this day, we've never had a year when we've lost money."

Although the company had to make tough choices, Baesman is also proud to say, "In the history of our company, we've never had a layoff."

He's quick to credit his employees for the ensuing turnaround. "With the help of all of our associates, we made up the lost sales within two years. In 2006, we made the Business First 'Fast 50' for the sixth time."

Baesman believes one of his leadership strengths is communication. "I'm confident in what I say, and I'm able to relate to people at different levels. I can communicate what I need so they understand what they need to do."

Baesman says others would describe him as a "master of details" and admits this penchant for the particular often gets him in trouble. "I've always been a details person, and I have a tendency to stick my nose in where it doesn't belong," he laughed. "I probably should have learned to delegate earlier in my career."

For Baesman, success continues to be centered around family. "Frankly, I don't know how people run a business without family members. Running a business has its peaks and valleys, and it's really comforting to have someone to lean on or share ideas with. You know they have as much on the line as you."

"It takes years to grow and nurture a company and just moments to destroy it. I think this concept scared me into working a little harder. Fear of failure is a big motivator."

DOUG BORROR

CHAIRMAN AND CEO, DOMINION HOMES INC.

Words to live by:
"Do what you love, trust your instincts, never give up and don't be afraid to change."

Hometown: Columbus, Ohio
First job: working at McDonald's
Hobbies: golfing, boating, walking
Favorite books: "Who Moved My Cheese?" Spencer Johnson, "Hunt for Red October," Tom Clancy
Favorite movie: any James Bond movie
I am: "Energetic."

Not many sons directly challenge their father's career advice. When he joined the family's home-building company, Doug Borror's dad told him: "It's a great business. Don't change anything. Just go and run it." Nevertheless, the younger Borror trusted his own instincts and decided to embark on a path to upgrade both the company's products and service levels.

Borror does, however, live by a rule his father taught him: "Your word is your bond."

He explained that his entrepreneurial father focused initially on land—laying out, zoning and selling parcels of ground. Borror remembers attending zoning-commission meetings as a child, and from that experience, he knew that he wanted to work with his father one day. In 1976, when Borror was a junior in college, his father added a home-building business to his portfolio of companies and called it Beasley Homes, the predecessor of Dominion Homes.

Borror earned a history degree in 1977 from The Ohio State University. He describes himself as an "ordinary student," though his athletic skills in waterskiing were extraordinary. He competed from ages 9 to 30, and won the national men's championships in 1974 and 1975. Borror credits this experience with enhancing his self-motivation: "Nobody had to tell me to get up in the morning to practice. I have a very competitive spirit and strong desire to win."

Before joining his father's company, Borror worked for two years for Huntington Bancshares in its management-training program, specializing in residential mortgages and construction loans. This work helped prepare him to join his father in the real estate business as they built condominiums and apartment complexes together.

In the mid-1980s, the junior Borror stepped into the home-building side of the business and began to make aggressive changes to the company's business model, including new architectural designs, the use of higher-quality products and significant improvements in service. This started the company's rapid growth—the Borror family took the company public in 1994.

In 1997, Borror renamed the entire operation Dominion Homes Inc., which today operates in Ohio and Kentucky. He's quick to credit those who helped him along the way. "The person I looked up to the most was my dad, who was an accomplished entrepreneur. To round out my skill set, I looked to Bill McCauley, head of operations for my dad's company, for mentorship in organizational skills and business management. I learned sales techniques from the late Lloyd Peale, a former executive of Huntington Bank, who was a consummate salesman."

"Success is doing what you love and making a positive difference," Borror said. He loves to create new products, watch them come to fruition and see them become accepted by the consumer. Expanding on this philosophy, Borror quotes advice from the Young President's Organization (YPO): "Don't confuse your self-worth with your net-worth." He credits YPO for helping him to become more open to new ideas and to be a better listener.

Borror notes that his enthusiasm and his ability to listen to all viewpoints and yet make timely decisions are his top leadership skills. He also thinks others may say he's strong-willed with a "can-do" attitude. "Some might even say, 'If Doug wants to get it done, get out of the way!' I was born with a positive attitude. I'm basically full of energy. I can't drink regular coffee—it would make me vibrate out the door!" Borror said.

Life has challenged Borror's upbeat perspective. In May 1994, Borror was injured in a serious automobile accident, which required neck surgery. Recuperation kept him away from work for four months. "The accident caused me to re-evaluate my management style. I realized that I had to build a strong, competent team and to learn to trust them," he said.

2006 has been challenging both personally and professionally for Borror, as the local and national housing markets have experienced a significant cyclical downturn. The company has also weathered a rash of negative publicity. However, Borror believes, "We continue to build the best homes. We're always improving our steadily rising levels of customer satisfaction. We currently have the highest customer satisfaction ratings in the history of the company."

"You have to operate with the highest integrity and have the self-confidence to know in your heart that you did all the right things. I've kept my positive attitude and continue to motivate my team to be the best we can be."

Underscoring this, Borror adds, "Every day is a great day! You have to measure happiness and success in your overall life, not just in business." He enjoys life with his wife, Kim, and his children—daughter Dani, 19, who attends Vanderbilt University, and son Donald, 18, who was one of 12 men accepted to the ballet program at The Julliard School in 2006. "It's great watching your kids grow up and achieve their own success."

The thing Borror wants to do most is create successful, thriving communities. "I work on it every day. I get a charge out of being able to make it possible for each family to move into the home they've always wanted."

Larry Abbott

Retired President, Abbott Foods

Words to live by:
"Consider the path of an entrepreneur for a career."

Hometown: Columbus, Ohio
First job: driving a meat delivery truck
Hobbies: scuba diving, golfing, photography
Favorite books: "Debt of Honor," Tom Clancy; "Good to Great," Jim Collins
Favorite movies: "Running Scared," "The Sting"
I am: "Balanced."

Larry Abbott became president of his family business when he was 21 years old. "My dad retired, threw me the keys and said, 'Here.' And I worked there for 36 years," Abbott said.

Abbott had just graduated with a degree in finance from The Ohio State University (he earned an MBA from there as well). He originally thought he would follow his grandfather and uncle into architecture but decided to join his father's business instead. "I truly liked 'the game' of managing and succeeding in business," he said.

He joined the family business at a pivotal time. During his father's tenure, there was still a strong demand for local meat-cutting and delivery services. When Abbott came along, full-service grocery stores had been developed, along with very good in-store butcher shops. "They were making our business obsolete," Abbott explained.

Undaunted by the new trend, Abbott found alternative markets for their products. He explained, "I took our business away from selling to 'Mrs. Housewife' and started selling to restaurants, schools, institutions, hospitals, nursing homes, vendors and that sort of thing. We built the business over 35 years from a volume of a little over $1 million to $240 million and sold it to SYSCO in 2003. I stuck with the business for three more years and decided to move on to another chapter in my life."

The secret to Abbott's success is twofold. He said he credits his parents with teaching him to "do a job right and don't cut corners." He's also quick to credit others in the company.

"I believe in people. The vast majority of people want to do what's right. I believe the CEO's job is to set the vision, provide the resources and get out of the way. I also believe in generously sharing the profits of business with those who most contributed to the success. The right profit sharing plan can greatly benefit all parties," he said.

Regarding his success, Abbott said, "When you're young, you're more monetarily motivated, and it's by necessity because you have to pay the grocery bill. Now success is having a good family, good relationships and good friends. It isn't in having the most toys or the most money."

Asked if there's anything he would change, Abbott said that as a younger business person, "I would have been more aggressive in holding certain people accountable to produce and less tolerant when they didn't do their job." He hopes his legacy at Abbott Foods was that he "did a good job of building a good, solid team."

Today Abbott admires "people who seem to have a reasonably good balance for life. That's something I've always strived for." He continued, "I can say very honestly that business was never number one for me. I was blessed to be successful in business, but if you keep it in perspective, you should get God, family, self and business in that order.

"So to a certain extent, since I retired I really haven't missed it an iota because it was not my life. I have a lot of other things I enjoy doing," Abbott said.

One of those things is scuba diving. Abbott and his family have dived all over the world, including the Caribbean, Indonesia, Fiji, the Galapagos Islands, the Red

Sea and Papua, New Guinea. One of his favorite spots is Palau, a remote island north of New Guinea.

Abbott's also had the good fortune to be able to indulge his passion for diving with a new business venture. He and his investment partners plan to open a scuba diving business in Columbus. They visited what they thought to be the four best dive shops east of the Mississippi to get some new ideas. "From that perspective I guess I'm just a carpetbagger," he laughed. "Why do you remake the wheel when you don't have to?"

In addition to his church, family and friends, Abbott spends his time with philanthropy and mentoring young business professionals. "The best times are usually not about business," Abbott said. "I have lived a pretty good life."

Kathy Gatterdam

CEO and Executive Vice President, The Columbus Coal and Lime Company

Words to live by:
"Take one step forward every day to accomplish something you want and you'll be successful."

Hometown: Columbus, Ohio
First job: 13 years old, swimming instructor at a local pool
Hobbies: reading, painting, snow skiing
Favorite movie: "The Quiet Man"
I am: "Positive."

During her youth, Columbus Coal and Lime CEO Kathy Gatterdam dreamed she'd be an artist. "I always wanted to have a loft and a lot of great artwork from all around the world. I still paint. With my current job, I still get to use my creativity in dealing with issues that come up every day."

"Creative" certainly describes Gatterdam's path leading to her role as CEO. From the ski slopes in Colorado to the library stacks in law school, she explored many interests before returning to her roots and assuming a leadership role at her family's company.

The Columbus Coal and Lime Co. was formed in 1888 by Gatterdam's great-great-grandfather, Carl Henry Niermeyer, and three local businessmen to supply coal to residential and commercial customers. Today it employs 40 people and sells concrete coatings, restoration materials and masonry supplies. Their business lines include the Archway Ohio and CPR (Concrete Protection and Repair) divisions, Granville Builder's Supply in Newark, Ohio, and a retail store called Patios, Walks & Walls in Grove City, Ohio.

Today the company remains a family endeavor. Gatterdam joined Columbus Coal and Lime in 1995, during the company's 107th year in business. Her father, John L. Niermeyer, is chairman of the board. Her husband, Rich, is president.

Her family has always exerted a strong influence on Gatterdam. She grew up in Bexley, Ohio, with an older brother and a twin brother. "My whole life, I've been one of a pair. Growing up was wonderful because I had a best friend since birth," she said.

"I grew up with two parents who were always a 'step ahead' and very forward thinking. My dad was into garage doors and tiles before they were big. My mother believed in diversity and freedom of thought. She was very progressive. She was one of two women in her day to graduate from Ohio State with a degree in finance," Gatterdam said. "Hard work was important to my family."

Before coming to Columbus Coal and Lime, Gatterdam was a practicing attorney. She remembers the best time of her life as completing her law degree. "I never planned to go to law school, but I went and flourished. I loved the learning and the friendships."

Before law school, she was skiing in Colorado and working as a cocktail waitress. "My mother kept bugging me about what I wanted to do with my life. She wanted me to take the LSAT. I took it and it was a pretty good indicator of what I should be doing." She returned to Columbus to attend Capital University's law school.

Gatterdam has also experienced her share of life's hardships. "I can't think of one that didn't make me stronger," she reflected. The worst time of her life was losing a baby when she was five months pregnant. "That was the most life-changing event for me," Gatterdam said.

Her personal strength adds to her role as a CEO. Gatterdam describes her leadership style as "open minded and direct. Honesty's huge for me. I believe in always giving a straight answer, even when people don't want to hear it."

She continued, "I start each day with a goal that I make sure I accomplish. If you do that, then you're already one step ahead." That's how she defines success—as taking "one step at a time."

How would her employees describe her? "I asked one of my employees and they said 'wonderful. I aspire to be like you.' I would say that my employees continue to motivate me because we all work together as a team. They help me to be successful."

In turn, Gatterdam hopes her leadership legacy will be "that I helped my employees get one step better every day. I hope they remember me as a person they could rely on."

Niles Overly

Chairman and CEO, The Frank Gates Companies

Words to live by:
"Always have faith in the goodness of people."

Hometown: Columbus, Ohio
First job: cutting grass
Hobbies: reading, golfing
Favorite book: "Democracy in America," Alexis De Tocqueville
Favorite movie: "Lawrence of Arabia"
I am: "A doer."

Niles Overly is a dynamic, high-intensity person. "My brain's turned on all the time. I can't turn off. Most of the real thinking I do isn't done at work. I execute at work and think at home," he said.

Although Overly claims he never had a lot of goals, his primary ambition was a lofty one. He wanted to be the CEO of GM. "I was very confident I'd be successful."

Growing up in the 1950s and 1960s to Overly was a "golden time; a wonderful time to be a kid." He wanted to be a paleontologist in those days. "I'm kind of a combined creature. My father was very left-brained and my mother was very right-brained. Discovery was the piece that linked the two. But seeing my dad go to work six days a week influenced me to go into business," Overly said.

He graduated from the Columbus Academy and entered the University of

Virginia where he earned a law degree. "Education was very important in shaping my life."

Overly spent the first three years of his legal career at Arthur Anderson, where he worked as an international tax attorney. At the time, Arthur Anderson was rated as the number-one accounting firm in the world. "I was so proud of that on my résumé. It was like going into the Army. It was great duty," Overly said. Although he compared his work there to indentured servitude, Overly said he wouldn't have traded it for anything. "I decided I didn't want to write memos and briefs, and I realized business was more important."

After Overly left Arthur Anderson, he joined The Frank Gates Companies in 1979 as general counsel. He became CEO in 1983. He credits his success in part to the rich learning opportunities throughout his early career at Frank Gates. "The people were very generous and very compassionate. Every one of them was a role model," he said.

Frank Gates is a $200 million national holding company that specializes in employee benefits and risk-management services. Overly's family connection comes from his father, his uncle and great-uncle, Frank Gates.

Overly acknowledges that managing a family business has presented some conflicts, but they never stood in the way of a successful venture. "The hard part about family business is that I've always been judged as a brother, a cousin or a son," he said.

Overly has thrived at Frank Gates. His zeal comes from sharing a vision with a team of people, mentoring them and watching them grow. "I get excited by watching people who have started out at a certain level become successful."

He believes his strengths lie in his integrity and vision, and he adds, "I'm more of a populist leader. I'm one of the team—it's the servant-leader concept. We're here to serve our people."

Overly is passionate about his role as leader of the company. "The people here love the fact that we're a family business. Today it's not just about management: It's about leadership. If you're truly a great leader, you have empowered people and created great leaders under you who shouldn't miss a beat," he said.

Not missing a beat was critical in 2001 when the company underwent a huge nationwide expansion. Overly explained: "When we got bigger, we had to articulate our values. Even with new people, our aspiration was to make everyone successful by emphasizing integrity and commitment to our relationships."

"We also value personal responsibility, respect, creativity and innovation. We make all decisions based on this platform. This is my personal mission statement," Overly said.

However, Overly stops short of evaluating his own success. "I let other people define it. We live in a capitalistic society, and dollars do define success in some ways, but very little in my mind. It's not a motivator to me. I'm interested in developing a team and executing a vision," he said.

"Success in my mind relates to what other people think. If other people think you're a success, then you're a success."

Tom Flesch

President and CEO, Gordon Flesch Company Inc.

Words to live by:
"There's no substitute for hard work."

Hometown: Madison, Wis.
First job: 8 years old, rotating paper in a warehouse
Hobbies: golfing, snow skiing, boating, traveling
Favorite book: "The Pillars of the Earth," Ken Follett
Favorite movie: "The Godfather"
I am: "Fair."

Many years ago, Tom Flesch's paychecks came in the form of soda bottles. At age 8 he began working at his father's company. "My father would take me and my brothers to the warehouse on Saturday mornings to rotate paper. Back then, (copier) paper had a life span because it was coated; so Dad would have us move the old boxes out and put the new ones behind it so the paper would never expire. As a reward, we got a Coke," he said, and laughingly added, "In high school, we were the janitors."

His father founded the Gordon Flesch Company in 1956 with a $10,000 loan from his father-in-law. Flesch remembers that his parents were expecting a new baby when his father left a steady job as a typewriter salesman to start his own "one man" copier sales, service and delivery company.

Today the Gordon Flesch Company is one of the largest independent providers of office-equipment solutions in the United States, with offices in three states and more than 700 associates. The company prides itself on having a customer-approval rating of nearly 100 percent.

Flesch said his father was a big influence in his childhood. "He was an entrepreneur, a risk taker." Flesch said, "Dad brought great people into the business. He wasn't a micromanager; he hired great people and let them run it."

After graduating from the University of Wisconsin–Eau Claire, Flesch took a job at Liberty Mutual Insurance Company. He'd been working there for over a year when his father asked him to come into the family business in Madison, Wis.

Flesch fondly remembers his first boss, Ted Williams, as a great mentor. Flesch said, "The biggest lesson he taught me was that when you're in sales, you're all about selling yourself and getting the glory. But when you're a manager, you have to feel good about others getting the deals and the glory."

Flesch did so well in Wisconsin that his father asked him to repeat his success and open a branch in Columbus, Ohio. The first two years in Ohio were tough, both on the company and on Flesch personally. A security guard set a fire that destroyed the Madison, Wis., location; his father was hospitalized with a heart attack; and the Columbus branch was struggling. Flesch recalls, "It was a very difficult time in my career and in the business. We were doing everything we could just to survive."

Unfortunately, an even more difficult time would come several years later. Flesch had been president of the company for five years when his father died. He said even though his father had a succession plan, "Losing a founder is very difficult for a business. You have to overcome the fear people have about what will happen and what direction the company will take. Just maintaining the status quo was difficult, but we came through it just fine," Flesch said.

Overcoming his employees' fear and establishing trust was crucial. "If you want to be successful, people have to trust you."

"Anybody who defines success monetarily has their priorities in the wrong place," Flesch continued. "On the business side, success is giving employees opportunities to grow and become productive." When asked if this definition has changed over time, he replied, "When you're young, success is all about getting the numbers up. And you're also obsessed with providing for your family. But as you mature, you want to make sure your people are taken care of as well."

This commitment to "do the right things to help his employees" keeps Flesch motivated. "We have the most dedicated people you can find."

Flesch believes integrity is critical in a leader. "It's a fundamental element of managing people." He believes others in the company would describe him as "very involved in the business, but I'm not a micromanager." His guiding principles also involve treating people fairly and with respect. He adds, "There's too much arrogance in business today."

The best time of his life is now. "I never look to the past to say it was better then," Flesch said.

As for the future, he states, "I hope I leave behind a platform for a successful business for my children and for our people to grow and prosper in. I hope they feel they've been treated fairly."

KENT JOHNSON

CEO, HIGHLIGHTS FOR CHILDREN

Words to live by:
"Understand your motivation. Commit to what you want to do."

Hometown: Schenectady, N.Y.
First job: paper boy
Hobbies: reading, exercising, spending time with family
Favorite books: random nonfiction
I am: "Thoughtful."

You may have read *Highlights for Children* magazine as a child; you may subscribe for your own child or grandchild. You've certainly seen a copy if you've spent any time recently in a dentist's or pediatrician's office or in the children's section of the library. Since its first issue in June 1946, this "Fun with a Purpose®" publication has entertained children worldwide with its stories, poems, "Hidden Pictures®," readers' letters, jokes, riddles and science projects.

Founders Dr. Garry Myers and Caroline Clark Myers created *Highlights for Children* to help children learn and grow, because they believed "children are the world's most important people." Today CEO Kent Johnson, a fourth-generation family member in the business, devotes himself to this mission.

As CEO, Johnson leads eight individual companies under the Highlights mantle, including the magazine production. *Highlights for Children* boasts the largest paid, monthly circulation of any children's general-interest publication—without any advertising, now or ever. It recently celebrated the printing of its *billionth* issue.

Johnson first worked at Highlights in 1988 as a college intern. He later became intrigued with accepting a full-time position after serving two years on the company's board of directors in a rotating position offered to family members to develop their knowledge of the business. Through this position and the Myer Family Council, the extended family is kept actively informed about company happenings and asked for input. The position's role is essential. With only five family members among the 700 employees at Highlights, "We try to be fiercely anti-nepotism," Johnson said. "But if the company owners become absentee landlords, it won't work, because over time, the focus could become more about the money than the mission."

Indeed, family-owned businesses face unique issues. In 2005, just six months into his new, full-time job at Highlights, Johnson lost Garry Myers III, his mentor, second-cousin and then-CEO, who died unexpectedly.

Johnson reflects, "In a family business, such a death is both a personal tragedy and a difficult disruption to even an organized transition. I'm still working on it, but it went well because of our organization's preparation, maturity and shared commitment to the mission. "Internal confidence is critical in times of crisis."

Johnson credits his parents with influencing his life's direction, which at first seemed unlikely to transition to educational publishing. His mother was mayor of his hometown, and his father was a scientist working in research and development at General Electric.

Science lured Johnson as well. He earned a bachelor's degree in physics from Amherst College in 1991 and a doctorate in physics from Harvard University in 1998. He took a year off between degrees to teach physics at a private high school in Connecticut, where he supervised a dorm with eleventh-grade boys. "It was quite a harrowing experience!" he laughs.

After graduate school, Johnson realized he preferred interdisciplinary work to that of academic physics. He took a job at a biotech firm in Maryland, he says, "to try to have my work impact more people." Now at Highlights, Johnson thrives on the company's impact on an even larger community.

"Success is having the maximum positive impact on the world, balancing the local with the global," Johnson explained. "I've become more and more fond of large-scale, long-term projects, things that are much larger than what an individual can accomplish and that require the efforts of many exerted in the same direction to achieve."

"I'm a pretty internally motivated person. We don't have a lot of ego at Highlights about the 'score.' But we do have a lot of pride in the 'score' as it relates to our impact on children," he explained.

"We're a family company. If we had a culture that didn't respect people's families, it'd be a real inconsistency," Johnson said. "This job could take over my life, but my family helps me keep things in balance. I know I always have a date for dinner."

Perhaps his own experience with fatherhood fuels Johnson's pride in the company's launch of a new magazine for preschool children titled *Highlights High Five.*

Johnson adds, "We don't choose between short-term and long-term thinking. We have to make good decisions when viewed over all time scales. There is no choice between behaving ethically and maximizing profitability. You have to have both."

In addition to having integrity, Johnson also credits listening as one of his strongest leadership abilities, along with a commitment to and understanding of the company's mission. "Let your personality guide how you do things. If you're not true to your personality, people see through the lack of integrity, and it will interfere with your ability to lead."

Greg Overmyer

President and CEO, Hilb, Rogal & Hobbs

Words to live by:
"Try and get a clear vision of where you want to go, maintain flexibility and go after it hard."

Hometown: Columbus, Ohio
First job: photocopying, filing
Hobbies: exercising, hunting, playing guitar
Favorite book: "Good to Great," Jim Collins
Favorite movie: "Smokey and the Bandit"
I am: "Balanced."

Robert F. Kennedy said, "Only those who dare to fail greatly can ever achieve greatly." Greg Overmyer also subscribes to that philosophy. "It would scare me to look back and have people say, 'There's somebody who had a lot of potential and just didn't do all they could have done,'" Overmyer said.

"In my view, success is achieving potential. God gives you a certain amount of talents. Are you using those to the best of your abilities? Those who are given a lot should be giving back a lot."

Perhaps this value was inspired by Overmyer's father, Ed, who along with partner Joe Berwanger, formed the insurance company Berwanger Overmyer Associates in 1973. Referring to his father, Overmyer said, "He had a good grasp on understanding people. I always admired that."

Although Overmyer shared his father's fundamental philosophies, he wasn't so sure he would follow his father's career path. While attending Miami University in Oxford, Ohio, Overmyer had worked a few odd jobs at BOA, but planned to make a career in accounting. He didn't consider working at BOA professionally until a trip overseas changed his perspective.

Overmyer spent his senior year in Luxembourg where he completed his accounting degree. "It was probably the thing that matured me the most," he said. "It gave me a chance to get outside the bubble of Miami University and Upper Arlington, Ohio. I got to experience different things I never would have experienced. And I learned that 'if it's going to be, then it's up to me.'"

Armed with fresh determination, Overmyer started his career in Columbus at Continental Insurance. After completing their underwriting program. he went to work at BOA in property and casualty sales. Overmyer advanced through positions in personal and commercial insurance. In 2001, BOA was sold to insurance giant Hilb, Rogal & Hobbs; in 2002 Overmyer became president of the company's Ohio office.

Hilb, Rogal & Hobbs is the eighth-largest insurance and risk-management intermediary in the United States and 10th largest in the world, with offices throughout the United States and in London.

The toughest test of his career was merging a large acquisition. It caused real culture issues within the organization. "I didn't do a good job of listening and getting buy-in," Overmyer said.

He believes his sense of empathy helped him then and continues to guide him now. "I understand and have the ability to communicate with people, and the ability to prioritize," he said. "I would be described as hardworking and fair."

There are, however, things he would have done differently. "I would have listened to people who have experience. It's easy to think you know what ought to be done. But people who have been through situations have a much better insight as to what should be done. So even if you're 'book smart,' you can't beat experience.

"I heard a great saying—'Smart people know everything. Wise people know everyone.' Being able to call on those who have been through similar experiences is huge," he added.

What does Overmeyer think his leadership legacy will be? "I hope it's that I was someone who cared about his employees, his customers and the community and was able to drive a company that served its purpose."

R. ANDREW "ANDY" JOHNSON

CEO, THE JOHNSON FAMILY'S DIAMOND CELLAR

Words to live by:
"Fill your mind with positive thoughts. Think like a child and believe that all things are possible."

Hometown: Columbus, Ohio
First job: bagging groceries
Hobbies: skiing, mountain climbing, golfing
Favorite book: Bible
Favorite movies: "Dr. Zhivago," "MASH"
I am: "Dichotomous."

"We're in the perfect business. It's about happy occasions and pretty items."

Andy Johnson gets a thrill out of his work. And it's no wonder, because usually his customers are happy as soon as they walk in the door. Johnson is CEO of The Johnson Family's Diamond Cellar, established by his father, Robert W. Johnson, in 1946. The Diamond Cellar offers a comprehensive line of jewelry, watches, repair services, and customer and in-house jewelry design.

"My father had a huge influence on me. He was very kind and sweet. He was very life-smart," Johnson said.

Although Johnson always spent a lot of time with his father at the business, he was required to work outside it when he was growing up. "I was raised always thinking I had to make my own money. So I had many jobs. I scooped ice cream and worked at an A & P grocery store," he said.

He returned to the family business in college, when he approached his father about needing a flexible job that would fit his class schedule. "I had the opportunity to work with my dad at his first shop, Robert W. Johnson, Inc., where he serviced other Ohio jewelry stores. I did repairs and alterations. It gave me the background to start in this business," Johnson said.

The family business may have been an integral part of his childhood, but Johnson never thought it would be his career. "When I got out of high school, I thought I'd be an attorney. But I realized I probably didn't want to know everyone's problems. I truly loved the entrepreneurial side of the jewelry business. And I love consumer businesses."

It was this love of people that finally brought Johnson into the fold. He's made his own way by combining his passion for business with a knack for interpreting complex marketing information and capitalizing on trends. The result? Under Johnson's leadership, the Diamond Cellar is now one of the largest jewelry retailers in the country.

Relationships also played a vital role in making Johnson successful. "I've been truly blessed because my customers became friends. I didn't have suppliers, I had partners. Plus, I've always had the ability to go forward. I have a positive, can-do attitude," he said.

Johnson thinks his skills in building consensus and setting strategy are also strengths of his leadership. He said, "I think others would say I'm communicative. My mantra is I respect you enough to tell you the truth. You get exactly what you see. I'm consistent with this."

He readily admits he's had rough times along the way. "I fail all the time. But when I do get it right, it's the coolest thing. I still believe in the old adage of living by the Golden Rule."

Today Johnson defines success as achieving balance. "In the past, success was geared more to the tangible things I could see, touch and feel. But today it's much more cerebral. Part of my success today is harmony and happiness. Success is something I'll probably never find. I never thought of it as a destination," he said.

Balancing the spiritual, physical, personal and financial aspects of his life requires constant attention. Johnson said, "I try to read something every day that gives me a spiritual perspective. And I love to work out and spend time with my family. I try to incorporate some of those pieces every day."

Johnson said his best times are when he feels most alive. "With mountain climbing, it takes so much effort to reach a goal. You're scared and tired but energized. It's like being next to God. I remember running in the desert and watching the sunset. It just seared into my mind. It's that same feeling you get sometimes with your children," Johnson said.

"I've never been bored a day in my life. I'm afraid that if I die I might miss something. But I can make myself disengage, go home and be with my family. I hope my legacy will be that I believed in doing what was right and was good at what I did."

HARLEY E. ROUDA, JR.

CEO AND MANAGING PARTNER, HER REAL LIVING, INC.

Words to live by:
"Share the vision."

Hometown: Columbus, Ohio
First job: working in his father's office
Hobbies: golfing
I am: "Passionate."

"Ski the Alps." "Explore other religions in history." "Take an animal safari." "Learn Karate." "Climb a mountain." These are a few of Harley E. Rouda, Jr.,'s long-term goals, artistically portrayed in a print on his office wall.

Evidently, setting and achieving lofty goals is part of what makes Rouda tick. In 1997, he blazed a trail to be the first in his industry to build an Internet-based marketing platform. At the time, this was a radical move, because the industry's revered, traditional marketing tactics were daily newspaper ads and Sunday morning television shows. "This was a tough process because no company of our type in the country had taken this path. To do it and be first meant a lot of arrows in the back."

"It was like building the Empire State Building. At first you don't see anything, because the first 20 floors are underground. That's what we were doing—we were building the foundation," Rouda said.

Building the Web site meant that Real Living eventually expanded from Central Ohio to become a national company. Today Real Living, Inc., is the nation's fourth-largest independently owned residential real estate firm, with more than $8 billion in annual sales and nearly 130 offices and 4,000 agents nationwide.

This phenomenal growth occurred in part through acquisitions, including Rouda's successful 2001 bid to purchase a large consolidator, Insignia. It was a difficult deal to close; and just when things were almost finalized, Sept. 11 occurred. The economy changed, and Rouda's deal was delayed. Finally, after facing even more time-consuming financing obstacles, Rouda found himself just three weeks away from the deal's closing.

"I realized we had put everything on the line. They might have taken our house. I was gambling with our family's future. But I also realized that if you want to make it to the next level, you must take extraordinary risks."

Rouda backs away from defining success for anyone except himself. "As a society, sometimes we try to impose our definition of success on others. And that's unfair and unfortunate, because I don't really know anyone else's life. I don't really know about another individual's challenges."

"I think success is finding the balance that provides your happiness. Balance in family, work and personal well-being," he said.

Rouda's introduction to the concept of "work balance" came at a young age when he and his brothers did odd jobs at his father's office. "My father was very successful, very entrepreneurial. And I'm sure he violated lots of child labor laws putting his four children to work," he joked.

Rouda continued, "It was standard protocol that you'd chip in on weekends. There was this big conference table in the office, with tall stacks of paper all around. The kids were the collators. He'd tell us, 'Start here and go around the table and stack the papers.'" Rouda laughs, "It was a great experience, but I wouldn't say any of it made me think of doing what I do today."

Rouda's preparation for his future began with earning a bachelor's degree from The University of Kentucky, a law degree from Capital University, and a MBA from The Ohio State University. He worked at a Columbus law firm before entering the real estate industry.

"When you first get out of school, you just want a decent job. Doing well on the bar exam was a huge achievement for me."

"Once people become successful, sometimes they think they're the only ones responsible. And that may be true. But sometimes it's luck. Sometimes it's the motivation from friends and family. I'm motivated more by fear of failure rather than the desire to succeed—not that it's healthy."

Rouda said his father heavily influenced him growing up. But he also credits others for helping him along the way, including college professors and partners at his law firm. He believes his strongest leadership abilities are understanding business strategy, organizing the right people to do the work and delegating well. "Most people would say that I'm very intense."

He offers this advice to anyone wanting to succeed in business: "Be willing to share anything. Share without expecting to get anything back, and you usually will in the long run."

Though Rouda says he wishes he would have "partied less" in high school and focused more on academics, he keeps it in perspective. "I learned valuable lessons even through some bad times. So in a sense, I guess I wouldn't change anything because it's all part of the fabric of how I ended up here."

Rouda says the best time of his life is where he's at right now. "I admire and love my wife, Kaira. She's a great part of my life and my partner both in our business and personal lives. My kids are a great learning experience. If they turn out well and make an impact on the world, then I can say it's a job well done."

LISA INGRAM

VICE PRESIDENT OF RESTAURANT OPERATIONS, WHITE CASTLE

Words to live by:
"Figure out what you really like doing by trying a lot of different things first."

Hometown: Columbus, Ohio
First job: babysitting
Favorite books: "Execution," Jim Collins, "Freakonomics," Steven Leavitt
Favorite movie: "Wedding Crashers"
I am: "Analytical."

Every Friday, you can have lunch with Lisa Ingram at a local White Castle restaurant, though she'll be serving the food, not sitting down and enjoying it herself. Since taking her job in management, Ingram decided to work the Friday lunch crowd to stay connected to the restaurants' daily operations.

"Our team member loyalty is phenomenal," Ingram explained. "Many people have worked for us for 40 years, starting when they were 16 years old. You can't buy that kind of dedication."

Famous for its "Slyder®" hamburgers served in cardboard boxes, White Castle opened its first restaurant in 1921 in Wichita, Kan., with a $700 loan. The company has since earned its share of "first" designations: first fast-food chain, first industrial-strength spatula, first mass-produced paper hats, and first to sell one million burgers, as well as frozen fast food.

Today White Castle operates 400 Midwest locations, most of which Ingram has visited. Its annual revenues are over $600 million.

A fourth-generation family employee, Ingram aims to affect the company by "having us all moving toward specific goals as part of a clear, strategic plan. I want to ensure the company is nimble, able to adjust to environmental changes and to respond to challenges proactively, not reactively."

In fact, every year she meets with all general managers to ensure their locations' goals and performance are in line with the company's plan. When the two don't match, Ingram may need to explain to some staff why they weren't chosen for a promotion, a situation that has taught her to be more sensitive to employees' emotional reactions. In fact, her most difficult challenge was revamping White Castle's promotion process. Today the company uses a more objective system that enables more people to be considered for promotions.

As for herself, Ingram said she sees things as more black and white than gray, and believes that others see her as organized, objective and a "numbers" person.

"I really like to be challenged mentally. The intellectual stimulation I find at White Castle is what gets me going in the morning," Ingram said. "My ultimate personal goal is to become president of White Castle."

Part of Ingram's unique challenge at White Castle has been to establish herself in a historically patriarchal company. Of her 12 direct reports, 11 are men. She's the first female family member to be employed at the executive level of the organization. Eleven family members are on the payroll, including her father, White Castle President Bill Ingram.

Ingram identifies her objectivity as one of her strongest leadership skills, along with an ability to analyze issues from various viewpoints. "At other organizations, I thought I was 110 percent committed," she said. "But at White Castle, I wake up in the middle of the night thinking about ways to improve the company. I am deeply invested here."

The oldest of six children, Ingram credits her father for encouraging her to follow her own interests and not pressuring her to take a role at White Castle. Even though Ingram grew up play-pretending to be a lawyer—"probably because I like to argue!"—she quickly realized in college that her forte was numbers. Ingram earned a degree in marketing and finance from Southern Methodist University in Dallas. "I couldn't wait to get out of Ohio. I don't like the winters here!" she explained. She stayed in Texas to work for a computer-supply company named Daisytek.

Ingram later earned an MBA in consulting and operations from The Ohio State

University. She worked as an intern at Hewlett Packard in Boise, Idaho, to gain experience at a large corporation.

Today she seeks inspiration from several role models. "For my mentors I mostly seek successful women who also have families, and who have learned to balance all aspects of their lives," Ingram said. "I admire people who have it all together—career, community involvement and family life."

In fact, Ingram defines success by this barometer of balance: "Success to me is knowing where I am, and having a balance with my job, my family and the community."

Mike Schoedinger

Vice President, Schoedinger Funeral and Cremation Service

Words to live by:
"Always try your hardest, and be happy with the results."

Hometown: Columbus, Ohio
First job: paper carrier
Hobbies: golfing, spending time with family
Favorite book: Bible
Favorite movie: "The Blues Brothers"
I am: "Driven."

Mike Schoedinger hopes to continue the proud tradition of personal service, caring and compassion that five previous generations of his family have taken over 150 years to establish.

Schoedinger Funeral and Cremation Service is one of the three largest privately owned funeral services in the country, operating 11 chapels, one cemetery and three crematories. Philip Schoedinger emigrated to the United States in 1829 from Dorrenbach, Germany. He was a cabinet maker by trade and by 1855 was making caskets; 10 years later, he established Schoedinger & Brown on West State Street in Columbus.

Mike Schoedinger's father and grandfather were huge influences during his childhood, and he started working for the family business as a part-time driver in 1983 when he was 16. However, when he enrolled at Miami University in Oxford, Ohio, he intended to study medicine. His father had other ideas and encouraged his son to get a business degree instead.

By his junior year, Schoedinger had switched majors and earned two degrees in business from Miami. He finally decided to join the family business and earned his graduate degree from the Cincinnati College of Mortuary Science. He received his embalmer's and funeral director's licenses in 1990 and started working full-time with his family.

Schoedinger gradually grew into his new management role as his father stepped back from running the business. He explained the difficulty of changing from his old role as an employee to one of the bosses. "I felt disconnected from my staff. I'd been 'one of the guys' since I was 16. But there came a time when I was pulled off hourly wage, and that was a shift. That was a very painful time."

Since taking charge, Schoedinger has helped grow the company to 11 locations and 180 employees. Consensus building is one of the hallmarks of his leadership. "I think of everybody before I make a decision," Schoedinger said. He also said his ability to evaluate issues from a long-term perspective and his organizational skills are other qualities that make him successful. However, he doesn't really know what his employees would say about his style. "I wonder about that all the time." He joked, "I hope they would say I'm at least competent."

The most difficult time in his life came when his younger sister died of a liver disorder in 1980. Schoedinger said, "I was a very quiet, shy kid. My school was very supportive, and this response helped me become more outgoing. That was a positive change in my life resulting from the most negative thing I'd ever experienced."

Schoedinger said the best time in his life was meeting and marrying his wife, Lisa. In fact, he defines his success as having balance between his family, work and spirituality. "I feel I'm emotionally balanced. I've got a great family, a great home and a great job. I give back to the community. I manage stress very well."

Managing stress has proven especially important because his business has faced its toughest competition in recent years from a discount funeral operator who moved to Columbus.

"These are turbulent times. Our staff is scared. And we don't have all the answers yet. We've maintained our volume through five years of competition. But when it's all said and done, his prices are lower than ours. But the thing we have that he doesn't have is great people offering great service to families in need."

Joe Dager

President, Velvet Ice Cream Company, Inc.

Words to live by:
"We all want to help our family and children have more. It's important to give them what they need, and let them earn the rest."

Hometown: Utica, Ohio
Hobbies: spending time with family, golfing, fishing and traveling
Favorite books: those about American history and sports professionals like Woody Hayes
I am: "Fair."

When in Utica, Ohio, tour Ye Olde Mill, home of Velvet Ice Cream Company, Inc. to see how ice cream is produced and enjoy a sweet treat. You might even get lucky and have company president Joe Dager for your tour guide. He resumes his old role about once a month in order to interact with his customers.

"I always wanted to be an ice cream maker," Dager said. Beginning in the 1950s, he worked with his father in the family business, advancing from forming three-gallon containers to flavoring the product to making it. "I was always popular in school because we had a lot of ice cream to sample, and we hired a lot of my classmates in the summer," Dager remembers.

Dager's grandfather, also Joseph Dager, started Velvet Ice Cream in 1914 with one flavor, Original Vanilla. The recipe remains a favorite and is one of about 60 flavors produced today out of a bank of 500-plus recipes, including nearly 50 seasonal varieties. Velvet produces more than six million gallons of ice cream each year that are shipped throughout Ohio, Kentucky, Indiana and Florida.

Velvet remains a family stronghold. Three of Dager's four daughters work with him, as do his wife, his sister, a son-in-law and several grandchildren. "The best thing in my life is knowing that I can pass on the business to my family. They bring their own talents, skills and enthusiasm, just like I did when I was younger," he said.

In fact, the company is a source of pride and pleasure for the family. Dager says, "Success is when a person is pleased and content with what they're doing. It's an inner feeling of satisfaction. It's not all dollars and cents."

Caring deeply about the quality of their product tops Dager's list of leadership skills. He focuses on people, too, drawing out valuable traits in others that they don't see themselves. And, of course, Dager invests time with his customers. "It's all for them. Without them, we don't function."

"We make a lot of people happy," Dager said. "Our product is for little people—and big people, too. That's why we came up with a product that's naturally good for you." Only high-quality ingredients go into the ice cream, down to the vegetable-based colors.

Two of Dager's school-age grandsons, Justin and Devon, had customer satisfaction in mind when they suggested an addition be made to the Blue Moon ice cream, a summer specialty. "I told them it didn't really need anything, but to keep working on their idea. They already knew what they wanted—mini marshmallows, to be 'clouds' next to the 'moon.'" The improved formula debuted in May 2006, at the annual Utica Old Fashioned Ice Cream Festival.

Many other changes predated the "clouds." For example, in the late 1980s, Velvet experimented with sugar-free additives to make the ice cream an option for those with special dietary needs, including Dager's mother, who had diabetes.

"Ice cream makes a lot of people happy," Dager said. "It gives us satisfaction to know that we make a healthy, high-quality product that people of all ages enjoy."

Bob Weiler

CEO, The Robert Weiler Company

Words to live by:
"Don't pet the sweaty stuff, and don't sweat the petty stuff. Don't take yourself too seriously, but do pay serious attention to others."

Hometown: Bexley, Ohio
First job: grade-school paper carrier
Hobbies: playing tennis, sailing, reading
Favorite books: "Roots," Alex Haley, "The DaVinci Code," Dan Brown
Favorite movies: "Walk the Line," "The Sting"
I am: "Lucky."

"If you get help early from your parents, it really makes a difference," observes Bob Weiler, CEO of The Robert Weiler Company in Columbus, Ohio. He inherited the thriving real estate company, which offers appraisal, brokerage, consulting, development and property management services, from his parents.

"I recognize I was born on the high side of the playing field, and now I'd like to give back and help others have at least a portion of the advantage I had." This is probably one of the reasons Weiler has been so active on many community boards over the years, including serving as president of the Columbus Board of Education and as trustee or director for Capital University, the Center of Science and Industry, the Mid-Ohio Regional Planning Commission and the Columbus Metropolitan YMCA.

In all, Weiler learned, "Success is establishing noble goals and doing your best to reach them, always trying your hardest. Making the most money was never a goal of mine."

Early in life, Weiler's parents motivated him to succeed. They both graduated from college in the 1920s; his father from the University of Pennsylvania/Wharton and his mother from Smith College.

In the 1930s, his entrepreneurial father started a real estate and insurance business. Weiler remembers that as soon as he could walk, he accompanied his father to open houses. In later years, he worked the events on weekends. "I always knew that I would be involved in the real estate business somehow," he said.

Fortunately, Weiler and his older brother, Alan, didn't wind up wanting to run the same end of the family businesses. His brother took over the insurance business after returning home from serving in the Korean conflict, and Weiler stayed in real estate. "We're partners in each other's business, but we stay out of each other's hair," he said.

Before he joined the business in 1957, Weiler earned a degree from the University of Arizona. He also earned a master's in real estate in 1964 and a doctorate in finance in 1968, both from The Ohio State University. Amazingly, Weiler also earned a law degree from Capital University in 1983.

Weiler met his wife, Missy, in Arizona; they married in Ohio after his graduation. "Missy keeps me grounded. She's my greatest supporter. She's volunteered for the Columbus Public Schools and a local hospital for 30 years," he said admiringly. This steady couple has lived in the same house for the past 47 years and has played tennis on Thursday mornings with the same doubles partners for over 30 years. They've helped raise Pilot Dogs for many years as well.

One of his primary goals has been to lead by example, although Weiler claims he's a poor administrator who gets frustrated when he sees people not working up to their potential. "I had a personal secretary for 25 years who shouldn't have lasted past five, but I couldn't bring myself to let her go. I've always found it easier to hire than fire."

He added: "Being considered one of the team is important to me. I don't want to be put on a pedestal. I like to work from a non-threatening position."

Weiler cites another challenging experience from his service on the Columbus Public Schools' board of education in the 1980s. The board was helping the district downsize its staff because twice as many administrators worked in the main office than the budget allowed. "As we went through the process, everyone agreed it had to be done. But I regret the manner in which we did it. We probably should have phased the administrators out over six to 24 months and helped them with out-placement instead of just terminating them immediately."

When making tough decisions, Weiler says to consider this: "If it will bother you in five years, deal with it; if not, get over it! I've learned that people are much more important than things—people are what matters in life."

The people in Weiler's family continue to motivate him. "We have a great group from both sides, and we really enjoy being with each other." Strong family support helped him get through the worst time of his life when both of his parents died within 60 days of each other. His mother was 67 and his father was 71.

His best times were his youth and the time he enjoys now with his wife, their four children and 14 grandchildren, whom he sees as his most important legacy.

"When work is over I enjoy playing, but when I'm at work, I work. I have the ability to turn it off when I go home," Weiler said. "I'm lucky enough to say I love what I do. As much as I love going home at night after a long day, I can't wait to get to the office each day."

Part V
Out on the Town

Ken Schnacke

President and General Manager, Columbus Clippers

Words to live by:
"When the fear of failure is greater than the thrill of success, you have a situation that's not conducive for young people to play any kind of sport."

Hometown: Cleveland, Ohio
First job: paper carrier
Hobbies: baseball, his children's activities
I am: "Dedicated."

He dreams of the perfect night at the ballpark—good weather, a crowd of 10,000 or more, and of course, a victory. Yet Ken Schnacke, president and general manager of the Columbus Clippers, remains pragmatic about the game he loves: "Winning is never final—there's always another game to face; and losing is never fatal—there's always another chance to be successful."

Schnacke takes pride in his organization's vitality of the past 30 years. Success, he says, is measured by the team's perception in the community. "Is it an affordable, safe and fun night out?" and "Does Mom want to come?" are among the questions Schnacke poses to test for success.

Despite the club's longevity, Schnacke explained, "I'd be lying if I didn't recognize we've fallen a little on the register, but we've held our own for a long time." He said that attendance at the ballpark fell because of the closure of a main-access highway and the building of several new sporting venues. Within the past 10 years, for example, Columbus has welcomed new stadiums for a national hockey team, a major league soccer team, a Big-10 basketball arena and an updated football stadium.

He expects to even the playing field when a new downtown ballpark, Huntington Park, opens for the 2009 season. The team currently plays at Cooper Stadium, just west of downtown. "Our core audience will always be a family with kids in the home. Other groups have been less available to us because we aren't a multiple-entertainment destination. Now, with the new park, we'll be more attractive to all audiences, especially people who want to catch dinner, the game and after-dinner events, all without getting back in their car," said Schnacke.

The team's prospects are getting even better: In September 2006, the Clippers signed a two-year contract, affiliating with the National League's Washington Nationals beginning in 2007. The Nationals replace the New York Yankees, who decided to leave Columbus and the Clippers after 28 seasons. "We now have a new 'double-play' combination—the state capital of Ohio and the nation's capital in Washington," Schnacke said.

Baseball made an early imprint on Schnacke's life. "My dad loved it—he even played semi-pro ball. Mom was used to it. I was one of three brothers who played baseball. We never ate dinner together in the summers," Schnacke recalled, as he fondly described childhood pick-up games and school teams on Cleveland's east side. He's matter-of-fact about his own performance. "I tell everyone that I peaked out at age 16. I couldn't hit the curve ball."

Schnacke laments that sports in this country today are too serious and too organized. "It's frightening how much pressure is on young athletes to perform. Parents need to step back and not do that," Schnacke said.

Schnacke was impressed by his father, a metallurgical engineer who designed a special collar for space suits, attaching the faceplate to the body, which was worn by astronaut Alan Shepherd. This admiration clearly affected Schnacke's initial choice of career. A high school honors student who dreamed of becoming a professional baseball player, Schnacke earned a mechanical engineering degree from Ohio Northern University. He put the degree to use in designing plastic injection molding machinery at a company called HPM, a division of Taylor's Industrial Services LLC, in Mt. Gilead, Ohio.

Soon after, college friends convinced Schnacke to join them at the newly created Ohio Environmental Protection Agency in Columbus, where he would head

Air Pollution Control and be second in command of the wastewater section. "The U.S. EPA was trying to clean up 200 years of pollution in 200 days. These were contentious times. I just didn't see myself staying in the job for 30 years," Schnacke said.

Throughout college and his early career, Schnacke continued to nurture his love of baseball. In college he broadcast sports events for radio station WIMA in Lima, Ohio. He played semi-pro baseball for the Marion Titans while he worked for HPM. While working for the EPA, he was hired by radio station WDLR in Delaware, Ohio, to do a worldwide broadcast of the U.S. Service softball tournament at the former Lockbourne Air Force Base in Columbus.

Finally, baseball became the leading force in Schnacke's life. In 1976, Schnacke drove to Florida with a friend to network with baseball executives at training camps. He met Bobby Bragan, then-president of minor-league baseball, who recommended him as business manager for the Gold Sox in Amarillo, Texas. Schnacke took the job. Within two weeks, Bragan intervened again, and Schnacke accepted an offer to start a baseball team from scratch in Harlingen, Texas. With $800 and help from a college friend, Schnacke developed the Rio Grand Valley White Wings. "We lost money that year, but it was a lot less than others in the league," he said.

Schnacke baseball career led him to Columbus, Ohio, in 1977 to help manage the new home team, the Columbus Clippers. He became general manager in 1989 when his mentor George Sisler retired. Today Schnacke leads a core staff of 20 employees. "I've never been bored. I've always loved this job. Every day is different," he said. He often works 12-16 hour days when the team plays at home. "I'm afraid my family plays second fiddle to much of the schedule," he admits. He and his wife of 29 years, Sandy, have three children.

On the job, Schnacke juggles many projects, but this self-described "bulldog" reminds himself to follow his instincts when making decisions. "I try to be proactive, but often I'm reacting to suggestions and complaints from visitors to the ballpark. I have to sort out the good from all those messages," he said.

Because it is a public business, Schnacke said that the organization's mistakes are amplified, fueling his desire to keep anything from going wrong.

"We're the guardians of the franchise. The new ballpark should position the team for success for another 30 years. I want to make sure the people of Columbus have an affordable source of wholesome, fun, family entertainment."

JIM LORIMER

PRESIDENT, CLASSIC PRODUCTIONS

Words to live by:
"Do unto others as you would have them do unto you."

Hometown: Morrisville, Pa.
First job: hod carrier for a mason
Hobbies: reading, working out
Favorite books: anything related to Shakespeare and linguistics
Favorite movies: all James Bond films
I am: "Joyful."

In 1939, when he was 13, Jim Lorimer wrote to FBI director John Edgar Hoover and asked for advice on becoming an agent. Hoover's response advised him to first become an attorney or an accountant. Following Naval service in World War II, Lorimer did just that and earned a law degree. He served as law review editor at the Dickinson School of Law. He also spent four years working for the FBI.

He never imagined that his career would lead him to partnering with Arnold Schwarzenegger for more than three decades in creating what has become the largest multi-sport festival in America.

"Sports are life in a microcosm—they teach you to prepare, train, compete, win and lose," Lorimer said. He would know: In high school, he lettered in four sports, captained the football team and led the student council.

His journey to sports promotion began at the FBI, when Lorimer worked in the intelligence field. "My work involved considerable contact with Communist sympathizers who believed that the Soviet system was superior to ours. It was during the Cold War, and the United States and Russia were both competing for world leadership," he explains.

Moving four times in three years for FBI work prompted Lorimer to accept a job in Columbus, Ohio, with Nationwide Insurance because, "I wanted my children to know where they were from." Lorimer worked up the ranks at Nationwide to become vice president of government relations. He also helped raise three children and served for 39 years as mayor and vice mayor of the Columbus suburb of Worthington.

However, Lorimer's strong interest in sports continued. He remembers becoming particularly intrigued with an international track meet between the United States and the Soviet Union, which was held in Philadelphia in the summer of 1959. Lorimer was in Columbus and wanted to see the competition firsthand and survey the political ramifications. The event changed his life.

"I knew that the Soviets had undertaken a national sports development program with the intention of demonstrating the superiority of their society and system," he said.

After two days of track and field competition involving men's and women's teams from both countries, the Soviets declared a "National Team Victory," as the result of combining men's and women's team scores. Lorimer explained: "The U.S. men's team won, but our women's team performed poorly. I was concerned because the U.S. women clearly had no training and were totally unprepared for international competition."

"The field of sports competition catches the eyes of the world. The international publicity concerning a Soviet win did not take into account the lack of opportunity for U.S. women in sports. Given the opportunity, both our men and women could be the best in the world in any sport."

A few weeks later, Lorimer's hope was renewed when he attended a Junior Olympic competition at The Ohio State University. It was run by the Columbus Recreation Department and involved 1,500 teenagers, half of whom were girls. He was impressed with their performance and competitive spirit and decided to take action.

Lorimer proposed to the then-director of the Columbus Recreation Department, Nick Barrack, that a four-year, Olympic development program be started immediately for the top 12 females from the Junior Olympics. Barrack, who also led the Amateur Athletic Union, agreed. He, too, had been in Philadelphia and had witnessed the poor performance of the women's team and realized the importance of training.

After obtaining the support of the previously all-male Ohio Track Club, Lorimer went to OSU, where he met with both the OSU director of athletics, Richard Larkins, and the world-famous head track coach Larry Snyder. Both Larkins and Snyder were involved in international sports and agreed to allow the newly formed Ohio Track Club Girls' Team to train at the indoor track at OSU. Lorimer coached the team.

"I didn't know girls had such a competitive spirit," Lorimer said. "These girls wanted to compete and were thrilled at the possibility of joining an Olympic development program." Under Lorimer's leadership, the team won the national track championship two years later in 1961.

The rest is leadership history. In the summer of 1961, Lorimer was appointed Secretary of the U.S. Olympic Committee for Women's Athletics. He was also selected to manage the United States Track Team, which visited Moscow that year to again compete against the Soviet Union. In 1964, Lorimer was selected Chairman of the U.S. Olympic Committee and served in that capacity through 1968. Additionally, several of the OTC girls' team members won national championships, and all were on the cutting-edge of new opportunities that were emerging for women in the sports field.

Lorimer's work in the sports promotion field had only begun. In 1967, he was asked to run the National Weightlifting Championships and the Mr. America Contest in Columbus. Lorimer's success there was recognized, and he was then asked to chair the World Weightlifting Championships and Mr. World Contest in Columbus in 1970. Lorimer invited the top six bodybuilders in the world—including a young Austrian named Arnold Schwarzenegger.

After winning in Columbus, Schwarzenegger told Lorimer, "This is the best contest I've ever been in," and committed to help him create the world's largest, highest-paying contest. In 1975 the two men drew up plans, shook hands and became partners in the Arnold Classic.

Today the Arnold Sports Festival attracts 130,000 attendees and 17,000 athletes in 38 events, 14 of them Olympic sports. To manage the event, Lorimer leads four full-time staff, 600 volunteers including a medical staff of 150 doctors and nurses, and 30 committees.

Success to Lorimer is living a full and contributing life, and sharing love on that journey with family and friends. He advises others to find what they love doing, without regard to financial considerations. Lorimer said, "Arnold would agree that to be successful, you must set goals and follow your dream!"

JACK HANNA

DIRECTOR EMERITUS, COLUMBUS ZOO AND AQUARIUM; HOST, "JACK HANNA'S ANIMAL ADVENTURES"

Words to live by (from his father):
"If you work hard and have enthusiasm, you will succeed."

Hometown: Knoxville, Tenn.
First job: working for my family vet
Hobbies: hiking, eating cookies, causing chaos, listening to country music
Favorite book: "Born Free," Joy Adamson
Favorite movie: "Born Free"
I am: "Hard-Working."

"Jungle Jack Hanna" is a national authority on wildlife and conservation. He's traveled to every continent at least twice. He's met presidents and mingled with celebrities. Nevertheless, he says, "My biggest thrill is the building of the Columbus Zoo. Those are my proudest times."

Hanna's path to directing the Zoo began on a small farm in Tennessee, where, with his parents' blessing, he grew up taking care of many animals, including goats and rabbits. He enjoyed exploring tadpoles and water life in the creek. He even brought baby ducks into his mother's commode and bathtub.

"You must have a passion for what you do," he said. "I was not a bright student, but I always worked hard—twice as hard as anybody else." Hanna knew at age 16 that his passion was zookeeping. By then he'd already spent five years working for the family vet, Dr. Roberts, in Knoxville, Tenn. "He thought I wouldn't last a day. He had me clean doorknobs, mop floors. He saw I wouldn't quit."

After studying at Kiski boarding school in Pennsylvania, Hanna earned a degree from Muskingum College in Ohio, where he met his wife, Suzi. Hanna took his wife and love of animals back to Knoxville, where they opened a pet shop. In 1973 they moved from Tennessee to Florida, where Hanna directed the Central Florida Zoo in Sanford, and in 1978 they relocated to Columbus, where Hanna began updating the Columbus Zoo and creating programs to boost a sagging attendance rate.

Hanna admires his wife "for putting up with all this stuff for 37 years. We moved 12 times. We lived in mobile homes. I even asked her once to breastfeed a sick chimpanzee. That was the only time she told me no. But she only said no because she said I'd tell everybody, and I'm telling you now anyway," he laughed. "She put up with a lot, put it that way."

Life for Hanna has not always been as upbeat as that of his "Jungle Jack" character. While Hanna was working at the Knoxville Zoo in 1972, a close friend's son lost his arm to an African lion. Hanna quit his job. "I didn't want to do anything else for the rest of my life," he said. However, a visit from family friend Dr. Albert Chesney helped change his perspective. Chesney had recently hit a child with his car while backing out of his driveway, and the child had died. Of such traumatic times in life, Hanna says, "They're going to be unbearable."

Hanna then moved his family to Florida, where they faced their next life-and-death challenge: The youngest of his three daughters, Julie, developed leukemia, which she eventually beat. Meantime, Hanna had quit his zoo job, had major back surgery and was trying to make a living selling real estate.

The family's prospects brightened in 1978, when a friend in New Jersey told Hanna about an ad for a zoo director in Columbus, Ohio. "It was just fate that got us there," he reflected. In addition to a challenging new position for Hanna, Columbus held promise for Julie, as Children's Hospital there was one of four in the country treating her type of cancer.

In 1996, Julie faced death again, this time due to a massive brain tumor, which she survived. By then, Hanna had also lost his parents. "Life is life, you know? It's going to have its changes. If you have a strong family, you'll make it through those changes," he said.

Looking back, Hanna said, "I would've spent a lot more time with my family. That's the biggest regret I have." But in the late '70s, Hanna said the Columbus Zoo job required seven days a week, 15-20 hours a day. It was a fun job for his kids, though. On Sundays, they'd pick up litter in the zoo and have family picnics. "I admire people who have been successful who are family people—they teach good values, build their organization on pride and hard work and passion," he said.

Hanna resists being called a star or a celebrity. "I'm a character who loves to talk about conservation and animals in a fun way and an educational way. That's what Jack Hanna is all about," he said. He views his high-profile TV career as an outlet for his goals. Hanna is a regular guest on "The Late Show with David Letterman" and "Good Morning America"; his "Jack Hanna's Animal Adventures" reaches 96 percent of TV households in the country.

He hopes others describe him as fair and hard-working. "That's all I care about. There is no easy solution to success in life. It takes a lot of hard work, and it takes a lot of passion."

Jerry Borin

Executive Director, Columbus Zoo and Aquarium

Words to live by:
"Find something you enjoy doing."

Hometown: Cincinnati, Ohio
First job: dairy processing plant
Hobbies: traveling, photography, reading
Favorite books: "The Catcher in the Rye," J.D. Salinger, "Catch 22," Joseph Heller
Favorite movies: "Old Yeller," "Patton"
I am: "Low-Key."

Jerry Borin is a laid-back kind of guy who doesn't need the glare of the spotlight to feel satisfied. "I'm fine operating under the radar," he said. "I actually enjoy the work tremendously. I have great satisfaction in making the Zoo better."

Borin came to the Columbus Zoo and Aquarium in 1985, just after the passage of the Zoo's first city property-tax levy. The Zoo was poised for tremendous growth, and director Jack Hanna's career was taking a new direction with public speaking and television appearances. The Zoo board knew they needed someone to step in and run the daily operations. The call went to Jerry Borin.

"Never in my life did I think I'd be working at a zoo," Borin said. "But the timing was right. I was ready for a change." Borin had spent 13 years at the Columbus Department of Recreation and Parks and had reached the level of assistant director. Although he didn't have zoo experience, he did have extensive experience in administration management, a perfect complement to Jack Hanna's exuberant public style.

Borin said, "Jack's popularity could only help the Zoo. To his credit, Jack never stepped back to try and run the Zoo. And I knew I was never going on 'David Letterman.'"

He continued, "From my survey of the landscape, we had this high-energy director who was all over the place telling everyone that we had a great Zoo. We'd better make sure everything works when they get here."

In 1992, the giant pandas came from China, and the Zoo had its highest attendance ever. Borin became executive director, and Hanna stepped back to emeritus status. Although the pandas met with great acclaim, Borin faced his worst pain as Zoo director with their procurement. The Zoo had started the process for securing a 100-day loan of the pandas from China in the 1980s. At the time, the process met with the local Zoo board's approval. "The Zoo community had been kept informed of what our plan was," Borin said.

However, by 1992 the atmosphere had changed. Borin remembers, "Even though we'd followed every procedure, our colleagues had turned against us. I had to go plead our case before a group that ended up being pretty hostile. They ended up suspending our organization a year from the national association."

"For a long time I was rather bitter about that and thought it was unfair. But I dealt with it by realizing it wasn't a unanimous decision but it just happened to be made by a couple of people in high authority. I overcame it. Since then this organization has been held in as high esteem by our colleagues as any zoological organization," Borin said.

Under Borin's leadership, the Zoo has continued to add exhibits, such as Asia Quest, which opened in June 2006. Today the Zoo has expanded to include 660 species of animals and 580 acres. According to Borin, the passage of a 10-year city-property tax in 2004 was the "pinnacle of success."

"No matter how popular you think you might be, you have to approach it like you're behind. Never take anything for granted," Borin said. "The public's approval of what we do is my marker for success."

Borin feels that his inclusionary and quiet style makes him an effective leader. "I think others find that I have the interest of the organization as my top priority; there's no hidden agenda. But I'm decisive when decisive action's called for," he said.

"I was raised to do the right thing. Be honest with people. If you don't know something, don't be afraid to go ask someone who does know."

Borin never had "someone to ask" growing up. Opportunities for discovering new interests were limited in his blue-collar hometown near Cincinnati. "As a younger person, I wish I would have tried to get more exposure," he said. Neither of his parents were high school graduates, but somehow Borin knew he'd go to college. He earned a bachelor's degree in history and a graduate degree in public administration from The Ohio State University.

Borin said he loves his work at the Zoo and hopes others can discover their life's passion as well. "I've never had a day here when I didn't want to go to work. If you can say that, then you've truly found it," he said. "I hope that when I leave, the Zoo continues to be this wonderful community asset that people enjoy for many years to come."

KATHRYN D. SULLIVAN

SCIENTIST, ASTRONAUT, EXPLORER

DIRECTOR, THE OHIO STATE UNIVERSITY'S BATTELLE CENTER FOR MATHEMATICS AND SCIENCE EDUCATION POLICY

Words to live by:
"Ask questions. Slow down and listen to what's really happening. Talk to people, and learn about their world."

Hometown: Woodland Hills, Calif.
First job: babysitting, wrapping gifts at a toy store
Hobbies: photography, scuba diving, reading, golfing
Favorite books: "Great Waters," Alister Hardy, "Carrying the Fire," Michael Collins
Favorite movies: "Four Seasons," "Star Trek," "Star Wars," "Indiana Jones"
I am: an "Explorer."

Kathy Sullivan dreamed of travel and exploration when she was a girl. Though her family traveled along the west coast and to Mexico and Canada, she wanted to see more of the world. A fervent reader, she spent hours devouring books about early explorers and their discoveries, without a concern that they were all men. She's been fascinated by this planet for as long as she can remember.

The opportunity to be part of earth's ultimate exploration arose when Sullivan was in graduate school. NASA was accepting applications for its new shuttle missions. She applied, knowing this might be her only chance to see the world from such an exceptional vantage point. "If you have a deep passion and interest about something, then you owe it to yourself to say 'yes' first. Walk toward it; you can always change your mind later if it's not right," she said.

Her choice was right. Sullivan became the first American woman to walk in space, making her mark in history and fulfilling her lofty dream.

"I've had so many 'best moments' in my career—walking in space, flying a jet, scuba diving around the world—it's hard to pick 'the' best one. I've learned that these kinds of accomplishments are short-lived, and completing them doesn't make you happy or change how you look at yourself in the mirror. I truly believe happiness can only be found from within. I'm always more curious about how an event will change or alter my view of myself and the world versus what others think or say."

Based on this philosophy, it makes sense that Sullivan defines success not by her achievements but by asking this: What does a day or a lifetime well-lived mean? "It's about the completeness of you as a person and how you are linked with the world. If I have the opportunity to give one truly meaningful gift to another human being and they accept it and now it is growing within them, then that's success," said Sullivan.

Her mission in life wasn't always so clear. Sullivan and her older brother grew up in Southern California, where their aerospace-engineer father taught them to fly at a young age. Sullivan's brother, who now flies for United, knew his destiny early on. Sullivan thought she'd study languages at the University of California in Santa Cruz. Despite quite vociferous objections, she was compelled to take a marine biology class, and she was hooked. She changed her major to earth sciences, realizing she could have a career doing the things about which she once dreamed and read.

During her junior year, Sullivan studied in Norway to learn another language (she was already fluent in German and French) and expand her insight into that country's geography. Near the end of her studies there, Sullivan was offered a position as an assistant air-traffic controller, due to her background. Her application was rejected because she wasn't a native. She returned to the states, completed her degree and headed next to Nova Scotia to complete her doctorate in geology.

If Sullivan had been navigating air space in Norway, she probably wouldn't have applied to be part of the U.S. team rocketing into space. In January 1977, 8,500 qualified candidates, including Sullivan, applied for the space program. After her selection in 1978, Sullivan spent 15 years preparing for and completing three shuttle missions, which included earth-science experiments and work on the Hubble telescope.

Though space was challenging, it paled in comparison to the time when, at 12, Sullivan suffered the death of her grandmother, after which her mother fell into a deep depression and alcoholism. “There was no talking about therapies and treatments back in the ’60s. These issues are still hard for people to face today.” If she could change anything in her life, she said, “I would take away my mother’s pain, without changing the catalytic effect it had on me.”

In 1993, President George H. Bush asked Sullivan to accept the nomination as chief scientist of the National Oceanic and Atmospheric Administration. Although it meant leaving NASA, she accepted and was later confirmed under President Bill Clinton.

After NOAA, Sullivan explored three career options: aerospace work in the corporate world, academia or science museums. “These museums are very entrepreneurial and creative places, but they’re generally under-appreciated by the communities they serve.” To determine where she’d fit best, Sullivan made a list of people she knew and trusted in each sector and invited them to lunch to talk about their worlds, what motivated them and what was on the horizon.

Once again she acted as an explorer and chose the CEO position at the Center of Science & Industry in Columbus, Ohio, where she worked from 1996-2005. As her NASA biography notes, Sullivan has “a passion for igniting in others the wonder and importance of science, math and technology”—and that’s what she did at COSI. Under her leadership, COSI strengthened its impact on science teaching in the classroom and its national reputation as an innovator of hands-on, inquiry-based science learning resources.

Today Sullivan continues to focus on conveying the wonder and importance of science in her new position as director of the Battelle Center for Mathematics and Science Education Policy, in the John Glenn School of Public Affairs at The Ohio State University. She also continues to be actively involved with COSI as its science adviser.

Her curiosity continues to motivate her, along with her desire for personal growth, having “real” conversations and doing something about things that really matter. “I want to continue to help get things ‘unstuck!’” To that end, she’s writing a book that explores leadership and education. She’s also the vice chair of the National Science Board, an independent group that makes policy recommendations on science and engineering issues to the President and Congress.

Though she strives to be collegial, Sullivan confesses she may be more intense at times than she realizes. However, she believes her career arose from the combined forces of her intellect, situational awareness, ability to listen well (often hearing what was meant and not said), and being good at conveying care, concern and commitment to a shared mission.

Sullivan uses these qualities to act on her theory on life: "The 'grand scheme' is not about one thing or a thousand or even a hundred, but a few small items: honor, passion, integrity, dealing with conflicting loyalties, success and satisfaction—and the inward and outward dimensions of dealing with these concepts. Though we may have a different path or journey, we're all dealing with these same life lessons. I carry within me a lot of ideas and gifts from other people whom I admire. If I'm able to share a similar gift and make and impact on other human beings, then I have left an enduring legacy."

Earle Bruce

Former Head Football Coach, The Ohio State University

Words to live by:
"Honesty, truth, commitment, fidelity, loyalty and hard work."

Hometown: Cumberland, Md.
First job: assistant football and basketball coach, Mansfield Senior High School
Hobbies: golfing, watching thoroughbred racing
Favorite book: anything on Harry Truman
Favorite movies: "Sabrina," "It's a Wonderful Life," "Remember the Titans"
I am: "Passionate."

Former Ohio State University football coach Earle Bruce prides himself on his honesty, always "telling it the way it is." His common sense and good judgment served him well on the playing field and off, as did his focus on toughness. "I always said our team would not be outworked or out-hit."

Born in Pittsburgh in 1931, Bruce developed his aptitude for hard work while growing up in Cumberland, Md. "I had a great childhood. I'd go back there any time!" He, his three brothers and two sisters benefited from hard-working, caring parents, who ensured the family maintained traditions such as eating dinner together nightly. "The nights we ate stew were tough for me," Bruce laughed, recalling how he disliked the vegetables. After the meal, Bruce usually washed or dried the dishes. "We all had duties," he said, lamenting that many families today lack such discipline.

"I also had great teachers. I can't fault them for my poor English and spelling!" he said. To get to school, Bruce and half a dozen friends walked two miles. "I came out OK. It's educational to walk with your friends. You learn to get along with people."

Family and friendship influenced Bruce's take on life. "Family is everything," he explained. "The most critical thing is the people you associate with. If you have good friends, you can't help being a good person."

Early in life, Bruce held no aspirations for coaching—just for a college education. He earned a bachelor's degree from OSU and a master's degree from Kent State University. While at Ohio State, he played football until a knee injury ended his career. That's when his coach, the legendary Woody Hayes, asked Bruce to join the coaching staff, which he did until his graduation in 1953.

That experience launched 44 successful years for Bruce as a coach, starting at Ohio high schools such as Massillon High School, known for its football prowess. "That was the first time I woke up at 2 a.m. and worried about a game. I knew I didn't want to feel that way—I wanted to enjoy the game. That's when I learned to 'put a little more steam on' for special games." In 1964 and 1965, Bruce's teams at Massillon were undefeated.

From Massillon, Bruce rejoined Hayes, "who recommended me for any job I got." Jobs as head football coach at the University of Tampa and at Iowa State University preceded a final return to OSU. Bruce coached there from 1979 to 1987. (Current head coach Jim Tressel served as an assistant coach to Bruce from 1983 to 1985.) In Bruce's first season, the Buckeye team was undefeated until the Rose Bowl, which they lost.

"I worked to keep the integrity of the game of football at all costs, to never violate the rules," Bruce said. "Football offers a lesson for life, too." That's why Bruce encouraged all his players to go to class and earn their degrees. He'd even show up at a player's room at 7:30 in the morning to ensure he got to an early class if any absences had been noted.

"I taught my guys that you can knock a player down, but you can also help him up." He added, "I tried to do what was right by all of my players. I would tell the truth, whether people liked it or not. I don't care about being politically correct—I want to be correct."

The most challenging moment in Bruce's coaching tenure was in 1988, when he was fired by OSU on the Monday preceding the Saturday match-up with archrival University of Michigan.

Nonetheless, he said, "I loved coaching. I never had a feeling I didn't want to go to work." He authored two books that reflect this lifelong passion for the game.

After OSU, Bruce took his coaching talents to the University of Northern Iowa and Colorado State University, and then he led teams in the Arena Football League. Bruce was inducted into the College Football Hall of Fame in 2002, with a career coaching record of 154-90-2.

"My legacy is all the people I've been fortunate to have coached. Success is 85 percent attitude. Attitude is the thing that makes it go."

Bruce still hasn't completely left the OSU Buckeye sports scene. He stays busy each Saturday as one of the pre-and post-game commentators on Columbus radio station WTVN-610 AM. He and his wife of 51 years, Jean, also enjoy their four daughters and grandchildren.

"I've had a great, great life."

DICK REYNOLDS

ATHLETIC DIRECTOR AND HEAD COACH, MEN'S BASKETBALL, OTTERBEIN COLLEGE

Words to live by:
"You get from point A to point B by a series of good choices. Make the good ones and avoid the bad ones—that's what it's all about."

Hometown: London, Ohio
First job: 8 years old, paper carrier
Hobbies: spending time with grandchildren, boating, fishing
Favorite book: "The DaVinci Code," Dan Brown
Favorite movie: "Dances With Wolves"
I am: "Fair."

Dick Reynolds learned a winning philosophy early in life, and it's stood the test of time.

"Age has enlightened me. As you get older, you tend to scrutinize things more. I admire people, like my mother and grandparents, who have common sense and work to keep their family together and functioning," he said.

"I don't think I would change anything, because it would change who I am and what I've become."

What he's become is successful. After 34 seasons as head basketball coach at Otterbein College in Westerville, Ohio, he is ranked first among Ohio Athletic Conference coaches on the all-time career victory list with 595 (his overall record is 595-330). Nationally, Reynolds is fourth in victories among active coaches and fifth all-time in NCAA Division III. He's also a nine-time OAC "Coach of the Year" selection, and the first conference coach to take teams to different conference titles spanning four different decades. He earned a conference title outright 11 times and a national championship in 2002.

"I enjoy working with young people. I instill my 'old-time values' about right and wrong in my coaching because of what I see. Although kids today are brighter and have more things, they don't have common sense or a work ethic. They want things, but they're not willing to pay the price. So I push them," said Reynolds.

His guiding philosophy addresses students' overall development as well as athletic achievement. "I'm here to compete but also to graduate my athletes and guide them with a liberal-arts philosophy. We're here to emphasize the mental, physical, social, emotional and spiritual aspects of their lives. We have to first consider, 'What's in the best interest of the student?'"

Reynolds is proud that during his 34-year coaching career at Otterbein College, he's graduated all but two of his student-athletes. "I'm an educator who happens to be a coach," he said.

His childhood prepared Reynolds well for his adult roles. "My parents divorced when I was very young. It was tough, growing up in a single-parent home in a small town in the 1950s. Everyone was poor, but we didn't realize it. Athletics and work were the only two things to do."

"We worked very hard—it was just what you did. I worked all through school. When I was 8 years old, I delivered newspapers; then in high school I painted houses and worked with the county highway department in the summers," he said.

Reynolds' grandparents also helped support the family, which consisted of Reynolds, his mother and three older brothers. "Pop-aw taught me how to work and put food on the table. My mother taught me about budgeting and sacrificing for others. She worked several jobs."

Although he kept busy with work and academics, Reynolds, much like his older brothers before him, found time to play football, basketball and run track in high school. He recalls in those days, teachers didn't run the schools—the coaches did. "It was very different then. Athletics were the most important thing. The coaches taught us about loyalty, respect and about knowing your place," he said.

His high school basketball coach was a graduate of Otterbein and influenced

Reynolds to enroll there as well. He also credits his mother for instilling the value of education in him and his brothers. “I never doubted that I would be an educator. My mother realized that academics were the only way out,” he said.

Reynolds went to Otterbein and lettered 12 times in football, basketball and track. He was also active in the ROTC. Reynolds graduated in 1965 and returned to London, Ohio, on a one-year military deferment to teach seventh-grade science and serve as an assistant coach. Reynolds went to Vietnam the following year and served as an officer in the U.S. Air Force until 1969.

After the Air Force, Reynolds returned to Ohio and taught physical education for four years in Westerville and Columbus Public schools. He landed at Otterbein in 1970 as part-time assistant coach to head coach Curt Tong for the men's junior varsity team. Reynolds helped the squad achieve a 31-20 record before taking over as head coach in 1972; he became athletic director in 1991.

Reynolds is “no-nonsense” when it comes to his leadership. “I have a good work ethic. I'm loyal to my people, and I follow the chain of command. And I can solve problems,” he said. “I hope when I leave people say that I brought balance, fairness and leadership to the program.”

About his leadership style, Reynolds said, “Others would probably say I'm militaristic. I hope they also say I'm supportive and expect them to have common sense.”

Interestingly, when asked to define success, Reynolds doesn't speak in athletic terms. “When I was a kid, success was being able to keep our family functioning. It was just getting to the next day. We may have had a tough life, but we didn't think of it that way. The deaths of my mother and grandparents were much harder,” he reflects.

Reynolds' best times are those spent with family. “Athletic performance is important, but it's my job—it's what I'm supposed to do. Today success is having everyone together and happy, and seeing my kids and grandkids become successful.”

Sherri Geldin

Director, Wexner Center for the Arts

Words to live by:
"Go for it. Don't trust conventional wisdom; trust your instincts and your heart."

Hometown: Los Angeles, Calif.
First job: supermarket bakery counter
Hobbies: reading, traveling, hiking, biking
Favorite book: "House of Mirth," Edith Wharton
Favorite movie: "The Rules of the Game"
I am: "Persistent."

Sherri Geldin is a true believer in the power of the written word. A letter she crafted to a prominent Los Angeles attorney helped her land a spot of her own in California's art history. She became one of the three founding staff members of the Museum of Contemporary Art in Los Angeles. "I can remember when MOCA was literally a stack of four file folders on a desk," she said.

A Los Angeles native, Geldin received both a bachelor's degree in art history and an MBA in arts management from UCLA. She was one of 18 people to complete a new and somewhat controversial graduate program in arts management offered through the business school.

Geldin describes the day during her last week of finals she read a particularly interesting article in the *Los Angeles Times*. "At the time, Los Angeles was the only major U.S. city without a museum devoted to modern and contemporary art. The article described how a committee of private citizens had been formed by the mayor to explore the feasibility of creating just such a contemporary museum for the city," Geldin recalled.

The committee was comprised of some of Los Angeles' best-known civic, corporate and cultural leaders, including nationally prominent art collectors. "These were very fancy people and I was a 'nobody,' but I couldn't resist the impulse to contact them," she remembers. "The opportunity seemed so perfect, however unlikely."

In fact, Geldin was so excited about the prospect of working with the committee that she immediately wrote a letter to the committee chair, attorney Bill Norris, a close friend of then-mayor Tom Bradley. It got Norris' attention. "He told me there were two things that persuaded him to call: first and foremost that I had written a 'great letter,' and second, he was intrigued with my dual degrees in art history and business because the combination was so unique, especially then," Geldin said.

Geldin was invited to join the committee on the spot, and within just two months, she was on the payroll. Her immediate task was to work on the request for proposals for a parcel of land near Bunker Hill in downtown Los Angeles, where it was proposed that the museum would be located. "I became the shuttle between the mayor's committee, the community redevelopment agency, a newly created artist advisory group and other interested parties," she said.

MOCA was established in 1979, and for the next 13 years, Geldin played an integral role in virtually every aspect of the museum's development, including artistic, educational and administrative functions. She served as the museum's deputy director for nine years.

By 1993, Geldin realized she was ready to try something different, but being in the number-one spot wasn't necessarily what she envisioned for herself. "I always considered myself a supremely capable 'number two,' but I wasn't entirely confident about being the one in charge," she said.

Geldin gave her notice to MOCA and ended up with three job offers to run museums, one of which was from the Wexner Center for the Arts in Columbus, Ohio. "I had never imagined living 'between the coasts,' but after visiting the center and talking with the search committee, I came away thinking, 'Wow, this place has enormous potential, and it's more intriguing than I thought.' By the third interview I decided the Wexner Center represented the greatest challenge but also the greatest potential reward. So I did it, and I've never regretted it," she said.

The transition from California to Ohio was difficult but made somewhat easier by the Columbus community. "They were very welcoming, encouraging, and seemed to have a genuine desire for me to succeed. That modest Midwest hospitality really existed, and I realized the city had a healthy cultural appetite and many ingredients that made ambitious thinking possible on an institutional level," Geldin said.

Under her leadership, the Wexner Center has become one of the country's foremost contemporary museums with an eclectic array of visual, film, media, performing and design arts programs. Geldin also guided the museum through a comprehensive three-year renovation of its landmark building, completed in October 2005.

"Success for me is largely about finding a way to merge your personal passions with your professional pursuits. It's about waking up each day with the potential to make a difference in a sphere that I care about. I hope that people would say I've made a difference and that I've conducted myself with the utmost intelligence, integrity, honesty and empathy—with a healthy dose of humor thrown in for good measure," Geldin said.

Geldin believes she's fair but tough. "I'm sure there are times when my staff thinks of me like I'm Meryl Streep's character in 'The Devil Wears Prada,'" she laughed.

Humor aside, Geldin is uncompromising when it comes to upholding high standards for herself and her team as well as the Center: "Standards exist for a reason, and there is no point reaching for any but the highest." Knowing all her options and remaining open to what she describes as the "wild card" is key. "I'm inclusive but decisive. And I love seizing the moment."

Geldin obviously loves her job. "The best thing is having the opportunity on any given day to meet and work with some of the most illustrious artists, critics and thinkers in their respective fields." She also thrives on the creative energy at the Wexner Center.

"It's always surprising and unpredictable. There's a feeling of creative combustion all around. I've been able to surround myself with people who share my values and enthusiasm for the arts and culture, people who appreciate and want to advance the creative success of others," she said.

"I also enjoy the fact that you don't have to park your individuality at the door."

MERIBAH MANSFIELD

DIRECTOR AND CLERK-TREASURER, WORTHINGTON LIBRARIES

Words to live by:
"Follow your heart.
Do what matters to you."

Hometown: Rochester, N.Y.
First job: working on the line in a Kodak camera repair facility
Hobbies: photography, nutrition, studying the Bible, spending time with family
I am: "Passionate."

Meribah Mansfield is too restless to enjoy movies, but she loves reading. She's a librarian who insists she has no favorite book. She said, "I've decided there's no such thing as a favorite book. It's just too hard to choose."

Her passion for books and libraries led to a 34-year career that's been marked along the way by many community and professional accomplishments. She's touched many lives through her work at the Columbus Metropolitan Library, the Fairfield County District Library, and the Upper Arlington and Bexley public libraries, both in Columbus, Ohio. She also helped form the Ohio Public Library Information Network (OPLIN) to ensure that all Ohio residents have fast, free, public Internet access throughout the state's 251 independent local libraries. Mansfield was also involved in the renovation and addition to Columbus' Main Library in 1991, the Northwest Library in 1996 and the Old Worthington Library in 1998.

Mansfield has spent the past 15 years at the Worthington Libraries. "I'm the 'Library Lady' wherever I go in the community. There's no dividing line between my work and my personal life," she said.

Despite her many successes as an adult, Mansfield grew up scared not to do well. Her alcoholic father was a salesman for Kodak, and the family moved all over the country as his career dictated. During that time, Mansfield didn't have any dreams about her future—she just wanted to stay out of trouble. "I was the typical child of an alcoholic. I just wanted to be good and do the right thing. I didn't have anyone who really inspired me to do well. I was extremely self-driven."

The family finally settled in Rochester, where Mansfield graduated from high school. She completed a bachelor's degree in English in 1971 from Wittenberg University in Springfield, Ohio, and a master's degree in library science in 1972 from Western Michigan University. Her library career began that same year at the Bexley Public Library.

Surviving her father's alcoholism was hard, but the most difficult time of Mansfield's life came in 1978 when she and her first husband separated. "I was 28 and on my own with my six-week old daughter. I survived it one day at time. And the days eventually grew into nine years. I'm a survivor. I don't suffer fools easily," Mansfield said.

Her experiences took their toll, but she isn't bitter about them. She credits therapy and her spirituality for helping her through. "I wouldn't change anything about my life. My experiences have made me who I am today. For me now, God is at the center of my life."

She continued: "When I was younger, success meant getting the next job. I always blew through the next challenge. Today success means balance. My work life and my personal life are so intertwined. I want to give enough to do my best at work but also take care of myself and my family."

Mansfield believes her vision and passion, combined with a roll-up-her-sleeves and "just do it" attitude, are marks of her leadership. "I've been described as 'hard to keep up with,' and a 'dreamer and a doer.' I'm not good at maintenance mode; I'm always looking ahead to the next thing," she added.

The next great thing came in 1986 when Mansfield met her second husband in a Leadership Columbus class. "That was my best time. I've learned that intimacy is a good thing," she said.

Today Mansfield is happy spending time with her husband, Bruce, and their 17-year-old son, Matthew. Her daughter, Jessica, is also a librarian. She lives in Tennessee with her husband and Mansfield's recent joy, new grandson Owen. "I really admire the new generation today. They're so smart and so willing to work hard. They embrace the future."

Mansfield not only admires the younger generation, but believes her legacy will be that she involved them in the process of making the library relevant for future generations. "I want to develop my stars," she said.

About Diabetes

Diabetes is a chronic, debilitating disease affecting every organ system. There are two major types of diabetes: Type 1 and type 2. Type 1 diabetes is an autoimmune disease in which a person's pancreas stops producing insulin, a hormone that enables people to get energy from food. Type 1 diabetes usually strikes in childhood, adolescence or young adulthood, but it lasts a lifetime. People with type 1 diabetes must take multiple injections of insulin daily or receive a continuous infusion of insulin through a pump to survive. Type 2 diabetes is a metabolic disorder in which a person's body still produces insulin but is unable to use it effectively. Type 2 is usually diagnosed in adulthood and does not always require insulin injections. However, increased obesity has led to a recent epidemic in cases of type 2 diabetes in young adults. Taking insulin does not cure any type of diabetes nor prevent the possibility of its devastating effects: kidney failure, blindness, nerve damage, amputation, heart attack and stroke.

Following are a few examples of examples of the impact of diabetes:

- More than 21 million Americans have diabetes—that's 7 percent of the population.
- Close to 200 million people have diabetes worldwide.
- Diabetes is the single-most costly chronic disease.
- In 2002, diabetes accounted for $132 billion in health-care costs in the United States alone.
- Diabetes accounts for 32 percent of all Medicare expenditures.
- People with diabetes in the United States incur medical expenses that are about 2.4 times higher than people without diabetes.

From The Desk Of William B. Zipf, MD, FAAP

The diagnosis of diabetes is a life-changing event. This is a serious chronic illness and requires that the patient and family become biochemists in order to manage the body's energy system. This would be a difficult task for any adult, but we ask this of children. Over time, the family and the children begin to understand this, but this growing understanding of their tasks and obligations occurs as they also acquire new and more sophisticated skills.

We have hundreds of books that discuss diabetes from the point of view of the glucose molecule, muscle cell, pancreas and organs that are affected by chronically elevated glucose. These books have taught me a lot and have given me tools to help patients understand how to control the body's glucose levels. However, it has been the children who have taught me about diabetes as a disease. If you live with diabetes, you are face to face with this daily, and know very quickly what it does to you as a person or is doing to your child's life. As a diabetes care provider, you can get a sense of what our children and our parents see if you allow yourself to get very close to them, not just as patients, but as separate and distinct individuals. Only then can you be put in a position to learn what they have to teach you about the extremely complex nature of this life-long disease.

Allowing this connection creates a sense of further obligation and, in that respect, is associated with some risk. But if you allow this connection, both you and your patients benefit. Your skills at managing this condition improve, helping the children you're responsible for. You begin to see in the children and families how capable we, as people, are in dealing with adversity. The way our children and families manage this chronic disease shows how adaptable, how strong and how compassionate we all can be.

Dr. Zipf is a clinical professor of pediatric medicine at The Ohio State University College of Medicine and has held two other academic appointments with The Ohio State University as professor of physiology and professor of pediatrics in the college of medicine. He is director of Central Ohio Pediatric Endocrinology and Diabetes Services (COPEDS) and vice president of B/W Research Consulting.

Juvenile Diabetes Research Foundation

The Juvenile Diabetes Research Foundation International is the leading charitable funder and advocate of type 1 diabetes research worldwide. The mission of JDRF is to find a cure for diabetes and its complications through the support of research.

Since its founding in 1970 by parents of children with type 1 diabetes, JDRF has awarded more than $900 million to diabetes research, including more than $98 million in 2005. More than 85 percent of JDRF's expenditures directly support research and research-related education. In 2005, the Foundation funded 500 centers, grants and fellowships in 19 countries.

JDRF plays a unique role in setting the global direction of diabetes research resources, to ensure that they are used as effectively as possible as a "cure enterprise" to bring about a world without diabetes and its complications. To that end, the organization has developed six therapeutic targets on which to focus over the next five years:

1. Perfecting islet transplantation without chronic immunosuppression.
2. Creating safe and widely available "universal donor" supplies of insulin-secreting cells for transplantation.
3. Regenerating the body's own beta cells without islet transplantation
4. Perfecting a closed-loop artificial pancreas.
5. Creating novel therapeutics for predicting preventing, and reversing complications.
6. Maintaining or restoring immune tolerance in new-onset patients and those at-risk for developing diabetes.

"Beyond any shadow of a doubt, leadership at JDRF is solidly aligned in our urgent mission to find a cure for type 1 diabetes. Many organizations never reach this basic plateau of understanding. While money and research tools are important, this alignment of our people—our volunteers, our donors, our staff, our partners, and our scientists who are incredible leaders unto themselves—enables them to set ever-higher standards and expectations. They approach every day with passion and a renewed sense of urgency. They constantly reorient based on the results achieved and those new ones yet to be achieved to make contributions that move the ball down the field."

Arnold W. Donald, CEO - Juvenile Diabetes Research Foundation

"As executive director of our chapter, I am impressed time and again with the passion our families have in finding a cure for type 1 diabetes. As a mother of a son with type 1, I am humbled and extremely grateful for the selflessness and altruism of all those involved with JDRF. What Chip has done with this book is give hope to all of us. Not just in finding a cure for diabetes, but in becoming the leaders that will make a better tomorrow. Chip and his family have my deepest and most sincere thanks for allowing JDRF to be a part of this project."

Staci Perkins, Executive Director - JDRF Mid-Ohio Chapter

lacelet™
a statement with every step
"The Original"

within reach

THE KNOWLEDGE GROUP

WHERE ARE YOU ON YOUR LEADERSHIP JOURNEY?

At The Knowledge Group, we define a successful leader as someone who guides people on an unfamiliar journey toward an uncertain but desirable vision. More simply, a leader is a person who sets goals, takes action and achieves results.

We find that the work of leaders is two-fold: First, they fend off the forces of distraction, procrastination, anxiety and doubt; and second, they make sure they and their teams are taking action and moving toward the organization's purpose and vision.

"Leadership Within Reach" was not designed to define what leadership is or exactly how it works. It was intended to explore the personal attributes and journeys that leaders demonstrate and experience. All the leaders profiled in this book, regardless of their situation, saw opportunities in their lives and chose to take action to make things happen.

Such leaders may be found at any level of a given organization, and many will ultimately rise to the proverbial "top" as did the majority of the people interviewed for this book. However, many true leaders will never become president or CEO but will instead find a niche that suits their strengths and allows them to continue to have a critical impact on their teams and their organization.

Besides having a passion for what they do, at least five other qualities enable some leaders to be more effective than others. Most of these qualities are reflected in every leader we interviewed. These effective leaders:

1. Know themselves and have a sense of their values and beliefs.

2. Are willing to take action and have the courage to engage their fears.

3. Demonstrate willpower—the discipline to persevere to reach their goals.

4. Believe in lifelong learning—it's their way of life.

5. Have the ability to pause—to reflect and attempt to balance their lives.

Self-Analysis

Following is a list of questions intended to help you analyze your own experiences. Most of these questions were posed during interviews for "Leadership Within Reach." Use the questions to reflect on past experiences and then project how those experiences will shape your plan for the future.

- Do you think leaders are born or are they made? After reading "Leadership Within Reach," do you still feel the same way?
- What or who were your early influences? Who inspired you?
- When you were younger, what did you want to be when you "grew up"? Did these thoughts include where you are now?
- Who do you admire now and why?
- What motivated and continues to motivate you?
- How do you define success?
- Has your definition of success changed over the years? If so, how? If not, why not?
- What do you feel are the key factors or components of your own personal and/or professional success?
- Who has helped you along the way? Do you currently have a mentor or a peer group?
- What are your top three leadership skills?
- How would others describe your leadership style?

- When times were hard, how did you see your way through?
- What guidelines (personal and/or professional) have you established for yourself?
- If you could change one thing on your path so far, what would it be?
- What's been the most difficult situation in your life, and what lessons have you learned from it?
- What's been the best time of your life, and what did you learn from it?
- What other life-changing events have influenced and helped define who you are today?
- What will be your legacy?

ORGANIZATIONAL QUESTIONS

Now, keeping in mind the definition of leadership, consider the following questions in lieu of your "organization"—which could be a business, a nonprofit agency, a school or even your own family.

- In your opinion, what role does leadership play in the success of your organization?
- On a scale of 1-10 (10 being the highest), how would you rate the overall effectiveness of leadership in your organization today?
- What are the risks to the organization if you answered anything less than a "10?"
- What would it mean to your organization if your rating were to rise by 1 point? By 2 points?
- What actions are you going to take to get these results?

Resources

Sign up for your free subscription to *Winning Ways,* an online newsletter that will provide you with strategies, ideas, techniques and inspiration for taking action and creating success.

Sign up today at:
www.GrowCompeteWin.com

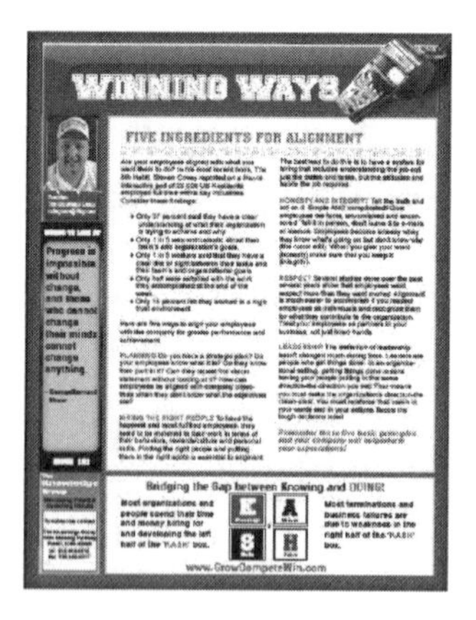

Visit The Knowledge Group Team in their online office at:
www.GrowCompeteWin.com

Get a peek at The Knowledge Group Strategic Playbook and learn how you can leverage your hidden marketing, people and technology assets to grow, compete and win!

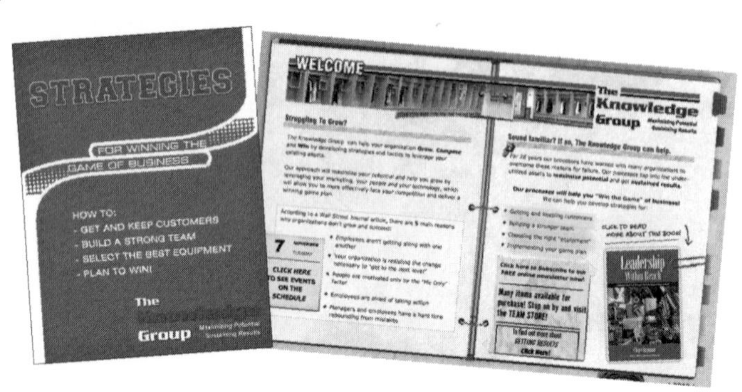

ABOUT THE AUTHORS

From left: Allison West, Chip Chapman, Rebecca Chapman

CHIP CHAPMAN

With 23 years of experience as a business owner, sales manager and consultant, Chip Chapman has developed unique insight into how organizations can actually solve their own problems. His expertise has been recognized with numerous business achievement awards, including the Wall Street Journal Entrepreneurial Award.

In addition to his leadership roles on several community service organization boards, Chip also speaks to businesses and organizations about how they can leverage their existing marketing, people and technology assets for improved results.

Chip holds a master's degree in business administration, with a marketing focus, from Capital University in Columbus, Ohio. Undergraduate work at the prestigious Transylvania University in Lexington, Ky., led Chip to complete a double major in business management and computer science.

ALLISON WEST

Allison West is a seasoned marketing professional with 18 years of experience in advertising, corporate communications and marketing. Most recently she acted as a strategic marketer for a well-known national brand, where she delivered annual planning, day-to-day management and innovative tactics to drive sales through five business lines.

Allison holds a master's degree in journalism, with an advertising focus, and a bachelor's degree in sociology from Marshall University in Huntington, W.Va.

REBECCA CHAPMAN

Delivering results through words and actions—that's the hallmark of Rebecca Chapman's career in public relations. For eight years, she influenced the public voice about education through her work at the Ohio Department of Education. While there, she promoted their message that "Every Child Counts" through the production of newsletters, speeches, press releases, annual reports, videos and statewide communications with more than 600 school districts.

Rebecca holds a bachelor's of science degree in journalism, with a specialty in public relations, and an honors distinction from Bowling Green State University in Bowling Green, Ohio.

LEADERSHIP WITHIN REACH ORDER FORM

Profits to Support Juvenile Diabetes Research Foundation

Shipping Info

Name ______________________

Address ______________________

City ______________________

State ______________________

Zip ______________________

Contact Info

Email address ______________________

Phone Number ______________________

Order Info

Qty of books ordered ______________________

Order Total $ ______________________

Pricing

Qty 1-9.......... $19.95 + S&H   Qty 50-99.............$16.50 + S&H

Qty 10-49...... $18.50 + S&H   Qty 100+................$14.95 + S&H

Shipping & Handling

Base S&H $4.05 per order plus an additonal $4.05 per $100 ordered

Mail or Fax To The Knowledge Group
1464 Manning Parkway
Powell, Ohio 43065
614.985.4815 Phone
614.985.4817 Fax

We accept
Personal or
Company Checks.

You may also order by credit card @ www.LeadershipWithinReach.com

INDEX

R

S

T

U

V

W

Z